# A Century of War

D1339915

# A Century of War

## Anglo-American Oil Politics and the New World Order

Revised Edition

William Engdahl

Pluto Press

LONDON • ANN ARBOR, MI

First published in English 1992

Revised edition first published 2004 by Pluto Press
345 Archway Road, London N6 5AA
and 839 Greene Street, Ann Arbor, MI 48106

www.plutobooks.com

British Library Cataloguing in Publication Data
A catalogue record for this book is available from the British Library

ISBN   0 7453 2310 3 hardback
ISBN   0 7453 2309 X paperback

Library of Congress Cataloging in Publication Data applied for

10   9   8   7   6   5   4   3   2   1

Designed and produced for Pluto Press by
Chase Publishing Services, Fortescue, Sidmouth, EX10 9QG, England
Typeset from disk by Stanford DTP Services, Northampton, England
Printed and bound in Canada by Transcontinental Printing

# Contents

## LIST OF FIGURES

# Preface

The fall of the Berlin Wall at the end of the 1980s and the collapse
of the Soviet Union were hailed by many as the dawn of a new era
of peace and prosperity. Some authors, such as Francis Fukuyama,
proclaimed it as the beginning of the end of history. The entire
world seemed to open to economic cooperation, to investment, to
democratic ideas. Trade barriers fell, doors opened. Little more than
a decade later, the optimism was long forgotten as the outlines of a
very different world were emerging.

As this preface to the new edition of *A Century of War* was written,
the world was mired in a bloody series of wars, the most serious
being the war in Iraq. It soon became clear to the world that the
decision of President George W. Bush to go to war against Iraq had
little to do with the threat of weapons of mass destruction. It was also
increasingly clear that the U.S. agenda in Iraq had little to do with
the proclaimed effort to 'bring democracy' to a once despotic Iraq.
That naturally raised in many minds the question of why the United
States put so much of its credibility, of its reputation, of what some
call its soft power, at risk, for apparently so little. The answer to the
question was a short one: it was about oil. But not about oil in the
simple sense many believed. This war was not an issue of corporate
greed. It was about power, and geopolitical power above all.

War in Iraq was about the very basis of America's 'national security,'
of future American power. America's role as the sole hegemon was the
unspoken reason for the war, and for this reason neither of the major
presidential candidates offered an alternative to American military
occupation of the vast oilfields of Mesopotamia. Iraq, as hawkish
Pentagon strategists put it, was part of the American post-cold war
agenda, U.S. pursuit of 'full spectrum dominance.' The role of oil in
the war, and the role of oil in most of the wars of the past century
or more forms the heart of this study of power and geography. It is
the thread running through the chapters of this book.

In 1904, a British geographer, Halford Mackinder, presented a
series of theses to the Royal Geographic Society in London under
the title 'The Geographical Pivot of History.' Almost a century later,
American security adviser and strategist Zbigniew Brzezinski spoke
in admiration of the work of Mackinder and his theory of Eurasian

geopolitics. It quietly but clearly guided American global strategy. The occupation of the oilfields of Iraq, the war in Kosovo and the Balkans, endless civil wars in Africa, financial crises across Asia, the dramatic collapse of the Soviet Union and the subsequent emergence of a Russian oligarchy, blessed by the International Monetary Fund and by Washington, all assumed coherence in a world where geopolitics, power and control dictated relations.

This book is no ordinary history of oil. The bare facts can be found elsewhere. The causal force driving the events is rarely spoken of. Here we present a sometimes controversial description of power and war, finance and economic warfare, and the relation of oil and finance to that power. One year after the U.S. occupation of Baghdad, the goals and aims of the world's only superpower were being questioned as they had not been since the Vietnam War. Degrading scenes of Iraqis being tortured filled the pages of world media. Allegations of corruption and collusion reaching up to the highest levels of Washington officialdom were commonplace. Outrage across the Islamic world was growing against a Washington foreign policy that had little in common with the policies of the U.S. Founding Fathers. Yet too much of the debate failed to take into account the fundamentals of American national security or its power. In 1945, the sun finally set on the British Empire. A year later in Fulton, Missouri, Winston Churchill helped light the spark of what came to be four decades of cold war. It was the emergence of the system which Henry Luce termed the American Century.

The American Century, stripped of the rhetoric of freedom, peace and democracy, was based on clear US hegemony among nations. It rested on two pillars. The one pillar was the uncontested role of US military power, a dominance which no combination of powers had been able to challenge since the end of the Second World War in 1945. The Soviet Union ultimately collapsed amid ruin in the effort to challenge that hegemony. In 1979 China decided to cooperate with that hegemony and realized, perhaps too late, that it had been a double-edged sword. The second pillar of American power was the uncontested role of the dollar as world reserve currency. The United States created the Bretton Woods System in 1944, in order to establish this unique role. The dollar served as reserve currency long after it had not one ounce of gold to back it.

The combined power of its military dominance and monetary dominance allowed the United States the enviable luxury of printing endless paper certificates, its dollars, and giving them to the rest of the world in exchange for well-engineered cars, machinery, textiles and every imaginable product. It was the greatest confidence game the world had ever seen. Americans bought the imports with more dollar debt, creating an edifice of dollar debt on which the entire world was dependent. This special hegemony also allowed the United States to become the world's largest debtor, to run endless trade imbalances, to inflate its currency beyond imagination, to create a buildup of private and public debt unprecedented in world history. So long as other nations depended on American markets for their trade, and on American military protection for their national security, the game appeared endless. Japan's role as 'lender of last resort' to the U.S. was supplemented at the turn of the century by China. Hundreds of billions of dollars in Japanese, Chinese and other foreign purchases of U.S. Treasury debt, U.S. real estate debt, and other assets, propped up the American economy long after it made any economic sense.

The power of the dollar and the power of the U.S. military had been uniquely intertwined with one commodity, the basis of the world economic growth engine, since before the First World War. That commodity was petroleum, and in its service British, American, German, French, Italian, and other nations called their soldiers to war. As Henry Kissinger once expressed this importance: 'control energy and you control the nations.' Oil played a decisive role in the collapse of the Soviet Union. Oil defined American foreign policy in much of the world during the cold war. And oil defines American military actions since the end of the cold war as never before. The how and why of that process define our theme here.

In 1919 Mackinder termed the winning of a British Mandate over Palestine the most important geopolitical outcome of the First World War. In the first decade of the third millennium, Palestine and Israel and Middle East geopolitics were still at the heart of world power politics, even if the players in the power complex had changed. How the destiny of the American Century was tied to the destiny of this small part of the world was a question of heated debate and discussion. A group of ultra-conservative ideologues largely around the Republican Party of George Bush were been accused of turning American foreign policy into a unilateral pursuit of military empire. Some defenders boasted of being democratic imperialists. Other Republicans and Democrats called for a return to traditional American foreign policy, a hegemony in which consensus among its Allies was essential. Both sides of this debate were misleading. Both factions accepted the underlying assumptions of an economic and political power which was no longer sustainable nor healthy for the United States nor for the rest of the world.

This book seeks to shed light on some lesser known aspects of our history, in an effort to provoke thinking beyond the moment, beyond embedded journalist impressions of reality, or major media sound-bite versions of reality, to encourage ordinary citizens to reflect on longer-term consequences of what our governments do with our mandate. If it leads to some critical questions being asked, its aim will have been met.

F. William Engdahl
Hochheim am Main
June 2004

# 1
# The Three Pillars of the British Empire

## THE EMPIRE NEEDS A NEW STRATEGY

No other element has shaped the history of the past 100 years so much as the fight to secure and control the world's reserves of petroleum. Too little is understood of how political and economic power around the raw material, petroleum, has been shaped by interests principally under the control of two nations—the United Kingdom and, later, the United States of America.

Britain, approaching the end of the 1890s, was in all respects the preeminent political, military and economic power in the world. British gold, under the jealous, guarding eye of the Bank of England, was the basis for the role of the pound sterling as the source spring of world credit, since 1815. Prussian military superiority was the actual key to the defeat of Napoleon's army at Waterloo. But Wellington and the British took the credit, and with it the lion's share of world gold reserves, which subsequently flowed into London. 'As good as sterling' was the truism of that day. After a law of June 22, 1816, gold was declared the sole measure of value in the British Empire. British foreign policy over the next 75 years or more would be increasingly preoccupied with securing for British coffers—the vaults of the Bank of England—the newly mined reserves of world gold, whether from Australia, California or South Africa. The corollary of this minerals policy was a policy of 'strategic denial' of those same identified gold reserves to competitor nations whenever possible.

After 1815, British naval superiority was unchallenged on the world's seas. British ships carried British steel, coal and exports of the Manchester textile industry. British manufactures had led the world for decades.

But behind her apparent status as the world's pre-eminent power, Britain was rotting internally. The more the British merchant houses extended credit for world trade, and City of London banks funneled loan capital to build railways in Argentina, the United States and Russia, the more the domestic economic basis of the United

Kingdom deteriorated. Few understood how ruthlessly lawful was the connection between the two parallel processes at the time.

Since the 1814–15 Congress of Vienna, which carved up post-Napoleonic Europe, with the diplomatic maneuvering of British Foreign Minister Lord Castlereagh, the British Empire had exacted rights to dominate the seas, in return for the self-serving 'concessions' granted to Habsburg Austria and the rest of the Continental European powers, which served to keep central Continental Europe divided, and too weak to rival British global expansion. British control of the seas, and with it control of world shipping trade, was thus to emerge after Waterloo as one of the three pillars of a new British Empire. The manufacturers of Continental Europe, as well as much of the rest of the world, were forced to respond to terms of trade set in London by the Lloyd's shipping insurance and banking syndicates. While Her Royal Britannic Majesty's Navy, the world's largest in that day, policed the world's major sea-lanes and provided cost-free 'insurance' for British merchant shipping vessels, competitor fleets were forced to insure their ships against piracy, catastrophe and acts of war, through London's large Lloyd's insurance syndicate.

Credit and bills of exchange out of the banks of the City of London were necessary for most of the world's shipping trade finance. The private Bank of England, itself the creature of the preeminent houses of finance in London's 'City,' as the financial district is called—houses such as Barings, Hambros, Rothschilds—manipulated the world's largest monetary gold supply, in calculated actions which could cause a flood of English exports to be dumped mercilessly onto any competitor market at will. Britain's unquestioned domination of international banking was the second pillar of English Imperial power following 1815.

The third pillar, more and more crucial as the century wore on, was British geopolitical domination of the world's major raw materials—cotton, metals, coffee, coal and, by the century's end, the new 'black gold,' petroleum.

## FREE TRADE AND THE SINEWS OF BRITISH POWER

In 1820, Britain's parliament passed a declaration of principle which was to usher in a series of changes that had as one consequence the outbreak, almost a century later, of the First World War and its tragic aftermath.

Acting on the urgings of a powerful group of London shipping and banking interests centered around the Bank of England, and Alexander Baring of Baring Brothers merchant bankers, parliament passed a statement of principle in support of the concept advocated several decades earlier by Scottish economist Adam Smith: so-called 'absolute free trade.'

By 1846, this declaration of principle had become formalized in a parliamentary repeal of domestic English agriculture protection, the famous Corn Laws. The Corn Laws repeal was based on the calculation of powerful financial and trade interests of the City of London that their world dominance gave them a decisive advantage, which they should push to the hilt. If they dominated world trade, 'free trade' could only ensure that their dominance would grow at the expense of other less-developed trading nations.

Under the hegemony of free trade, British merchant banks reaped enormous profits on the India–Turkey–China opium trade, while the British Foreign Ministry furthered their banking interests by publicly demanding China open its ports to 'free trade,' during the British Opium Wars.

A new weekly propaganda journal of these powerful City of London merchant and finance interests, *The Economist*, was founded in 1843 with the explicit purpose of agitating for the repeal of the Corn Laws.

The British Tory Party of Sir Robert Peel pushed through the fateful Corn Laws repeal in May 1846, a turning point not only in British but in world history, for the worse. Repeal opened the door for a flood of cheap products in agriculture, which created ruin among not only British but also other nation's farmers. The merchants simple dictum, 'Buy cheap, sell dear,' was raised to the level of national economic strategy. Consumption was deemed the sole purpose of production.

Britain's domestic agriculture and farmers were ruined by the loss of the Corn Laws protectionism. Irish farmers were enmiserated, as their largest export market suddenly lowered food prices drastically, as a result of the repeal of the Corn Laws. The mass starvation and emigration of Irish peasants and their families in the late 1840s— the tragic Irish Potato Famine of 1845–46 and its aftermath—was a direct consequence of this 'free-trade' policy of Britain. Britain's prior policy toward Ireland prohibited development of a strong self-sufficient manufacture, demanding it remain the economically captive breadbasket to supply England's needs. Now that breadbasket itself was destroyed in pursuit of the fictional free trade.

After 1846, Hindu peasants from Britain's Indian colony, with their dirt-poor wages, competed against British and Irish farmers for the market of the British 'consumer.' Wage levels inside Britain began falling with the price of bread. The British Poor Laws granted compensation for workers earning below human subsistence wage, with income supplement payment pegged to the price of a loaf of wheat bread. Thus, as bread prices plunged, so did living standards in Britain.

In effect, repeal of Corn Laws protectionism opened the floodgates throughout the British Empire to a 'cheap labor policy.' The only ones to benefit, following an initial surge of cheap food prices in Britain, were the giant international London trading houses, and the merchant banks which financed them. The class separations of British society were aggravated by a growing separation of a tiny number of very wealthy from the growing masses of very poor, as a lawful consequence of 'free trade.'[1]

E. Peshine Smith, an American economist and fierce opponent of British free trade, writing at the time, summarized the effect of the British Empire's free trade hegemony over the world economy of the 1850s:

Such has been the policy which still controls the legislation of Great Britain. It has, in practice, regarded the nation collectively as a gigantic trader, with the rest of the world, possessing a great stock of goods, not for use, but for sale, endeavoring to produce them cheaply, so that it might undersell rival shopkeepers; and looking upon the wages paid to its own people as so much lost to the profits of the establishment.[2]

Peshine Smith contrasted this 'nation as giant shopkeeper' doctrine of the Britain of Adam Smith and company to the growing national economic thinking emerging on the Continent of Europe in the 1850s, especially under the German *Zollverein*, and other national economic policies of Friedrich List.[3]

Their policy will be dictated by the instincts of producers, and not that of shopkeepers. They will look to the aggregate of production, not to the rate of profits in trade, as the test of national prosperity. Accordingly, the great Continental nations, France, Russia and the

German States—united in the Zollverein or Customs Union—have practically repudiated the idea which has so long controlled the commercial policy of England. What England has gained by that policy is thus described by one of her own learned and respected writers, Joseph Kay, who speaks of that nation as the one 'where the aristocracy is richer and more powerful than any other country in the world, the poor are more oppressed, more pauperized, more numerous in comparison to the other classes, more irreligious and very much worse educated than the poor of any other European nation, solely excepting uncivilized Russia and Turkey, enslaved Italy, mis-governed Portugal and revolutionized Spain.'[4]

So a campaign began to shape ruling English ideology in 1851, using a viciously false Malthusian argument of overpopulation, rather than admit the reality of a deliberate policy of forced underinvestment in new productive technologies. The name given the political doctrine which rationalized the brutal economic policy was British liberalism. In essence, British liberalism, as it was defined towards the end of the nineteenth century, justified development of an ever more powerful imperial elite class, ruling on behalf of the 'vulgar ignorant masses,' who could not be entrusted to rule on their own behalf.

But the underlying purpose of the liberal elites of nineteenth-century British government and public life was to preserve and serve the interests of an exclusive private power. In the last part of the nineteenth century, that private power was concentrated in the hands of a tiny number of bankers and institutions of the City of London.

## BRITAIN'S 'INFORMAL EMPIRE'

Such free-trade manipulation has been the essence of British economic strategy for the past 150 years. Britain's genius has been a chameleon-like ability to adapt that policy to a shifting international economic reality. But the core policy has remained—Adam Smith's 'absolute free trade,' as a weapon against sovereign national economic policy of rival powers.

By the end of the nineteenth century, the British establishment began an intense debate over how to maintain its global empire. Amid slogans about a new era of 'anti-imperialism,' beginning the last quarter of the nineteenth century, Britain embarked on a more sophisticated and far more effective form for maintaining its dominant world role, through what came to be called 'informal empire.' While maintaining core imperial possessions in India and the Far East, British capital flowed in prodigious amounts especially into Argentina, Brazil and the United States, to form bonds of financial dependence in many ways more effective than formal colonial titles.

The notion of special economic relationships with 'client states,' the concept of 'spheres of influence' as well as that of 'balance-of-power diplomacy,' all came out of this complex weave of British 'informal empire' towards the end of the last century.

Since the British defeat of Spain's Armada in 1588, Britain had used the special circumstance of being an island apart from Continental Europe. She was saved the costs of having to raise a large standing army to defend her interests, leaving her free to concentrate on mastery of the seas. Britain's looting of the wealth of the vast reaches of the world allowed her to maintain, as well, a balance of power on the Continent, creating or financing coalitions against whichever nation seemed on the verge at a given time of dominating the European land mass, stretching from Russia to Spain.

In the aftermath of the 1815 Congress of Vienna, in the reorganized Europe following the defeat of Napoleon, England had perfected the cynical diplomatic strategy known as 'balance of power.' Never was it admitted by Her Majesty's Foreign Office establishment that, as on a scale, with weights added to equalize opposite sides of a center 'balance point,' British balance-of-power diplomacy was rigorously defined, always, from the fulcrum or center point of London, that is, how Britain could play off rival economic powers to her own unique advantage.

After 1815, the peculiar 'genius' of British foreign policy lay in her skill in shifting alliance relations, abruptly if necessary, as her perception of strategic power in Europe or globally shifted. British diplomacy cultivated this cynical doctrine, which dictated that Britain should never hold sentimental or moral relations with other nations as sovereign respected partners, but rather, should develop her own 'interests.' British alliance strategies were dictated strictly by what she determined at any given period might best serve her own 'interest.' The shift from hostile relations with France in Africa to the 'Entente Cordiale' after the Fashoda showdown in 1898, or the shift from Britain's decades-long backing for Ottoman Turkey to blocking the expansion of Russia, in what was known in Britain and India as the 'Great Game,' were indicative of such dramatic alliance shifts.

Increasingly during the last decades of the nineteenth century, British capital flowed into select capital-deficit countries such as

Argentina, in order to finance, build, then run their national rail and transport infrastructure, a role usually encouraged by generous concessions from the host government. British capital also went to develop the local countries' steamship lines and their ports. So were the economies of Argentina and other British 'client states' effectively made into an economic captive, with terms of trade and finance dictated from the City of London by British merchant houses and trade finance banks. These client states of Britain thereby found that they had surrendered control over their essential economic sovereignty far more completely than if British troops had occupied Buenos Aires to enforce tax collection in support of the British Empire.

During the 1880s Argentina's new railroads brought her goods, especially beef and wheat, to her ports for export. Exports doubled and her external debts, mainly to London banks, increased 700 per cent. The country was a debt vassal of the British Empire, 'imperialism on the cheap' as one commentator dubbed it. It was manifestly not the intent of British policy to develop strong sovereign industrial economies from these client-state relationships. Rather, it was to make the minimum investment necessary to control, while ensuring that other rival powers did not gain coveted raw materials or other treasures of economic power.

During this time, in order first to safeguard her sea-lanes to India, British troops occupied Egypt in 1882. The Suez Canal must not be allowed to fall into rival French hands. The British military occupation so destroyed any structure of Egyptian rule that, after 1882, British soldiers remained a permanent presence in this nodal point of empire between London and India.

Similarly, the British presence in South Africa was initially in order to safeguard the southern route to India, preventing foreign rival powers from securing bases there that could flank British shipping trade. British control in the 1840s and 1850s over South Africa was not formal. Instead, Britain shut the Boer Republics from access to the Indian Ocean in stages, beginning with their annexation of Natal in 1843, keeping the Boers out of Delagoa Bay and intervening to block the union of the Boer Republics under Pretorius in 1869. The goal was to ensure, by the least means necessary, British supremacy in the entire southern African region. Secure monopoly for Britain's control of trade was primary in this nineteenth-century era of British Imperialism.

British secret intelligence services at this time also evolved in an unusual manner. Unlike the empires of France or other nations, Britain modelled its post-Waterloo empire on an extremely sophisticated marriage between top bankers and financiers of the City of London, government cabinet ministers, heads of key industrial companies deemed strategic to the national interest, and the heads of the espionage services. Representative of this arrangement was City of London merchant banking scion, Sir Charles Jocelyn Hambro, who sat as a director of the Bank of England from 1928 until his death in 1963. During the Second World War Hambro was executive chief of British secret intelligence's Special Operations Executive (SOE), inside the government's Ministry of Economic Warfare, which ran wartime economic warfare against Germany and trained the entire leadership of what was to become the postwar American Central Intelligence Agency and intelligence elite, including William Casey, Charles Kindelberger, Walt Rostow, Robert Roosa, later Kennedy's Treasury deputy secretary and partner of Wall Street's elite Brown Brothers, Harriman.

Rather than the traditional service providing data from agents of espionage in foreign capitals, Britain's secret intelligence services operated as a secret, Masonic-like network which wove together the immense powers of British banking, shipping, industry and government. Because all this was secret, it wielded immense power over credulous and unsuspecting foreign economies. In the Free Trade era after 1846, this covert marriage of private commercial power with government was the secret of British hegemony. British foreign policy was based on the cultivation, not of good neighborly relations with allies, but rather of calculated 'interests,' which could dictate shifting alliances or national allies, abruptly if required.

## THE GREAT DEPRESSION OF 1873

However, as a direct consequence of this British free-trade transformation, by the early 1870s a deep economic depression had begun in Britain following a financial panic. The free-trade doctrine had been premised on the assumption that British influence could ensure that same dogma became economic policy in all the world's major trading nations. That homogeneity was not to be won.

Following a severe London banking panic in 1857, the City of London banking establishment including the directors of the Bank of England, resolved on a novel device intended to prevent future outflows of gold from London banks. The panic of 1857 resulted from a foreign run on the international gold reserves held by the Bank of

England. The run collapsed bank credit in the City and across the country. In response to the crisis, the British authorities devised a policy which resulted in a simple if dangerous evolution of central bank practice.

The Bank of England, a private holding controlled not by the government at the time but rather by the financial interests of the City, realized that if it merely raised its central bank discount or interest rate to a sufficiently high level relative to rates in competing trading countries, which at any time might be draining Britain's gold reserves, then the drain would cease and if rates were driven sufficiently high, gold would eventually flow back into the banks of the City of London from Berlin, or New York or Paris or Moscow.

This interest-rate policy was a powerful weapon in central banking, which gave the Bank of England a decisive advantage over rivals. No matter that the usurious high interest rates created devastating depressions in British manufacture or agriculture; increasingly after the 1846 Corn Laws repeal, the dominant faction in British economic policy was not industry or agriculture, but finance and international trade. In order to insure the supremacy of British international banking, those bankers were willing to sacrifice domestic industry and investment, much as happened in the United States after the Kennedy assassination in the 1960s. But the consequences for British industry of this new Bank of England interest rate policy came home with a vengeance with the Great Depression which hit Britain in 1873 and lasted until 1896.

Beginning with a financial crisis in the British banking world, as the pyramid of foreign lending for railway construction to the Americas, North and South, collapsed, the British Empire entered what was called then the Great Depression. Reflecting the rising unemployment and industrial bankruptcies of that depression, British prices collapsed by almost 50 per cent in nominal terms, in an unbroken fall from 1873 to 1896. Unemployment became widespread.

The lack of capital investment into British manufactures was evident already at the International Exhibition of 1867. Products from entirely new manufactures of machinery, even textiles from Germany and elsewhere, clearly overshadowed the stagnant technological levels of British manufacture, the world leader only two decades before. Export of British iron and steel, coal and other products declined in this period. It was a turning point in British history which signaled that the onset of 'free trade' some three decades earlier, with the repeal of the Corn Laws, had doomed English industrial technology to decadence in order that finance assume supremacy in the affairs of the Empire. The period of Britain's easy leadership among the world's industrial nations was clearly over by the 1890s.

The free-trade dogma of nineteenth-century British Empire, and its Malthusian rationalizations, were doomed to eventual failure. Its foundations were based on cannibalizing the economies of increasing parts of the globe in order to survive. Only a quarter century after the repeal of the Corn Laws, the British Empire as a consequence sank into the worst and longest economic depression of its history. After 1873, British efforts to spread the virus of the 'English disease,' Adam Smith's 'cosmopolitan economic model' of absolute free trade, became markedly less successful, as nations of Continental Europe, led by Germany, initiated a series of national economic protectionist measures which allowed them to unleash the most dramatic rates of industrial growth seen in the past 200 years.

This all set the stage for a new debate amongst the British elite over how to maintain empire and power in a rapidly changing world. The geopolitics of petroleum was introduced into this debate in 1882. Now the debate was about how to maintain British naval supremacy.

# 2
# The Lines are Drawn: Germany and the Geopolitics of the Great War

## GERMANY'S *WIRTSCHAFTSWUNDER*

Growing divergence after 1873 between the depressed economy of the British Empire and the emerging industrial economies of Continental Europe, above all the German Reich, created the background to the outbreak in 1914 of the Great War. The role of petroleum in this conflict had already become central, though to a degree that few outside a tiny elite of London and New York bankers and financiers realized until years later.

Towards the final decade of the nineteenth century, British banking and political elites had begun to express first signs of alarm over two specific aspects of the impressive industrial development in Germany. The first was the emergence of an independent, modern German merchant and military naval fleet. Since 1815 and the Vienna Congress, the British Navy had been unchallenged lord of the seas. The second strategic alarm was sounded over an ambitious German project to construct a railway linking Berlin with, ultimately, Baghdad, then part of the Ottoman Empire.

In both areas, the naval challenge and the construction of a rail infrastructure linking Berlin to the Persian Gulf, oil figured as a decisive, if still hidden, motive force for both the British and the German sides. We shall see why these two developments were regarded as virtual *casus belli* by the Anglo-Saxon establishment at the turn of the century.

By the 1890s, British industry had been surpassed in both rate and quality of technological development by an astonishing emergence of industrial and agricultural development within Germany. With the United States concentrated largely on its internal expansion after its Civil War, the industrial emergence of Germany was seen increasingly as the largest 'threat' to Britain's global hegemony during the last decade of the century. By the 1870s, decades of piecemeal German

11

adoption of the economic reforms of Friedrich List, in creation of a national modern rail transport infrastructure and tariff protection for emerging domestic industries, began to bring notable results, more so in the context of the political unity of the German Reich after 1871.

Until approximately the 1850s, imitation of the apparently successful British economic model was the dominant policy followed in Germany, and the free-trade economics of such British economists as Adam Smith and David Ricardo were regarded as holy gospel in German universities. But increasingly, after England went into prolonged depression in the 1870s, which hit Germany and Austria as well, Germany began to realize the serious flaws in continuing faithfully to follow the 'British model.' As Germany, in building up national industrial and agricultural production, turned increasingly to a form of national economic strategy, and away from British 'free trade' adherence, the results were remarkable.

As one indication of this shift away from the British model, from 1850 to the eve of the First World War in 1913 German total domestic output increased fivefold. Per capita output increased in the same period by 250 per cent. The population began to experience a steady increase in its living standard as real industrial wages doubled between 1871 and 1913.

But the heart of the German industrial revolution was the explosion of technological progress. Germany established a national system of technological schools (*Technische Hochschulen*) and colleges, modelled on the French *Ecole Polytechnique*, for the education of scientific and engineering personnel for industry, and a system of *Handelshochschulen*, organized with support from the various chambers of commerce and industry, for education of business personnel. Moreover, German universities placed emphasis on natural sciences in the university curriculum. German engineering and science began to blossom. This was paralleled by a nationwide system of *Fachschulen* for training of skilled tradesmen. The net result of it all was a dramatic increase in the technological competence of the German working population after the 1870s.

As late as 1870, British large industrial companies dwarfed their young German rivals. But that was to change drastically over the next three to four decades. In the decades before 1914, in terms of fueling world industry and transportation, coal was king. In 1890, Germany produced 88 million tons of coal, while Britain produced more than double as much, 182 million tons. But by 1910, the German output of coal had climbed impressively to 219 million tons, while Britain had only a slight lead at 264 million tons.

Steel was at the center of Germany's growth, with the rapidly emerging electrical power and chemicals industries close behind. Using the innovation of the Gilchrist Thomas steelmaking process, which capitalized on the high-phosphorus ores of Lorraine, German steel output increased 1,000 per cent in the 20 years from 1880 to 1900, leaving British steel output far behind. As late as 1890, Britain still led Germany in production of pig iron, producing 7.9 million tons against Germany's 4.6 million tons. But by 1910, German pig iron output was 50 per cent greater than Britain's at 14.6 million tons to 10 million tons. At the same time, the cost of making Germany's steel dropped to one-tenth the cost of the 1860s. By 1913, Germany was smelting almost twice the amount of pig iron as British foundries.[1]

The rail infrastructure to transport this rapidly expanding flow of industrial goods was the driving force behind Germany's first *Wirtschaftswunder* (economic miracle). While the initial expansion of the German railway system began in the 1840s and 1850s, under the initial influence of List's *Zollverein* and his national railway plan, state-backed rail infrastructure fully doubled the kilometers of track between 1870 and 1913.

Following the development of centralized electric power generation and long-distance transmission under the impulse of Oskar von Miller and others, the German electrical industry grew from an infant industry employing 26,000 in 1895 to dominating fully half of all international trade in electrical goods by 1913. The German chemical industry, under the impulse of great researchers such as Justus von Liebig and others, grew from one vastly inferior to both the French and the British industries, to become the world's leader in analine dye production, pharmaceuticals and chemical fertilizers.

Introduction of scientific agriculture chemistry by von Liebig and others led to astonishing rates of productivity increase during this period for German agriculture. Going from a situation in the early decades of the 1800s which was literally desperate, with outbreaks of famine and harvest failure, when it seemed more economical to import grain from Russia or even Argentina, Germany reimposed a protective tariff blocking imports of cheap grain in the 1890s.

The mechanization of farming began to show progress, going from 20,000 harvesting machines in 1882 to some 300,000 by 1907. Despite often inferior and sandy soils, German chemical fertilizer development led to improving harvest yields. Grain harvest yields had improved as a result, by 80 per cent at the time of the Great War, compared with the period before 1887 when fertilizers were first introduced on a significant scale. By contrast, Russia, at the outbreak of the war, with 3 million acres more under grain cultivation, produced 19 million fewer tons of grain than Germany. By 1913, Germany was 95 per cent self-sufficient in meat production, despite per capita meat consumption having doubled since 1870, while Britain in 1913 imported 45 per cent of her meat requirements. Paralleling the expansion of its industry and agriculture, Germany went from a net emigration country in the early 1800s, to a country with strong population growth by the end of the century. Between 1870 and 1914 Germany's population increased almost 75 per cent, from 40,000,000 to more than 67,000,000. Large industry grew after the 1880s in a symbiosis with large banks such as Deutsche Bank, under what became known as the *Grossbanken* model, or simply the 'German model' of interlocking ownership between major banks and key industrial companies.[2]

Germany's *Wirtschaftswunder* arose in this period after 1870. The much-proclaimed industrial recovery from the devastation of war and world depression in the late 1950s represented, to a very significant degree, the recovery of the foundations laid during the 1880s up to 1914.

## A BERLIN BANK PANIC

The development of an independent national economic policy in Germany took its second impetus from the consequences, ironically, of a banking panic. In 1890, as a result of the near failure of the prestigious London merchant bank, Baring Brothers, arising from their huge losses in Argentine bond speculation and investment, and the ties of German banking to this Argentine speculation, a Berlin bank panic ensued, as the dominoes of an international financial pyramid began to topple.

Berlin, and German investors generally, had been caught up in international railroad speculation mania in the 1880s. With the crash of the elite Baring Bros., with some $75,000,000 invested in various Argentine bonds, down came the illusions of many Germans about the marvels of financial speculation.

In the wake of the financial collapse of Argentina, a large wheat exporter to Europe, Berlin grain traders Ritter & Blumenthal had foolishly attempted a 'corner' on the entire German wheat market, planning to capitalize on the consequences of the financial troubles in Argentina. This only aggravated the financial panic in Germany as their scheme collapsed, bankrupting in its wake the esteemed private banking house of Hirschfeld & Wolf, and causing huge losses at the Rheinisch-Westphaelische Bank, further triggering a general run on German banks and a collapse of the Berlin stock market, lasting into the autumn of 1891.

Responding to the crisis, the Chancellor named a Commission of Inquiry of 28 eminent persons, under the chairmanship of Reichsbank President Dr. Richard Koch, to look into the causes and to propose legislative measures to prevent further such panics from occurring. The Koch Commission was composed of a broad and representative cross-section of German economic society, including representatives from industry, agriculture, universities, political parties, as well as banking and finance.

The result of the commission's work, most of it voted into law by the Reichstag in the Exchange Act in June 1896, and the *Depotgesetz* of that July, was the most severe legislation restricting financial speculation of any industrial country of the time. Futures positions in grain were prohibited. Stock market speculation possibilities were severely constrained, one result of which has been the relative absence of stock market speculation since then as a major factor affecting German economic life.

The German Exchange Act of 1896 established definitively a different form of organization of finance and banking in Germany from that of Britain or America—Anglo-Saxon banking. Not only this, but many London financial houses reduced their activity in the restrictive German financial market after the 1890s as a result of these restrictions, lessening the influence of City of London finance over German economic policy. Significantly, to the present day, these fundamental differences between Anglo-Saxon banking and finance, and a 'German model' as largely practiced in Germany, Holland, Switzerland and Japan, are still somewhat visible.[3]

## THE NECESSITY FOR SHIP AND RAIL INFRASTRUCTURE

Thus, while Britain's national industrial and finance policy, especially after 1873, fostered industrial retardation of technological progress, that of Germany fostered quite the opposite. By 1900, the trends of divergence between the two countries were evident to all. But a growing friction between Germany and England in the years before 1914 was centered on two special aspects of Germany's impressive overall economic development. First and foremost was the dramatic emergence of Germany as a preeminent modern shipping nation, ultimately threatening the decades-long British domination of the seas.

So long as Germany did not control her own modern merchant ship fleet, and have a navy to defend it, she could never determine her own economic affairs. Britain was still the sovereign on the world's oceans, and intended to remain so. This was the heart of British geopolitical strategy. Under such conditions, argued an increasing majority in Germany, the nation's economic life would be ever subject to the manipulations of a foreign shipping power for the essential terms of its vital international trade.

In 1870, the total merchant fleet of the German Reich barely totaled 640,000 tons. The German merchant fleet at the time was the fifth largest in the world, behind the British, American, French and Norwegian. By 1914, Germany's fleet had risen to second place, just behind Britain's and gaining rapidly.

German export goods in 1870 were subject to both the rates and the ships of other nations, above all Britain. By 1914, this had changed dramatically. Already by 1901, 9,000,000 tons on 52,000 different ships left German ports sailing under the German flag. By 1909, these figures had increased to 65,000 vessels totaling 13,000,000 tons under the German flag. In this time, fully 70 per cent of all German trade was dependent on the sea. Control of the terms of this trade was clearly vital for the economic security of Germany. But few in London finance and shipping circles welcomed that prospect.

The parallel developments in German steel and engineering were directly applied to construction of a modern merchant shipping fleet. Replacement of sailing ships with steam propulsion and of wooden hulls, first with iron reinforcement and later with steel hulls, allowed Germany's merchant fleet to become larger and more efficient. In 1891, the German fleet could count three steamers of size over 7,000 DWT (dead weight tons). By 1914, the German flag carried five steamers above 20,000 DWT, nine between 15,000 and 20,000 DWT, and 66 between 7,000 and 10,000 DWT.

During this time, German sea transport developed with extraordinary rapidity and efficiency. By 1914, two large companies, the Hamburg-American and the North German Lloyd, held some 40 per cent of all Germany's commercial marine fleet. Organization, economies of scale and emphasis on construction of the most efficient and modern ships were the secrets of the spectacular growth during this period.

A French observer of the day, commenting on the extraordinary success of German marine transport in this period, noted,

> It is this concentration which makes possible the rapid amortization of capital and, in consequence, the 'scrapping' of ships which have become old, the perpetual rejuvenation of the floating machinery. You do not find in the German mercantile marine old vessels of thirty or forty years. What the German industries, properly speaking—metallurgy, electro-technique, etc.—secure by standardized production, the German merchant service obtains by the frequency and regularity of sailings ... In the case of the Germans, the creation of shipping lines does not follow trade, it precedes it, and in preceding it, it brings it into existence.[4]

Following the final incorporation of Hamburg into the German Reich in 1888, Hamburg, and later Bremen-Bremerhaven, became the centers for construction of the most modern and efficient port facilities in all Europe, drawing the rail freight of much of central Europe north, to be shipped out to world markets. Through establishment of a national infrastructure policy that encouraged the cheapest possible transport communications, Germany in the decade and a half before 1914 expanded its shipping presence throughout the world, including the traditional market monopolies of Britain's colonies and other traditional 'spheres of influence', such as Egypt and even the Americas. In 1897, little more than one year after the Reichstag passed the restrictive financial speculation controls, Grand Admiral von Tirpitz announced the first German naval construction program, which the Reichstag approved in 1898, followed in 1900 by a second law doubling the number of naval ships to be built.

By 1906, Britain had launched a superior new, all-big-gun battleship class, with the Dreadnought, which was swifter and carried more firepower than any existing battleship. In response, Germany in 1906 passed a little-publicized law mandating replacement of the German naval fleet every 20 years. By 1909, to the astonishment of the British, Germany launched its Nassau series with four ships superior to the Dreadnought class ships; these were soon superseded by both British and German shipbuilders with an even more advanced Super Dreadnought series. Britain had never imagined that Germany could develop such a modern fleet in its own naval yards, and in such a short time. Reviewing the background of the 1914 Great War in an Oxford University lecture in 1951, Sir Llewellyn Woodward tersely stated, 'Germany, like every other power, was free to build for herself as large a fleet as she might wish. The question was one of expediency and of realist calculation. A German battle fleet could not be other than a challenge to Great Britain, the dominant sea power.'[5]

It was becoming clear to some in Britain by about 1910 that dramatic remedies would be required to deal with the awesome German economic emergence. For the first time, as we shall now see, petroleum also emerged as a significant factor in the geopolitical calculus of war.

# 3
# A Global Fight for Control
# of Petroleum Begins

In 1882, the black heavy sludge we today know as petroleum had little commercial interest other than as fuel to light the new mineral oil lamps, a technique developed in Berlin in 1853 by a German lamp manufacturer named Stohwasser. The fuel was then known as 'rock oil' because it seeped through rocks in certain oil areas such as Titusville, Pennsylvania, or Baku in Russia, or in Galicia, now part of Poland. In 1870, John D. Rockefeller created the Standard Oil Company to exploit this market for lamp oil and various oil medicine 'cures' in the United States. The development of the internal combustion engine had not yet revolutionized world industry.

But at least one man understood the military–strategic implications of petroleum for future control of the world seas. Beginning with a public address in September 1882, Britain's Admiral Lord Fisher, then Captain Fisher, argued to anyone in the British establishment who would listen that Britain must convert its naval fleet from bulky coal-fired propulsion to the new oil fuel. Since 1870, Russian steamers on the Caspian Sea had burned a heavy fuel oil the Russians called 'mazut.' Fisher and a few other farsighted individuals began to argue for adoption of the new fuel. He insisted that oil power would allow Britain to maintain decisive strategic advantage in future control of the seas.

Fisher had done his homework on the qualitative superiority of petroleum over coal as a fuel, and knew his reasoning was sound. A battleship powered by a diesel motor burning petroleum issued no tell-tale smoke, while a coal ship's emission was visible up to ten kilometers away. Where some four to nine hours were required for a coal-fired ship's motor to reach full power, an oil motor required a mere 30 minutes and could reach peak power within five minutes. To provide oil fuel for a battleship required the work of twelve men for twelve hours. The same equivalent of energy for a coal ship required the work of 500 men for five days. For equal horsepower propulsion, the oil-fired ship required one-third the engine weight, and almost one-quarter the daily tonnage of fuel, a critical factor for a fleet, whether commercial or military. The radius of action of an oil-powered fleet was up to four times as great as that of the comparable coal ship.[1] But at the time, Fisher was regarded by his English peers as an eccentric dreamer.

Meantime, a German engineer, Gottlieb Daimler, had by 1885 developed the world's first workable petroleum motor to drive a road vehicle. Although automobiles were regarded as playthings of the ultra-rich until the turn of the century, the economic potentials of the petroleum era were beginning to be more broadly realized by many beyond Admiral Fisher and his circle.

## D'ARCY CAPTURES THE SECRET OF THE BURNING ROCKS

By 1905, the British secret services and the British government had finally realized the strategic importance of the new fuel. Britain's problem was that it had no known oil of its own. It must rely on America, Russia or Mexico to supply it, an unacceptable condition in time of peace, impossible in the event of a major war. A year before, in 1904, Captain Fisher had been promoted to the rank of Britain's First Sea Lord, the supreme commander of British naval affairs. Fisher promptly established a committee to 'consider and make recommendations as to how the British navy shall secure its oil supplies.'

Britain's presence in Persia and the Arabian Gulf—the latter still part of the Ottoman Empire—was at this time quite limited. Persia was not part of the formal British Empire. For some years, Britain had maintained consulates at Bushire and Bandar Abbas, and kept British naval ships in the Gulf to deter other powers from entertaining designs on strategic waters so close to Britain's most vital colonial source of looting, India. In 1892, Lord Curzon, later viceroy of India, writing on Persia, stated, 'I should regard the concession of a port upon the Persian Gulf to Russia, by any power, as a deliberate insult to Great Britain and as a wanton rupture of the status quo, and as an international provocation to war.'[2]

But in 1905, His Majesty's Government, through the agency of the notorious British 'ace of spies,' Sidney Reilly, secured an extraordinarily significant exclusive right over what were then believed to be vast untapped petroleum deposits in the Middle East. In early 1905, the British secret services sent Reilly (born Sigmund Georgjevich

Rosenblum, in Odessa, Russia) on a mission to extract the rights to exploit the mineral resources of Persia from an eccentric Australian amateur geologist and engineer named William Knox d'Arcy.

D'Arcy, a devout Christian who had studied history deeply, became convinced that accounts of 'pillars of fire' in the holy sites of the ancient Persian god of fire, Ormuzd, derived from the practice of the priests of Zoroaster lighting naptha—oil—seeping from the rocks in those select sites. He spent years wandering the areas where these ancient Persian temples existed, searching for oil. He made numerous visits to London to secure financial support for his quest, with diminishing support from British bankers.

Sometime in the 1890s, the new Persian monarch, Shah Muzaffar al-din, a man committed to modernizing what today is Iran, called on d'Arcy as an engineer who knew Iran thoroughly, asking him to aid Persia in the development of railways and the beginnings of industry.

In 1901, in exchange for a significant sum of cash up front, the Shah awarded d'Arcy a 'firman,' or royal concession, giving him

> full powers and unlimited liberty, for a period of sixty years, to probe, pierce and drill at their will the depths of Persian soil; in consequence of which all the sub-soil products sought by him without exception will remain his inalienable property.

D'Arcy paid the equivalent of $20,000 cash and agreed to pay the Shah a 16 per cent royalty from sales of whatever petroleum was discovered. Thus the eccentric Australian secured one of the most valuable legal documents of the day, granting him and 'all his heirs and assigns and friends' exclusive rights to tap the oil potential of Persia until 1961. D'Arcy's first successful oil discovery came in the region of Shushtar, north of the Persian Gulf.[3]

Sidney Reilly managed to track down d'Arcy in 1905, just as the latter was on the verge of signing a joint oil exploration partnership with the French through the Paris Rothschild banking group, before retiring back to his native Australia.

Reilly, disguised as a priest, and skillfully playing on d'Arcy's strong religious inclinations, persuaded d'Arcy instead to sign over his exclusive rights to Persian oil resources in an agreement with a British company which he claimed to be a good 'Christian' enterprise, the Anglo-Persian Oil Company. Scottish financier Lord Strathcona was brought in by the British government as a key shareholder of Anglo-Persian, while the government's own role in Anglo-Persian was kept secret. Reilly had thus secured Britain's first major petroleum source.

## BY RAIL FROM BERLIN TO BAGHDAD

In 1889, a group of German industrialists and bankers, led by Deutsche Bank, secured a concession from the Ottoman government to build a railway through Anatolia from the capitol, Constantinople. This accord was expanded ten years later, in 1899, when the Ottoman government gave the German group approval for the next stage of what became known as the Berlin–Baghdad railway project. The second agreement was one consequence of the 1898 visit to Constantinople by German Kaiser Wilhelm II. German–Turkish relations had become increasingly important over those ten years.

Germany had decided to build a strong economic alliance with Turkey, beginning in the 1890s, as a way to develop potentially vast new markets to the East for the export of German industrial goods. The Berlin–Baghdad railway project was to be the centerpiece of a brilliant and quite workable economic strategy. Potential supplies of oil were lurking in the background and Britain stood opposed. The seeds of the animosities tragically being acted out in the Middle East from the 1990s to the present day trace directly back to this period.

For more than two decades, the question of the construction of a modern railway linking Continental Europe with Baghdad was a point of friction at the center of German–English relations. By the estimation of Deutsche Bank director Karl Helfferich, the person responsible at the time for the Baghdad rail project negotiations, no other issue led to greater tension between London and Berlin in the decade and a half before 1914, with the possible exception of the issue of Germany's growing naval fleet.[4]

In 1888, under the leadership of Deutsche Bank, a consortium secured a concession for the construction and maintenance of a railway connecting Haidar-Pascha, outside Constantinople, with Angora. The company was named the Anatolian Railway Company, and included Austrian and Italian shareholders as well as a small British shareholding. Work on the railway proceeded so well that the section was completed ahead of schedule and construction was further extended south to Konia.

By 1896, a rail line was open from Berlin to Konia, deep in the Turkish interior of the Anatolian highlands, a stretch of some 1,000 kilometers of new rail in a space of less than eight years in an economically desolate area. It was a true engineering and construction accomplishment. The ancient rich valley of the Tigris and Euphrates rivers was coming into sight of a modern transportation infrastructure. Hitherto, the only rail infrastructure built in the Middle East had been British or French, all of it extremely short stretches in Syria or elsewhere to link key port cities, but never to open up large expanses of interior to modern industrialization.

For the first time, the railway gave Constantinople and the Ottoman Empire a vital modern economic linkage with its entire Asiatic interior. The rail link, once extended to Baghdad and a short distance further to Kuwait, would provide the cheapest and fastest link between Europe and the entire Indian subcontinent, a world rail link of the first order.

From the British side, this was exactly the point. 'If "Berlin–Baghdad" were achieved, a huge block of territory producing every kind of economic wealth, and unassailable by sea-power would be united under German authority,' warned R.G.D. Laffan, at that time a senior British military adviser attached to the Serbian Army. 'Russia would be cut off by this barrier from her western friends, Great Britain and France,' Laffan added.

German and Turkish armies would be within easy striking distance of our Egyptian interests, and from the Persian Gulf, our Indian Empire would be threatened. The port of Alexandretta and the control of the Dardanelles would soon give Germany enormous naval power in the Mediterranean.

Laffan hinted at the British strategy to sabotage the Berlin–Baghdad link.

A glance at the map of the world will show how the chain of States stretched from Berlin to Baghdad. The German Empire, the Austro-Hungarian Empire, Bulgaria, Turkey. One little strip of territory alone blocked the way and prevented the two ends of the chain from being linked together. That little strip was Serbia. Serbia stood small but defiant between Germany and the great ports of Constantinople and Salonika, holding the Gate of the East … *Serbia was really the first line of defense of our eastern possessions. If she were crushed or enticed into the 'Berlin–Baghdad' system, then our vast but slightly defended empire would soon have felt the shock of Germany's eastward thrust.'* [emphasis added][5]

Thus it is not surprising to find enormous unrest and wars throughout the Balkans in the decade before 1914, including the Turkish War, the Bulgarian War and continuous unrest in the region. Conveniently enough, the conflict and wars helped weaken the Berlin–Constantinople alliance, and especially the completion of the Berlin–Baghdad rail link, just as Laffan had urged. But it would be a mistake to view the construction of the Berlin–Baghdad railway project as a unilateral German move against Britain. Germany repeatedly sought British cooperation in the project. From the 1890s, when agreement was reached with the Turkish government to complete a final 2,500 kilometer stretch of rail which would complete the line down to what is today Kuwait, Deutsche Bank and the Berlin government made countless attempts to secure British participation and cofinancing of the enormous project.

In November 1899, following his visit to Constantinople, Germany's Kaiser Wilhelm II met with Britain's Queen Victoria in Windsor Castle, to personally intercede in favor of soliciting a significant British participation in the Baghdad project. Germany knew well that Britain asserted interests in the Persian Gulf and Suez in defense of her India passage, as it was known. Without positive British backing, it was clear that the project would face great difficulties, not least political and financial. The size of the final leg of the railway was beyond the resources of German banks, even one as large as Deutsche Bank, to finance alone.

From its side, however, for the next 15 years Britain sought with every device known, to delay and obstruct progress of the railway, while always holding out the hope of ultimate agreement to keep the German side off balance. This game lasted until the outbreak of war in August 1914.

But the trump card which Her Royal Britannic Majesty played in the final phase of the negotiations around the Baghdad railway was her ties with the Sheikh of Kuwait. In 1901, British warships off the Kuwait coast dictated to the Turkish government that henceforth they must consider the Gulf port located just below the Shaat al-Arab, controlled by the Anaza tribe of Sheikh Mubarak al-Sabah, to be a 'British protectorate.'

Turkey was at that point too economically and militarily weak to do other than feebly protest the de facto British occupation of this distant part of the Ottoman Empire. Kuwait in British hands blocked successful completion of the Berlin–Baghdad railway from important eventual access to the Persian Gulf waters and beyond.

In 1907, Sheikh Mubarak al-Sabah, a ruthless sort who reportedly seized power in the region in 1896 by murdering his two half-brothers as they slept in his palace, was persuaded to sign over, in the form of a 'lease in perpetuity,' the land of Bander Shwaikh to 'the precious Imperial British Government.' The document was co-signed by Major C.G. Knox, Political Agent of the Imperial British Government in Kuwait. There were reportedly generous portions of British gold and rifles to make the signing more palatable to the sheikh. By October, 1913, Lieutenant Colonel Sir Percy Cox had secured from the ever-obliging sheikh a letter wherein the sheikh agreed not to grant any concession for development of oil in the land 'to anyone other than a person nominated and recommended by the British government.'[6]

By 1902 it was known that the region of the Ottoman Empire known as Mesopotamia—today Iraq and Kuwait—contained resources of petroleum; how much and how accessible was still a matter for speculation. This discovery shaped the gigantic battle for global economic and military control which continues to the present day.

In 1912, Deutsche Bank, in the course of its financing of the Baghdad rail connection, negotiated a concession from the Ottoman emperor giving the Baghdad Rail Co. full 'right-of-way' rights to all oil and minerals on a parallel 20 kilometers either side of the rail line. The line had reached as far as Mosul in what today is Iraq.

By 1912, German industry and government had realized that oil was the fuel of its economic future, not only for land transport but for naval vessels. At that time, Germany was itself locked in the grip of the large American Rockefeller Standard Oil Company trust. Standard Oil's Deutsche Petroleums Verkaufgesellschaft controlled 91 per cent of all German oil sales. Deutsche Bank held a minority 9 per cent share of Deutsche Petroleums Verkaufgesellschaft, hardly a decisive interest. Germany in 1912 had no independent, secure supply of oil.

But geologists had discovered oil in that part of Mesopotamia today called Iraq, between Mosul and Baghdad. The projected line of the last part of the Berlin–Baghdad rail link would go right through the area believed to hold large oil reserves.

Efforts to pass legislation in the Berlin Reichstag in 1912–13 to establish a German state-owned company to develop and run the new found oil resources independently of the American Rockefeller

## AGREEMENT BY THE SHAIKH OF KUWAIT REGARDING THE NON-RECEPTION OF FOREIGN REPRESENTATIVES AND THE NON-CESSION OF TERRITORY TO FOREIGN POWERS OR SUBJECTS, 23RD JANUARY 1899.

The object of writing this lawful and honourable bond is that it is hereby covenanted and agreed between Lieutenant-Colonel Malcolm John Meade, I.S.C., Her Britannic Majesty's Political Resident, on behalf of the British Government on the one part, and Sheikh Mubarak-bin-Sheikh Subah, Sheikh of Koweit, on the other part, that the said Sheikh Mubarak-bin-Sheikh Subah of his own free will and desire does hereby pledge and bind himself, his heirs and successors not to receive the Agent or Representative of any Power or Government at Koweit, or at any other place within the limits of his territory, without the previous sanction of the British Government ; and he further binds himself, his heirs and successors not to cede, sell, lease, mortgage, or give for occupation or for any other purpose any portion of his territory to the Government or subjects of any other Power without the previous consent of Her Majesty's Government for these purposes. This engagement also to extend to any portion of the territory of the said Sheikh Mubarak, which may now be in the possession of the subjects of any other Government.

In token of the conclusion of this lawful and honourable bond, Lieutenant-Colonel Malcolm John Meade, I.S.C., Her Britannic Majesty's Political Resident in the Persian Gulf, and Sheikh Mubarak-bin-Sheikh Subah, the former on behalf of the British Government and the latter on behalf of himself, his heirs and successors do each, in the presence of witnesses, affix their signatures on this, the tenth day of Ramazan 1316, corresponding with the twenty-third day of January 1899.

| | |
|---|---|
| (Sd.) M. J. MEADE, | MUBARAK-AL-SUBAH. |
| *Political Resident in the* | |
| *Persian Gulf.* | (L.S.) |

### Witnesses.

| | |
|---|---|
| (Sd.) E. WICKHAM HORE, | MUHAMMAD RAHIM BIN |
| *Captain, I.M.S.* | ABDUL NEBI SAFFER. |
| (Sd.) J. CALCOTT GASKIN. | (L.S.) |

*Figure 1* Text of the remarkable 1899 agreement secured on behalf of the British government with Sheikh Mubarak al-Sabah of Kuwait. Since then, Britain has regarded Kuwait as its special sphere of interest in the Arabian Gulf.

## THE BAGHDAD RAILWAY.

(FROM OUR CORRESPONDENT.)

VIENNA, SEPT. 29.

My attention has been called to an important aspect of the rival Baghdad railway schemes. This is, that an arrangement between the three existing lines, that is to say, the German Anatolian Railway, the English Smyrna-Aidin line, and the French line from Smyrna to Afium Karahissar, via Kassaba, together with the adoption of the alternative German proposals for the extension of the Anatolian Railway to Baghdad and the Persian Gulf, would constitute the only project strategically acceptable and economically possible.

Two of the most essential strategic requirements of Turkey are an adequate system of communications radiating from the capital, which would facilitate the speedy despatch of troops to any point that may be threatened, and that the terminus of the Asiatic Railway system should be practically secure from possible attack by a hostile fleet. A terminus on the Bosporus fulfils that condition. Until this primary necessity has been provided it is not to be expected that the Sultan will ever consent to the construction of a line from the coast, and least of all from such an important strategic position as Alexandretta, the existence of which would enable a Power holding the sea to pour troops into the centre of his Asiatic dominions. This consideration will have been emphasized by the Padisha's German military advisers. On the other hand, one of the alternative extensions proposed by the Germans—namely, that starting from the present Angora terminus of the Anatolian railway—would place Constantinople in direct communication with the city of Diarbekr, which is recognized as the strategic centre of resistance to Russian designs upon Kurdistan and the Tigris valley. The second alternative route, proceeding from the present Konieh terminus through Aintab and Orfah, would also bring troops to the scene of action, while it is fairly secure from attack by a force landed on the coast.

## THE BAGDAD RAILWAY INTRIGUE.

The German railway interests in Asia Minor are trying very hard; and if Dr. Zander and his friends fail to get their project through it will not be for any lack of assiduity in playing every available card. Naturally, the press is not being neglected, and correspondents here, there, and everywhere are answering like marionettes to the wirepuller, and inserting in their journals convenient bits of information concerning the latest phase of the German Bagdad Railway scheme. The latest communication hails from Vienna, and as the *Times* correspondent in that city has passed on to his readers the inspired information he received, without any apparent exercise of his own critical faculty, it may assist the general knowledge if we supplement his letter by a few comments. The "important aspect" to which he says his attention has been called is "that "an arrangement between the three existing "lines—that is to say, the German Anatolian "Railway, the English Smyrna-Aidin line, "and the French line from Smyrna to Afium-"Karahissar, viá Kassaba — together with "the adoption of the alternative German "proposals for the extension of the Ana-"tolian Railway to Bagdad and the "Persian Gulf, would constitute the only "project strategically acceptable and eco-"nomically possible." This is a very inspired sentence, for it is not likely that the correspondent would have arrived at its conclusions on his own independent investigations, and it does not cost much cogitation to guess the source of the inspiration; and though the conclusion, measured by the standpoint of a regard for accuracy, falls short of the desired standard, it nevertheless does furnish us with an "important aspect" of the case. For it clearly intimates that Dr. Zander's scheme (announced from Berlin some two months ago, and commented on at the time in our columns) for constructing the

*Zeitungsartikel über die Bagdadbahn in der »Times« vom 3. 10. 1899 und den »Financial News« vom 6. 10. 1899.*

*Figure 2* The London *Times* (October 3, 1899) and *Financial News* (October 6, 1899) reveal the strong geopolitical views of leading British foreign-policy circles towards Germany's Baghdad Railway project.

combine were stalled and delayed until the outbreak of war in August 1914 pushed it from the agenda. The Deutsche Bank plan was to have the Baghdad rail link transport Mesopotamian oil over land, free from possible naval blockade by the British, thereby making Germany independent in its petroleum requirements.

## THE NEW DREADNOUGHTS

It was not until 1909 that Admiral Fisher's plans for Britain's oil-fired navy began to be implemented. Germany had just launched the first of its advanced improvement on the British Dreadnought series. The German *Von der Tann* carried 80,000 horsepower engines, which, while still coal-fired, were capable of a then-astounding 28 knots. Only two British ships could meet that speed. Britain's coal-fired fleet was at its technological limit and British naval supremacy was decisively threatened by the rapidly expanding German economic marvel.

By 1911, a young Winston Churchill had succeeded Lord Fisher as First Lord of the Admiralty. Churchill immediately began a campaign to implement Fisher's demand for an oil-fired navy. Using Fisher's arguments, Churchill pointed out that with ships of equal size, oil gives far greater speed, and per equal weight gives a decisive advantage in the domain of action without refueling.

In 1912, the United States produced more than 63 per cent of the world's petroleum, Russia's Baku 19 per cent and Mexico about 5 per cent. Britain's Anglo-Persian Exploration Co. was not yet producing major supplies of petroleum, but British government strategy had determined even then that a British presence in the Persian Gulf was essential to the national interest. As we have seen, Germany's relentless extension of the Berlin–Baghdad railway line played a significant role in this determination.

By July 1912, Prime Minister Asquith's government, on Churchill's urging, appointed a Royal Commission on Oil and the Oil Engine, chaired by the retired Lord Fisher. By early 1913, acting secretly, again at Churchill's urging, the British government bought up majority share ownership of Anglo-Persian Oil (today British Petroleum). From this point, oil was at the core of British strategic interest.[7]

If Britain could not only secure her own direct petroleum needs for the transport and energy technology of the future, but perhaps more decisive, if she could deny economic rivals their access to secure petroleum reserves in the world, her dominant role might be maintained into the next decades. In short, if Britain's stagnating industry could not compete with Germany's emerging Daimler motors, then she would control the raw material on which the Daimler motors must run. Just what this policy of British petroleum control implied for the course of world history will become clear.

## SIR EDWARD GREY'S FATEFUL PARIS TRIP

Why would Britain risk a world war in order to stop the development of Germany's industrial economy in 1914? The ultimate reason she declared war in August 1914 lay fundamentally 'in the old tradition of British policy, through which England grew to great power status, and through which she sought to remain a great power,' stated German banker Karl Helfferich in 1918. 'England's policy was always constructed against the politically and economically strongest Continental power,' he stressed.

Ever since Germany became the politically and economically strongest Continental power, did England feel threatened from Germany more than from any other land in its global economic position and its naval supremacy. Since that point, the English–German differences were unbridgeable, and susceptible to no agreement in any one single question.

Helfferich sadly notes the accuracy of the declaration of Bismarck from 1897: 'The only condition which could lead to improvement of German–English relations would be if we bridled our economic development, and this is not possible.'[8]

In April 1914, King George VII and his foreign minister, Sir Edward Grey, made an extraordinary visit to meet French President Poincaré in Paris. It was one of the few times Sir Edward Grey left the British Isles. Russia's ambassador to France, Iswolski, joined them and the three powers firmed up a secret military alliance against the German and Austro-Hungarian powers. Grey deliberately did not warn Germany beforehand of its secret alliance, whereby Britain would enter a war which engaged any one of the carefully constructed web of alliance partners she had built up against Germany.[9]

Many in the British establishment had determined well before 1914 that war was the only course suitable to bring the European situation under control. British interests dictated, according to her balance-of-power logic, a shift from the traditional 'pro-Ottoman and anti-Russian' alliance strategy of the nineteenth century, to a 'pro-

Russian and anti-German' alliance strategy. This shift was evident as early as the late 1890s, when the emerging alliance between France's Gabriel Hanotaux and Russia's Sergei Witte, together with an emerging industrial Germany, seemed imminent.

## FASHODA, WITTE, GREAT PROJECTS AND GREAT MISTAKES

Indeed, fear of the emerging German economic challenge towards the end of the 1890s was so extreme among the leading circles of the British establishment that Britain made a drastic change in her decades-long Continental alliance strategy, in a bold effort to tilt European events back to her own advantage.

A seminal event which crystallized this alliance shift was, oddly enough, an eyeball-to-eyeball military confrontation over Egypt, where historically both Britain and France had major interests through the Suez Canal Company. In 1898, French troops marching across the Sahara to the east, under Colonel Jean Marchand, encountered British forces under the command of General Kitchener at Fashoda on the Nile. A tense military showdown ensued, with each side ordering the other to withdraw, until finally, after consultation with Paris, Marchand withdrew. The Fashoda Crisis as it became known, ended in a de facto Anglo-French balance-of-power alliance against Germany, in which France foolishly ceded major opportunities to industrialize Africa.

The decision to send the French Expeditionary Force under Marchand to Fashoda for a head-on military confrontation with Britain in Africa came from Colonial Minister Théophile Delcassé. Britain had steadily moved to what became a de facto military occupation of Egypt and the Suez Canal, despite French claims to the area going back to Napoleon. Since 1882, British troops had 'temporarily' occupied Egypt, and British civil servants ran the government in order to 'protect' French and British interests in the Suez Canal Company. Britain was stealing Egypt from under the eyes of France.

Delcassé acted against the better interests of France and against the explicit policy design of French Foreign Minister Gabriel Hanotaux. Hanotaux, who was absent from government for a critical six months when the Fashoda folly was decided, had a conception of development and industrialization of France's African colonies. A republican who was known as an Anglophobe, Hanotaux had a conception of an economically unified French Africa centered around development of

Lake Chad, with a railroad linking the interior from Dakar in French Senegal to French Djibouti on the Red Sea. The idea was referred to in France as the Trans-Sahara railway project. It would have transformed the entirety of Saharan Africa from west to east. It would also have blocked major British strategic objectives to control the entire region from Africa, across Egypt and into India.

Hanotaux had carefully pursued a policy of normalizing relations between France and Germany, a most threatening development to British balance-of-power machinations. In early 1896, the German foreign secretary asked the French ambassador in Berlin if France would consider joint action in Africa for 'limiting the insatiable appetite of England ... [It] is necessary to show England that she can no longer take advantage of the Franco-German antagonism to seize whatever she wants.'

But then the infamous Dreyfus affair erupted in the French press. Its direct aim was to rupture the delicate efforts of Hanotaux to stabilize relations with Germany. A French army captain named Dreyfus was prosecuted on charges of spying for the Germans. Hanotaux intervened in the initial process in 1894, correctly warning that the Dreyfus affair would lead to 'a diplomatic rupture with Germany, even war.' Dreyfus was exonerated years later, and it was revealed that Count Ferdinand Walsin-Esterhazy, in the pay of the Rothschild banking family, had manufactured the evidence against Dreyfus. By 1898, Hanotaux was out of office and had been succeeded by the malleable Anglophile, Théophile Delcassé.

After Fashoda in 1898, Britain had skillfully enticed France, under Foreign Minister Delcassé, to give up fundamental colonial and economic interests in Egypt and concentrate on a French policy against Germany, in which Britain secretly agreed to back French claims on Alsace-Lorraine, as well as British support for French ambitions in other areas not vital to British designs. Describing these British diplomatic machinations around Fashoda some years later (in 1909), Hanotaux remarked:

It is an historical, proven fact that any colonial expansion of France has been seen with fear and concern in England. For a long time, England has thought that, in the domination of the Seas, she has no other rival to consider than that power endowed by nature with a triple coastline of the Channel, the Atlantic and the Mediterranean Sea. And when, after 1880, France, induced by the circumstances and stimulated by the genius of Jules Ferry, began to reconstitute her dismembered colonial domain, she came up against the same resistance. In Egypt, in Tunisia, Madagascar, Indo-china, even the Congo and Oceania, it is always England she confronts.

After Fashoda, the Entente Cordiale was fashioned, and ultimately formalized in a secret agreement between France and Britain, signed by Delcassé, Hanotaux's successor, in 1904. Germany's economic threat was the glue binding the two unlikely allies. Commenting on this sad turn of events afterwards, Hanotaux noted the success with which Britain had imposed a new foreign policy on France, 'a marvelous invention of English diplomatic genius to divide its adversaries.'

Over the next eight years, Britain reversed its geopolitical alliance policy in another profound matter as well, and shifted developments in Russia to British advantage. Beginning in 1891, Russia had embarked on an ambitious industrialization program, with the passage of a stringent protective tariff and a railroad infrastructure program. In 1892, the man responsible for the railroad plan, Count Sergei Witte, became minister of finance. Witte had enjoyed close relations with France's Hanotaux and a positive basis for Franco-Russian relations developed around the construction of the railway system in Russia.

The most ambitious project initiated in Russia at that time had been the construction of a railroad linking Russia in the west to Vladivostock in the Far East—the Trans-Siberian railway project, a 5,400 mile-long undertaking, which would transform the entire economy of Russia. This was the most ambitious rail project in the world. Witte himself was a profound student of the German economic model of Friedrich List, having translated into Russian List's 'National System of Political Economy', which Witte termed 'the solution for Russia.'

Witte spoke of the rail project's effect on uplifting the culturally backward regions of the interior. In 1890, he wrote:

The railroad is like a leaven which creates a cultural fermentation among the population. Even if it is passed through an absolutely wild people along the way, it would raise them in a short time to the level requisite for its operation.

A central part of Witte's plan was to develop peaceful and productive relations with China, independent of British control of China's ports and sea-lanes, through the overland openings which the Siberian rail line would facilitate.

As finance minister from 1892 until he was deposed during the suspiciously timed 1905 Russian 'revolution,' Witte transformed Russia's prospects dramatically from its former role as 'breadbasket' to British grain-trading houses, into a potentially modern industrial nation. Railroads became the largest industry in the country and were inducing a transformation of the entire range of related steel and other sectors. Furthermore, Witte's friend and close collaborator, the scientist Dimitri Mendeleyev, who had founded Russian agrochemistry based on the ideas of the German Justus von Liebig, was appointed by Witte to head a new Office of Standard Weights and Measures, in which he introduced the metric system to further facilitate trade with the Continent of Europe.

Britain energetically opposed the economic policies of Witte and the Trans-Siberian railway project with every means at its disposal, including attempts to influence reactionary Russian landed nobility linked to the British grain trade. Shortly after the inception of the Trans-Siberian rail project, a British commentator, A. Colqhum, expressed the dominant views of the British Foreign Office and the City of London. Referring to the new Russian rail project, undertaken with French financing and which would ultimately link Paris to Moscow to Vladivostok by rail, Colqhum declared:

> This line will not only be one of the greatest trade routes that the world has ever known, but it will also become a political weapon in the hands of the Russians whose power and significance it is difficult to estimate. It will make a single nation out of Russia, for whom it will no longer be necessary to pass through the Dardanelles or through the Suez Canal. It will give her an economic independence, through which she will become stronger than she has ever been or ever dreamed of becoming.

For decades, the British balance-of-power alliance strategy in Europe had been built around support for Ottoman Turkey's empire, as part of what British strategists called the Great Game—blocking the emergence of a strong and industrialized Russia. Support for Turkey, which controlled the vital Dardanelles access to warm waters for Russia, had been a vital part of British geopolitics until that time. But as German economic links with the Ottoman Empire grew stronger at the end of the century and into the early 1900s, so too did British overtures to Russia, and against Turkey and Germany.

It took a series of wars and crises, but following unsuccessful British attempts to block Russia's Trans-Siberian railway to Vladivostok, which the Russians largely completed in 1903, Russia was badly humiliated in the Russo-Japanese War in 1905, in which Britain had allied with Japan against Russia. After 1905, Witte was forced to resign his position as chairman of the Council of Ministers under Czar Nicholas II. His successor argued that Russia must come to terms with British power, and proceeded to sign over to the British the rights to Afghanistan and large parts of Persia, and agreed to curtail Russian ambitions in Asia significantly. Thus, a British–French–Russian Triple Entente in effect had been fully established by 1907. Britain had created a web of secret alliances encircling Germany, and had laid the foundations for the coming military showdown with the Kaiser's Reich. The next seven years were ones of preparation for the final elimination of the German threat.[10]

Following British consolidation of its new Triple Entente strategy of encirclement of Germany and her allies, a series of continuous crises and regional wars were unleashed in the Balkans, the 'soft underbelly' of Central Europe. In the so-called First Balkan War of 1912, Serbia, Bulgaria and Greece, secretly backed by England, declared war against the weak Ottoman Turkey, resulting in stripping Turkey of most of her European possessions. This was followed in 1913 by a second Balkan War over the spoils of the first, in which Romania joined to help crush Bulgaria. The stage was being set for Britain's great European war.

Three months after Edward Grey's Paris talks, on July 28, 1914, Archduke Franz Ferdinand, heir to the Austrian throne, was assassinated in Sarajevo by a Serb, setting off a predictably tragic chain of events which detonated the Great War.

# 4
# Oil Becomes the Weapon, the Near East the Battleground

One of the better kept secrets of the 1914–18 world war was that on the eve of August 1914, when Britain declared war against the German Reich, the British Treasury and the finances of the British Empire were in effect bankrupt. An examination of the actual financial relations of the principal parties to the war reveals an extraordinary background of secret credits, coupled with detailed plans to reallocate the raw materials and physical wealth of the entire world after the war, especially those areas of the Ottoman Empire believed to hold significant petroleum reserves.

By most accounts, the trigger detonating the Great War was pulled by a Serbian assassin on June 28, 1914, at the Bosnian capital Sarajevo, when he murdered Archduke Franz Ferdinand, heir to the Austro-Hungarian throne. Following a month of frenzied negotiations, Austria declared war on July 28 against the tiny state of Serbia, holding her responsible for the assassination. Austria had been assured of German support should Russia back Serbia. The following day, July 29, Russia ordered mobilization of her army in the event of war becoming necessary.

That same day, the German Kaiser sent a telegram to Czar Nicholas begging the czar not to mobilize, and causing the czar momentarily to rescind his order. On July 30, the Russian High Command persuaded the hesitant czar to resume the mobilization. On July 31, the German ambassador to St. Petersburg handed the czar a German declaration of war against Russia, then reportedly burst into tears and ran from the room.

The German General Staff, having been prepared for possible war on both eastern and western fronts, implemented its Schlieffen plan. As France and Russia had mutual defense commitments, Germany decided that France must be defeated swiftly, correctly calculating that Russia would be slower to mobilize. On August 3, 1914, Germany declared war on France, and German troops entered Belgium en route to attack France.

Then, on August 4, only eight days after Austria's declaration of war against tiny Serbia, Britain announced it had declared war against Germany. The nominal reason given was Britain's prior commitment to protecting Belgian neutrality. The actual reasons were far from any spirit of neighborly charity.

Britain's decision in August 1914 to go to war against Germany on the Continent was remarkable to say the least, given that the British Treasury and the pound sterling system, the then-dominant currency system of world trade and finance, were de facto bankrupt. Recently declassified internal memoranda from the British Treasury staff of then-Chancellor of the Exchequer Lloyd George raise further questions. In January 1914, a full six months before the nominal *casus belli* at Sarajevo, Sir George Paish, senior British Treasury official, was asked by the chancellor to make a definitive study of the state of the all-important British gold reserves.

In 1914, the sterling gold standard was the prop of the world monetary system. In fact, sterling had been so much accepted in international commerce and finance for more than 75 years that sterling itself was considered 'as good as gold.' Sterling in 1914 played a role comparable to that of the US dollar before August 15, 1971.

Sir George's confidential memorandum reveals the thinking of the highest levels of the City of London at the time:

> Another influence fanning the agitation for banking reform has been the growing commercial and banking power of Germany, and the growth of uneasiness lest the gold reserves of London should be raided just before or at the beginning of a great conflict between the two countries.

This confidential report was written more than six months before the heir to the Austrian throne was assassinated in Sarajevo.

Paish then discussed his concern over the growing sophistication of the large German trade banks following the 1911–12 Balkan crisis, which had led the German banks to stock up their gold reserves. Sir George warned his chancellor that any future run on the banks of London, under prevailing conditions, 'might seriously hamper a nation in raising money to conduct a great war.'[1]

On May 22, 1914, a senior British Treasury official, Basil Blackett, drafted another confidential memorandum for Lloyd George.

This memo dealt with the 'Effect of War on Our Gold Reserves.' Blackett writes,

> It is of course impossible clearly to forecast what would be the effect of a general European war in which most of the Continental countries as well as Great Britain were engaged, leaving only New York (assuming the neutrality of the United States) among the big money markets of the world available from which gold could be attracted to the seats of war.

Equally astonishing, in light of Britain's decision to go to war that fateful August 4, was a letter from Sir George Paish to Lloyd George dated 2 A.M., Saturday morning, August 1, 1914:

> Dear Mr. Chancellor,
> The credit system upon which the business of this country is formed, has completely broken down, and it is of supreme importance that steps should be taken to repair the mischief without delay; otherwise, we cannot hope to finance a great war if, at its very commencement, our greatest houses are forced into bankruptcy.[2]

Specie payments (gold and silver bullion) were promptly suspended by the Bank of England, along with the Bank Act of 1844. This decision placed large sums of gold into the hands of the Bank of England, in order that Britain's government could finance food and war *matériel* purchases for the newly declared war against Germany. Instead of gold, British citizens were given Bank of England notes as legal tender for the duration of the emergency. By August 4, the British financial establishment was ready for war.

But, as we shall soon see, the secret weapon was to emerge later: the special relationship of His Majesty's Treasury with the New York banking syndicate of Morgan.

## OIL IN THE GREAT WAR

Between 1914 when fighting began and 1918 when it ended, petroleum had emerged as the recognized key to success of a revolution in military strategy. In the age of air warfare, mobile tank warfare and swifter naval warfare, abundant and secure supplies of the new fuel were becoming increasingly essential.

Under the foreign policy guidance of Sir Edward Grey, Britain, in the months leading up to August 1914, precipitated what was to become the bloodiest, most destructive war in modern history. According to official statistics, deaths due to the war, directly or indirectly, numbered between 16,000,000 and 20,000,000, with the great majority, 10,000,000 or more, being civilian deaths. The British Empire itself incurred more than 500,000 dead and total casualties of almost 2,500,000 in the four-year-long world 'war to end all wars.'

Rarely discussed, however, is the fact that the strategic geopolitical objectives of Britain, well before 1914, included not merely the crushing of its greatest industrial rival, Germany, but, through the conquest of war, the securing of unchallenged British control over the precious resource which, by 1919, had proved itself as the strategic raw material of future economic development—petroleum. This was part of the Great Game—the creation of a new global British Empire, whose hegemony would be unchallenged for the rest of the century, a British-led New World Order.

A study of the major theatres of the 1914–18 war reveals the extent to which securing petroleum supplies was already at the center of military planning. Oil had opened the door for a terrifying new mobility in modern warfare during the course of the war. The German campaign in Romania, under Field Marshal von Mackensen, had the priority of reorganizing into a single combine, Steaua Romana, the previously English, Dutch, French and Romanian oil-refining, production and pipeline capacities. Romania during the course of the war was the only secure German petroleum supply for her entire air force, tank forces, and U-boat fleet. The British campaign in the Dardanelles, the disastrous defeat at Gallipoli, was undertaken to secure the oil supplies of the Russian Baku for the Anglo-French war effort. The Ottoman sultan had embargoed the shipping out of Russian oil via the Dardanelles.

By 1918, the rich Russian oil fields of Baku on the Caspian Sea were the object of intense military and political effort on the part of Germany, and also of Britain, which pre-emptively occupied them for a critical period of weeks in August 1918, denying the German General Staff vital oil supplies. Denial of Baku was a decisive last blow against Germany, which sued for peace some weeks later, only months after it had seemed that Germany had defeated the Allied forces. Oil had proved to be at the center of geopolitics.

By the end of the First World War, no major power was unaware of the vital strategic importance of the new fuel, petroleum, for future military and economic security. At the end of the war, fully 40 per cent of the British naval fleet was oil fired. In 1914, at the onset of the war, the French army had a mere 110 trucks, 60 tractors and 132 airplanes. By 1918, four years later, this had increased to 70,000 trucks and 12,000 airplanes, while the British, and in the final months the Americans, put 105,000 trucks and over 4,000 airplanes into combat service. The final British–French–American offensives of the war on the Western Front consumed a staggering 12,000 barrels of oil per day.

By December 1917, French supplies of oil had become so low that General Foch pressed President Clemenceau to send an urgent appeal to President Woodrow Wilson. 'A failure in the supply of petrol would cause the immediate paralysis of our armies, and might compel us to a peace unfavorable to the Allies,' Clemenceau wrote to Wilson.

> The safety of the Allies is in the balance. If the Allies do not wish to lose the war, then, at the moment of the great German offensive, they must not let France lack the petrol which is as necessary as blood in the battles of tomorrow.

Rockefeller's Standard Oil group answered Clemenceau's appeal, giving Marshall Foch's forces vital petrol. Lacking a sufficient Romanian oil supply, as well as access to Baku, German forces were unable to successfully mount a final offensive in 1918 (despite the Russian–German Brest–Litovsk agreement to cease hostilities) as the trucks necessary to bring sufficient reserves were unable to secure petrol.

Britain's foreign minister, Lord Curzon, commented, quite accurately:

> The Allies were carried to victory on a flood of oil ... With the commencement of the war, oil and its products began to rank as among the principal agents by which they [the Allied forces] would conduct, and by which they could win it. Without oil, how could they have procured the mobility of the fleet, the transport of their troops, or the manufacture of several explosives?

The occasion was a November 21, 1918, victory dinner, ten days after the Armistice which ended the war. France's Senator Henry Berenger, director of the wartime Comité Général du Petrole, added that oil was the 'blood of victory. Germany had boasted too much of its superiority in iron and coal, but it had not taken sufficient account of our superiority of oil.'[3]

With this emerging role of petroleum in the war, we should now follow the thread of the postwar Versailles reorganization, with a special eye to British objectives.

Britain's creation of the League of Nations through the Versailles Peace Conference in 1919 became a vehicle for giving a facade of international legitimacy to a naked imperial seizure of territory. For the financial establishment of the City of London, the expenditure of hundreds of thousands of British lives was a seemingly small price to pay in order to dominate future world economic development through the control of raw materials, especially of the new resource, oil.

## BRITAIN'S SECRET EASTERN WAR

If anything demonstrated the hidden agenda of the Allied powers in the 1914–18 war against the Central Powers grouped around Germany, Austria–Hungary and Ottoman Turkey, it was a secret diplomatic accord signed in 1916, during the heat of battle. The signatories were Britain, France and later Italy and czarist Russia. Named after the two officials, British and French, who drafted the paper, the Sykes–Picot agreement spelled out betrayal and Britain's intent to grab commanding control of the undeveloped petroleum potentials of the Arabian Gulf after the war.

While France was occupied with Germany, in a bloody and fruitless slaughter along the French Maginot Line, Britain moved an astonishingly large number of its own soldiers, more than 1,400,000 troops, into the eastern theatre.

Britain's public explanation for this extraordinary commitment of scarce men and *matériel* to the eastern reaches of the Mediterranean and the Persian Gulf was that this would ensure the more effective fighting capacity of Russia against the Central Powers, as well as allowing Russian grain out through the Dardanelles into Western Europe, where it was badly in need.

This was not quite the reality however. After 1918, Britain continued to maintain almost a million soldiers stationed throughout the Middle East. The Persian Gulf had become a 'British Lake' by 1919. The angry French feebly protested that while millions of their forces bled on the Western Front, Britain took advantage of the stalemate to win

# THE PETROLEUM DEPOSITS OF MESOPOTAMIA.

## A SECOND BAKU IN THE MAKING.

According to all indications, the near future will witness the opening of the extensive oilfields of Mesopotamia, which have been mentioned in Babylonian railway, at last be opened for widespread use and international trade. The rôle to be played by Mesopotamian oil in the world's market may be of great

*Legend on map:*

Oilfields.
○ Asphalt Fields.
Bagdad Railway (in erection).
Projected Railway Lines.
Frontier of the Districts.
Frontier between Turkish and Persian Domains.

scriptures as well as in the Bible, and which in the form of asphalt contributed to the erection of the magnificent buildings of Babylon and Assyria.

The rich oil treasures of Mesopotamia will, with the aid of modern technical science and the new Bagdad magnitude and importance. The subject is also of political importance, as it is of great interest both to Germany and England, and if only the German bank which participates in the erection of the Bagdad railway line obtains concessions, the influence of Germany

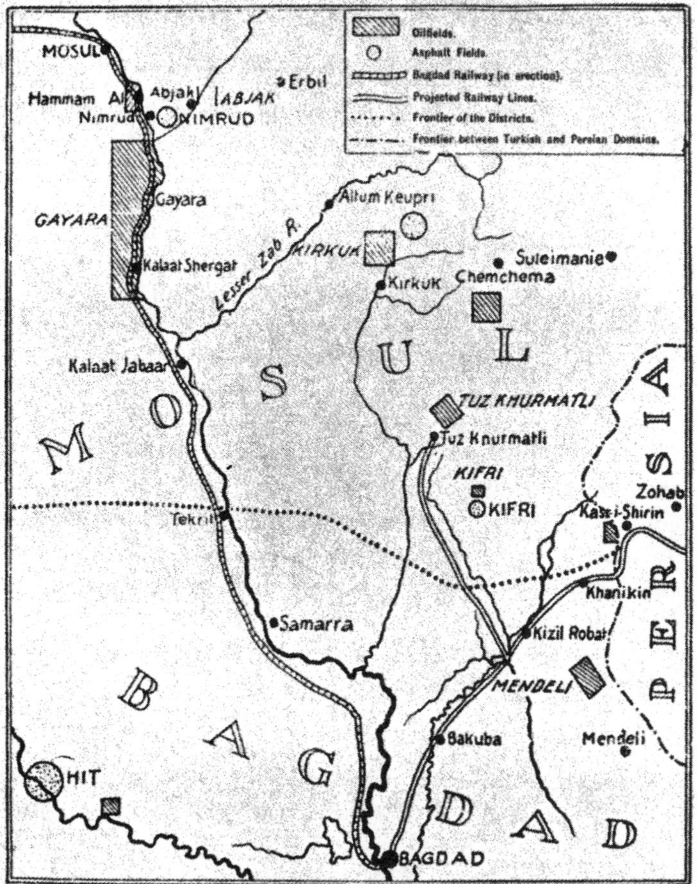

*Figure 3* Detailed map of the oilfields of Mesopotamia (present-day Iraq), from the London *Petroleum Review* dated May 23, 1914, before the outbreak of the First World War. These oilfields became British as a result of the war.

victories against the weaker Turkish Empire. France had lost almost 1,500,000 soldiers and another 2,600,000 were badly wounded.

In November 1917, following the Bolshevik seizure of power in Russia, Lenin's communists discovered among the documents of the czarist Foreign Ministry a secret document which they quickly made public. It was a plan of the great powers to carve up the entire Ottoman Empire after the war, and parcel out relevant parts to the victorious powers. The details had been worked out in February 1916, and were secretly ratified by the relevant governments in May 1916. The world at large knew nothing of this secret wartime diplomacy.

From the British side, Sir Mark Sykes, an adviser on eastern affairs to Lord Kitchener of Khartoum, secretary of state for war, drafted the document. The document was designed to secure French acquiescence to a huge diversion of British manpower from the European theatre into the Middle East. To get that French concession, Sykes was authorized to offer French negotiator Georges Picot, former consul general in Beirut, valuable postwar concessions in the Arab portion of the Ottoman Empire.

France was to get effective control over what was called 'Area A,' encompassing Greater Syria (Syria and Lebanon), including the major inland towns of Aleppo, Hama, Homs and Damascus, as well as the oil-rich Mosul to the northeast, including the oil concessions then held by Deutsche Bank in the Turkish Petroleum Gesellschaft. This French control paid nominal lip service to recognition of Arab 'independence' from Turkey, under a French 'protectorate.'

Under the Sykes–Picot accord, Britain would control 'Area B' in the region to the southeast of the French region, from what today is Jordan, east to most of Iraq and Kuwait, including Basra and Baghdad. Further, Britain was to get the ports of Haifa and Acre, and the rights to build a railway from Haifa through the French zone to Baghdad and to use it for troop transport.

Italy had been promised a huge section of the mountainous coastline of Turkish Anatolia and the Dodecanese Islands, while czarist Russia was to receive the areas of Ottoman Armenia and Kurdistan, southwest of Jerevan.[4]

Out of these secret Sykes–Picot paragraphs, the British created the arbitrary divisions which largely exist through the present day, including the creation of Syria and Lebanon as French 'protectorates,' and Trans-Jordan, Palestine (Israel), Iraq and Kuwait as British entities. Persia, as we have seen, had been in effective British control since 1905, and Saudi Arabia was considered at that point unimportant to

British strategic interests—one of their few major blunders, as they were later to realize to their great dismay.

Britain had been forced, through her relative weakness following the disastrous failure of the Gallipoli expedition in 1915, to grant France the oil concessions of the Mosul, in addition to recognition of previous French claims over the Levant. But Britain's loss of the Mosul oil riches was only a temporary tactical expedient in her long-term designs to dominate world petroleum supplies, as we shall see.

## 'SELLING THE SAME HORSE TWICE'

The major embarrassment for Britain, when details of the secret Sykes–Picot agreement became public, was the simultaneous and directly contradictory assurances England had given Arab leaders, in order to secure Arab revolt against Turkish rule during the war.

Britain had gained the invaluable military assistance of Arab forces under Sherif Husain ibn Ali, the Hashemite emir of Mecca, and guardian of the Muslim holy places of Mecca and Medina. Britain had assured the Arab forces who served under the command of T.E. Lawrence ('Lawrence of Arabia') that the reward for their help in defeating the Turks would be British assurance of full postwar Arab sovereignty and independence. The assurances were contained in a series of letters from Sir Henry McMahon, Britain's high commissioner in Egypt, to Sherif Husain of Mecca, then self-proclaimed leader of the Arabs.

Lawrence was fully aware of the British fraud to the Arabs at the time. As he admitted some years later in his memoirs,

I risked the fraud on my conviction that Arab help was necessary to our cheap and speedy victory in the East, and that better we win and break our word, than lose … The Arab inspiration was our main tool for winning the Eastern war. So I assured them that England kept her word in letter and spirit. In this comfort they performed their fine things; but of course, instead of being proud of what we did together, I was continually and bitterly ashamed.[5]

The loss of 100,000 Arab lives was part of this 'cheap and speedy victory.' Britain quickly betrayed her promises in a move to secure for herself the vast oil and political riches of the Arab Middle East.

To add insult to injury, once publication of Sykes–Picot had revealed a contrary commitment to France in the Middle East, Britain and France issued a new Anglo-French declaration on November 7, 1918, four days before the European Armistice ending the war with Germany. The new declaration insisted that Britain and France were fighting for 'the complete and definite emancipation of the peoples so long oppressed by the Turks, and the establishment of national governments and administrations deriving their authority from the initiative and free choice of the indigenous populations.'[6] That noble result was not to happen. Once the solemn pledges of Versailles had been signed, Britain, with its approximately 1-million-strong military force in the region, established its military supremacy over the French area of the Middle East as well.

By September 30, 1918, France had agreed to British terms for creating what were called 'zones of temporary military occupation.' Under this agreement, the British would occupy Turkish Palestine, under what was called Occupied Enemy Territory Administration, along with the other parts of the British sphere.

Recognizing the French inability to deploy sufficient troops into the designated French areas after the exhaustion of war in Europe, Britain generously offered to act as the overall supreme military and administrative guardian, with General Sir Edmund Allenby, commander-in-chief of the Egyptian Expeditionary Force, as the de facto military dictator over the entire Arab Middle East after 1918, including the French sphere. In a private discussion in London in December, 1918, British Prime Minister Lloyd George told France's Clemenceau that Britain wanted France to attach the 'Mosul to Iraq, and Palestine from Dan to Beersheba under British control.' In return France was said to have been assured of the remaining claims to Greater Syria, as well as a half share in the exploitation of Mosul oil, and a guarantee of British support in the postwar period in Europe, should France ever have to 'respond' to German action on the Rhine.[7] This private understanding set the stage for later events in a profoundly tragic manner, as we shall see.

## ARTHUR BALFOUR'S STRANGE LETTER TO LORD ROTHSCHILD

But postwar British designs for redrawing the military and economic map of the Ottoman Empire included an extraordinary new element— all the more extraordinary in that many of the most influential advocates of the creation of a Jewish homeland in Palestine, including Lloyd George, were British 'gentile Zionists'.[8]

On November 2, 1917, in the darkest days of the Great War, with Russia's war effort on behalf of the Anglo-French alliance collapsing under economic chaos and the Bolshevik seizure of power, and with the might of America not yet fully engaged in Europe as a combatant on the side of Britain, Britain's foreign secretary, Arthur Balfour, sent the following letter to Walter Lord Rothschild, representative of the English Federation of Zionists:

> Dear Lord Rothschild, I have much pleasure in conveying to you, on behalf of His Majesty's Government, the following declaration of sympathy with Jewish Zionist aspirations which has been submitted to, and approved by, the Cabinet:
> 'His Majesty's Government view with favour the establishment in Palestine of a national home for the Jewish people, and will use their best endeavours for the achievement of this object, it being clearly understood that nothing shall be done which may prejudice the civil and religious rights of existing non-Jewish communities in Palestine, or the rights and political status enjoyed by Jews in any other country.' I should be grateful if you would bring this declaration to the knowledge of the Zionist Federation. Yours sincerely, Arthur James Balfour.[9]

The letter formed the basis on which a post-1919 British League of Nations mandate over Palestine was established under whose guiding hand territorial changes of global consequence were to be wrought. The almost casual reference to 'existing non-Jewish communities in Palestine' by Balfour and the cabinet was a reference to the more than 85 per cent of the population who were Palestinian Arabs; in 1917, less than 1 per cent of the inhabitants of Palestine were Jewish.

It is notable that the letter was an exchange between two close friends. Both Balfour and Lord Rothschild were members of an emerging imperialist faction in Britain, which sought to create an enduring global empire, one based on more sophisticated methods of social control.

Also notable is the fact that Lord Rothschild spoke, not as head of any international organization of Jewry, but rather as a member of the English Federation of Zionists, whose president at the time was Chaim Weizmann. Rothschild money had essentially created that organization, and had subsidized the emigration to Palestine of hundreds of Jews, fleeing Poland and Russia since 1900, through the Jewish Colonisation Association of which Lord Rothschild was president for life. Britain was generous in offering lands far away from her shores, while in the same period she was far from open-armed in welcoming persecuted Jewish refugees to her own shores.

But more relevant than the evident hypocrisy in the Balfour–Rothschild exchange was the British Great Game, which lay behind the Balfour note. It is not insignificant that the geographical location for the new British-sponsored Jewish homeland lay in one of the most strategic areas along the main artery of the enlarged post-1914 British Empire, in a sensitive position along the route to India as well as in relation to the newly won Arab petroleum lands of Ottoman Turkey. The settlement of a Jewish minority under British protectorate in Palestine, argued Balfour and others in London, would give London strategic possibilities of enormous importance. It was, to say the least, a cynical ploy on the part of Balfour and his circle.

## BALFOUR BACKS THE NEW CONCEPT OF EMPIRE

Beginning approximately in the early 1890s, a group of British elites, primarily from the privileged colleges of Oxford and Cambridge, formed what was to become the most influential policy network in Britain over the next half century and more. The group denied its existence as a formal group, but its footprints can be found around the establishment of a new journal of empire, the *Round Table*, founded in 1910.

The group argued that a more subtle and efficient system of global empire was required to extend the effective hegemony of Anglo-Saxon culture over the next century.

At the time of its inception, this 'Round Table' group as it was sometimes called, was explicitly anti-German and pro-Empire. Writing in the *Round Table* in August 1911, three years before Britain declared war against Germany, the influential Philip Kerr (Lord Lothian) declared:

There are at present two codes of international morality—the British or Anglo-Saxon and the continental or German. Both cannot prevail. If the British Empire is not strong enough to be a real influence for fair dealing between nations, the reactionary standards of the German bureaucracy will triumph, and it will then only be a question of time before the British Empire itself is victimized by an international 'hold-up' on the lines of the Agadir incident. Unless the British people are strong enough to make it impossible for backward rivals to attack them with any prospect of success, they will have to accept the political standards of the aggressive military powers.[10]

In place of the costly military occupation of the colonies of the British Empire, they argued for a more repressive tolerance, calling for the creation of a British 'Commonwealth of Nations.' Members nations were to be given the illusion of independence, enabling Britain to reduce the high costs of far-flung armies of occupation from India to Egypt, and now across Africa and the Middle East as well. The term 'informal empire' was sometimes used to describe the shift.

This emerging faction was grouped around the influential London *Times*, and included such voices as Foreign Secretary Albert Lord Grey, historian and member of British secret intelligence Arnold Toynbee, as well as H.G. Wells, Alfred Lord Milner of the South Africa project, and the proponent of a new field termed geopolitics, Halford J. Mackinder of the London School of Economics. Its principal think tank, which was formed in the corridors of Versailles in 1919, became the Royal Institute for International Affairs (Chatham House).

The idea of a Jewish-dominated Palestine, beholden to England for its tenuous survival, surrounded by a balkanized group of squabbling Arab states, formed part of this group's concept of a new British Empire. Mackinder, commenting at the time of the Versailles peace conference, described his influential group's vision of the role a British protectorate over Palestine would play in the Great Game of British advance toward a post-1918 global empire, to be shaped around a British-defined and dominated League of Nations.

Mackinder described how the more far-thinking of the British establishment viewed their Palestine project in 1919:

> If the World-Island be inevitably the principal seat of humanity on this globe, and if Arabia, as the passage-land from Europe to the Indies and from the Northern to the Southern Heartland, be central to the World-Island, then the hill citadel of Jerusalem has a strategical position with reference to world-realities not differing essentially from its ideal position in the perspective of the Middle Ages, or its strategical position between ancient Babylon and Egypt.

He noted that

> the Suez Canal carries the rich traffic between the Indies and Europe to within striking distance of an army based on Palestine,

and already the trunk railway is being built through the coastal plain by Jaffa, which will connect the Southern with the Northern Heartland.

Commenting on the special significance of the thinking behind his friend Balfour's 1917 proposal to Lord Rothschild, Mackinder noted:

> The Jewish national seat in Palestine will be one of the most important outcomes of the war. That is a subject on which we can now afford to speak the truth ... a national home at the physical and historical centre of the world, should make the Jew 'range' [sic] himself ... There are those who try to distinguish between the Jewish religion and the Hebrew race, but surely the popular view of their broad identity is not far wrong.[11]

The Round Table group's grand design was to link England's vast colonial possessions, from the gold and diamond mines of Cecil Rhodes and Rothschild's Consolidated Gold Fields in South Africa, north to Egypt and the vital shipping route through the Suez Canal, and on through Mesopotamia, Kuwait and Persia into India in the East.

The British conquest of the German colony of Tanganyika (German East Africa) in central Africa in 1916, was not a decisive battle in a war to bring Germany to the peace table, but rather the completion of a vital link in this chain of British imperial control, from the Cape of Good Hope to Cairo.

The great power able to control this vast reach would control the world's most valuable strategic raw materials, from gold, basis of the international gold standard for world trade, to petroleum, in 1919 emerging as the energy source of the modern industrial era.

This remains a geopolitical reality every bit as much during the early years of the twenty-first century as it was in 1919. With such control, every nation on earth would fall under the scepter of the Britannic Empire. Until his death in 1902, Cecil Rhodes was the prime financial backer of this elite new 'informal empire' group.

The Boer War (1899–1902) was a project of the group, financed and personally instigated by Rhodes in order to secure firm British control of the vast mineral wealth of the Transvaal, at that time in control of the Boer minority, who were of Dutch origin. The war itself, in which Winston Churchill rose to public notice, was precipitated by Rhodes and Alfred Milner, and others of their circle, in order to bring what was believed to be the world's richest gold-producing region firmly under British control.

The Transvaal was the site of the world's largest gold discovery since the 1848 California Gold Rush, and its capture was essential to the continued role of London as the capital of the world's financial system and of its gold standard. Lord Milner, Jan Smuts and Rhodes were all part of the new empire faction which, as part of the Great Game, defeated the independent Boers and created a Union of South Africa.[12]

By 1920, Britain had succeeded in establishing firm control over all of southern Africa, including the former German South West Africa, as well as the vast newly discovered petroleum wealth of the former Ottoman Empire, by means of her military presence, conflicting promises and the establishment of a British protectorate over Palestine as a new Jewish homeland. But all accounts were not quite in order in 1920. The British Empire had come out of the war as bankrupt as she entered it, if not more so.

# 5
# Combined and Conflicting Goals: The United States Rivals Britain

## MORGAN FINANCES THE BRITISH WAR

Britain emerged from the deliberations of the 1919 Versailles conference in most apparent respects the dominant superpower in the world. One small detail, pushed to the background during the actual conduct of war between 1914 and 1918, however, was that this victory was secured on borrowed money.

American savings amounting to billions of dollars, organized by the Wall Street house of J.P. Morgan & Co., were a decisive component of the British victory. At the time of the Versailles peace conference in 1919, Britain owed the United States the staggering sum of $4.7 billion in war debts, while its own domestic economy was in a deep postwar depression, its industry in shambles, and domestic price inflation 300 per cent higher after the four years of war. The British national debt had increased more than ninefold, some 924 per cent between 1913 and the end of the war in 1918, to the then-enormous sum of £7.4 billion.

If Britain emerged as the territorial victor of Versailles, the United States, or at least certain powerful international banking and industrial interests, emerged in the early 1920s with the clear idea that they, and no longer Britain, were now the most powerful world economic power. For the next several years, a bitter power struggle took place between British and American international interests to settle this question.

By the beginning of the 1920s, the three pillars of British imperial power—control of world sea-lanes, control of world banking and finance, and control of strategic raw materials—were each under threat from a newly created American 'internationalist' establishment. Trained for decades by London, this once Anglophile American grouping decided it need no longer remain the docile pupil. Over the following decade, a bitter struggle was fought between the combined but conflicting goals of Britain and the United States. The seeds of the Second World War were planted in this same conflict.

The stakes were enormous. Would the United States emerge as the world's dominant political superpower by virtue of her economic status? Or would she remain a useful, but distinctly junior partner, in a British dominated Anglo-American condominium after Versailles? In other words, would the capital of the new world empire after Versailles remains London, or would it become Washington? The answer was not at all obvious in 1920.

Indicative of the intensity of this Anglo-American economic and political rivalry was a dispatch in 1921 from the British ambassador to Washington, who told his Foreign Office in London:

> The central ambition of the realist school of American politicians is to win for America the position of leading nation in the world, and also of leader among the English-speaking nations. To do this, they intend to have the strongest navy and the largest mercantile marine. They intend also to prevent us from paying our debt by sending goods to America and they look for an opportunity to treat us as a vassal state so long as our debt remains unpaid.[1]

Since the 1870s, Britain's most important market for foreign investment, in the form of railroad and other investments, had been the United States, through relations built up with select New York banking houses. Accordingly, in October 1914, the British War Office dispatched a special representative to neutral America, to arrange purchase of war materials and other vital supplies for what was then expected to be a relatively short war.

By January 1915, four months into the Great War, the British government had named a private New York banking house, J.P. Morgan & Co., to be its sole purchasing agent for all war supplies from the United States. Morgan was designated Britain's exclusive financial agent for all British war lending from private U.S. banks as well. In a short time, Britain in turn became the guarantor for all such war purchases and loans by the French, Italians and Russians in the war against the German–Austrian Continental powers. It was a giant credit pyramid on top of which sat the influential American house of Morgan. Never had a single banking house gambled on such high and risky global stakes.

The British Empire and Britain herself were virtually bankrupt at the outbreak of war in 1914, as we have noted. But British financial officials were confident of the backing of the United States and the Anglophile circles of New York banking.

The role of Morgan and the New York financial community was of supreme importance to the war efforts of the Entente powers. Under an exclusive arrangement, purchase of all American munitions and war materials, as well as necessary grains and food supplies for Britain, France and the other Allied powers in Europe, was funneled through the house of Morgan. Morgan also utilized its London affiliate, Morgan Grenfell & Co., whose senior partner, E.C. Grenfell, was a director of the Bank of England, and an intimate friend of Chancellor of the Exchequer Lloyd George. Morgan's Paris office, Morgan Harjes & Co., completed the essential Entente circle. Such power in the hands of a single investment house, given the scale of the British war requirements, was without precedent.

Morgan, with its franchise as sole purchasing agent for the entire Entente group, became virtual arbiter over the future of the U.S. industrial and agricultural export economy. Morgan decided who would, or would not, be favored with very sizeable and highly profitable export orders for the European war effort against Germany.

Firms such as DuPont Chemicals grew into multinational giants as a result of their privileged ties to Morgan. Remington and Winchester arms companies were also favored Morgan 'friends.' Major grain trading companies grew up in the Midwest as well, to feed Morgan's European clients. The relations were incestuous, as most of the Morgan loans raised privately for the British and French were raised through the corporate resources of DuPont and friends, in return for a guarantee of the huge European munitions market.

The position of this private banking house was all the more remarkable since Woodrow Wilson's White House at this time was professing strict neutrality. But that neutrality became a thinly veiled fraud, as billions of dollars of vital war supplies and credits flowed to the British side over the next years. As purchasing agent alone, Morgan took a 2 per cent commission on the net price of all goods shipped. The business grew so large that Morgan took in E.R. Stettinius, later to become Secretary of State, as a senior Morgan partner to handle war purchases for what was becoming a colossal operation.

All of this activity was in strict violation of international law regarding a neutral, which forbade allowing belligerents to build supply bases in neutral countries. Morgan himself was later charged in a U.S. Senate inquiry with having made excess profits, and with having directed purchases to firms in which Morgan partners had an interest. By 1917, the British War Office had placed purchase orders totaling more than $20,000,000,000 through the house of Morgan.

This is not to mention the direct loans raised by Britain, France and others through Morgan and his New York financial syndicate.

In 1915, U.S. Treasury Secretary McAdoo convinced a nervous President Wilson that such private American loans were necessary in order to 'maintain American exports.' The flows continued. By 1915, American exports to Britain had increased 68 per cent from the level of 1913. By the eve of the American entry into the war in 1917 on the side of Britain, the Entente powers had raised some $1,250,000,000 through the private efforts of Morgan, Citibank, and the other major New York investment houses, a staggering sum in that day. Morgan's relation to the financial powers of the newly created New York Federal Reserve Bank, under the control of former J.P. Morgan banker Governor Benjamin Strong, was essential to the success of the private financial mobilization. Even so, the risky enterprise several times threatened to break down.

The threat in January 1917 of British and French collapse, after Russia fell back in exhaustion from the war effort, provided more than enough incentive for Morgan and his New York financial syndicate to mobilize their combined propaganda and other resources. They did this with the careful assistance of the highest levels of British secret intelligence and friendly American press outlets, when it became clear that nothing else but American entry into the war would turn the looming disaster in Europe facing J.P. Morgan and Morgan's European clients. They organized that America would enter the European war on the 'right' side—in support of British interests. Morgan & Co., and Britain as well, faced complete financial ruin by early 1917 if they did not succeed.

Fortunately for Morgan and for London, German General Erich Ludendorff provided the basis for the Anglo-Morgan interests to avert financial ruin. In February 1917, Germany declared unrestricted submarine warfare, in an attempt to cut off the supply of American oil to the Allies, among other things. The sinking of American tankers was the excuse needed for the Morgan-controlled press to demand an end to American neutrality.[2]

Once the Congress of the United States declared war against Germany, on April 2, 1917, the New York financial community, with the backing of the New York Federal Reserve's Governor Strong, launched the most ambitious financial operation in history.

Had Woodrow Wilson not been persuaded to sign the Federal Reserve Act into law on December 23, 1913, it is questionable whether the United States would ever have committed the resources it did to a war in Europe. Without the new law, it is also doubtful whether Britain would have launched her bold designs against the rival empires of the Continent in August 1914. The house of Morgan and the powerful international financial interests of the City of London played the critical role in shaping a U.S. Federal Reserve System in the months just before outbreak of the European war.

In stark contrast to the German experience, with the Reichstag severely restricting financial speculation in the 1890s, the group of interests which shaped the Federal Reserve Act in 1913 were dominated by the elite circles of the house of Morgan, for the benefit of New York's emerging role as an international capital center. New York bankers were beginning to adopt the style of British imperial finance.

In August 1917, the Federal Reserve mobilized sales of Liberty Loans and bonds, to finance U.S. government war costs. Bonds of the U.S. Treasury sold to private investors in this great 'patriotic' mobilization were sold through Morgan and the other leading New York investment houses. The total of these Liberty Loans and bonds had reached the breathtaking sum of more than $21,478,000,000 by June 30, 1919. Never before in history had such sums been mobilized in so short a time. Morgan's commission on this business was handsome indeed.

By 1920, Morgan partner Thomas W. Lamont noted with obvious satisfaction that, as a result of the four years of war and global devastation, 'the national debts of the world have increased by $210,000,000,000 or about 475 per cent in the last six years, and as a natural consequence, the variety of government bonds and the number of investors in them have been greatly multiplied.' Lamont added, 'These results have made themselves manifest in all the investment markets of the world; but nowhere, perhaps, in greater measure than in the United States.'[3]

Once the house of Morgan and the allied New York investment community had tasted playing the role of the world's leading financial power, they seemed willing to do anything to keep their grip on that power.

Morgan's men, including Thomas Lamont, as well as fellow Wall Street crony Bernard Baruch, sat at the table during the closed-door Versailles sessions which drew up the 'bill' for the Great War. They jointly established a special Commission for Reparations, to be permanently established in order to devise the precise amount and means for Germany to repay its war damages to the Entente powers.

And, being good conservative bankers, Morgan and friends could not let the war loans of the Allied powers simply be forgotten in the euphoria of peace, despite the assumptions of A.J. Balfour and others in the British government that such magnanimity would follow. Morgan & Co. had quietly shifted their private British government loans over to the general debt of the U.S. Treasury as soon as the United States officially entered the war, in effect making the British debts the burden of the American taxpayers after the war. Despite this, Morgan interests made sure they had a major stake in the postwar Versailles reparations financing. As the U.S. war debt grew beyond anything known before in her history, the distinction between Morgan's interests and that of the government became blurred. The U.S. government increasingly made itself simply a useful instrument for the extension of the new power of New York's international bankers.

## NEW YORK BANKERS CHALLENGE THE CITY OF LONDON

During the course of the Versailles talks, a new institution of Anglo-American coordination in strategic affairs was formed. Lionel Curtis, a longtime member of the secretive Round Table or 'new empire' circle of Balfour, Milner and others, proposed organizing a Royal Institute of International Affairs. The proposal was made on May 30, 1919, in the midst of the Versailles deliberations, at a private gathering at the Hotel Majestic. Philip Kerr (Lord Lothian), Lord Robert Cecil and other members of the Round Table circle attended that formative meeting. The first nominal mission of the new institute would be to write the 'official' history of the Versailles peace conference. The Royal Institute received an initial endowment of £2,000 from Thomas Lamont of J.P. Morgan. Historian Arnold J. Toynbee was the institute's first paid staff member.

The same circle at Versailles also decided to establish an American branch of the London Institute, to be named the New York Council on Foreign Relations, so as to obscure its close British ties. The New York Council was initially composed almost entirely of the Morgan men, financed by Morgan money. It was hoped that this tie would serve to weld American interests into harmony with England's after Versailles. This was not to occur for some years, however.[4]

It took the entirety of the 1920s, in often bitter, almost military, conflicts over war-debt repayment terms, rubber agreements, naval accords, the parity of a new gold standard and most significantly, control of untapped oil regions of the world, before the Anglo-American condominium emerged in its present form, and before the policy harmony between the circles of Morgan's Council on Foreign Relations and London's Royal Institute could take hold. In 1922, a Wall Street lawyer, John Foster Dulles, a key participant at the Versailles talks, who had authored the Treaty's Article 231, the infamous German 'war guilt' clause, wrote in the Council on Foreign Affairs magazine *Foreign Affairs* about the thinking of Morgan and his fellow New York bankers. It was quite simple; he stated: 'There cannot be a war without losses. The resulting losses are measured by debts. The debt assumes varying forms—internal, reparations, Inter-allied, etc.—and is generally represented by bonds or notes.'

Dulles calculated that Britain and the other Allied powers owed the United States $12,500,000,000 at 5 per cent interest. Britain, France, and the other Entente countries, in turn, were owed by Germany, according to the Versailles demands, the sum of $33,000,000,000. The figures were beyond the scale of imagination at that time. The sum, 132 billion gold marks, was decided finally in May 1921. Germany was offered a six-day ultimatum to accept the terms; if she rejected them, the industrial Ruhr Valley would be militarily occupied. This latter issue was to reemerge soon afterwards with a global fight for oil playing a crucial motivating role in the background.

Germany, the main target of Versailles negotiators, had also lost valuable raw material resources, as all her colonial possessions had been taken away at Versailles. Her 25 per cent share of the Turkish Petroleum Gesellschaft was seized, and ultimately given over to France by Britain.

The American Congress refused to sign the Versailles Treaty and the included League of Nations apparatus to enforce it, but Morgan and the New York Federal Reserve axis proceeded to dominate the financial destiny of Europe in the postwar period. The combined burden of the Versailles German reparations debt, as well as the inter-Allied debts of the respective 'victors'—the war debts of France, Italy and Belgium to Britain, and in turn, of Britain to the United States—overwhelmed world finance and monetary policy from 1919 through to the October 1929 Wall Street crash. The entire pyramid of post-Versailles international finance was propped up on the edifice of the punitive war-debt structure. Morgan and the newly powerful New York banks refused to compromise on the debt issue.

The scale of the combined war debt burden of Europe was so large that its annual debt service demands on the world financial system were greater than the entire annual foreign trade of the United States during the 1920s. New York's international banking community redirected world capital flows to the service of this staggering debt burden. The debt servicing was carried out at the expense of the desperately needed investment in rebuilding and modernizing the war-torn economies of Europe.

J.P. Morgan & Co. enjoyed the competitive advantages provided by a devastated European economy, in which New York credit could dictate the terms. Profits from the new European lending were far greater than gains from investment in the postwar U.S. economic expansion. New York financial interests centered around Morgan and the New York Federal Reserve under Morgan's Benjamin Strong deliberately kept U.S. interest rates low. As a consequence, American loans flooded postwar Europe and the rest of the world, where capital earned a higher risk premium than at home, while London and a new Bank of England governor, Montagu Norman, looked on nervously at the American financial incursion into their traditional markets.

This early postwar Anglo-American rivalry in the vital area of banking reached an alarming level in 1924, when the United States threatened to co-opt the gold and raw materials center of the British Empire, secured only two decades earlier through the bloody Boer War. In late 1924, the South African government invited an international commission headed by American financial expert, Princeton Professor Edwin W. Kemmerer, to give advice on whether South Africa should return to an international gold standard, independently of Britain. As late as 1924, the devastation of the war had still prevented Britain from being able to return to a gold standard without suffering severe economic hardship, at a time when Britain still had one and a half million unemployed.

Kemmerer told the South Africans they should establish direct financial ties with New York banks and bypass their traditional dependence on London. As the powerful financial interests in the City of London well knew, this would open the door for the United States to economically co-opt what Britain had militarily fought to secure, and with it, gain dominant power over the world gold supply, and thereby power over world credit. London acted quickly to preempt this consequence, but the wound did not heal rapidly.[5]

British interests benefited from the much-discussed retreat of the United States during Versailles into a neo-isolationism. The U.S. Congress turned away from Wilson's support for the British League of Nations idea, as well as most features of the new world order emerging out of the Carthaginian Versailles deliberations. With America in the background, Britain could move aggressively in Europe, Africa and the Middle East to establish her vital long-term hegemony.

But it became increasingly clear that the powerful American banking and petroleum interests were anything but isolationist. British power must either defeat this threat, or effectively co-opt it into a new Atlantic union.

## BRITAIN MOVES FOR OIL SUPREMACY

The ink on the Versailles treaty had barely dried when the powerful American oil interests of the Rockefeller Standard Oil companies realized they had been skillfully cut out of the spoils of war by their British alliance partners. The newly carved Middle East boundaries, as well as the markets of postwar Europe, were dominated by British government interests through Britain's covert ownership of Royal Dutch Shell and the Anglo-Persian Oil Company.

In April 1920, without American participation, ministers of the Allied Supreme Council met in San Remo, Italy, to work out the details of which country got what oil interests in the former Ottoman Middle East. Britain's Prime Minister Lloyd George and French Premier Alexandre Millerand formalized the San Remo agreement, which gave France a 25 per cent share of oil exploited by the British from Mesopotamia (Iraq), while it was agreed that Mesopotamia would become a British mandate under the aegis of the new League of Nations.

The French were given what had been the 25 per cent German Deutsche Bank share of the old Turkish Petroleum Gesellschaft, which was 'acquired' from the Germans, as part of the spoils of Versailles. The remaining 75 per cent control of the huge Mesopotamian oil concession was directly in the hands of the British government through the Anglo-Persian Oil Company and Royal Dutch Shell. The French government created a new state-backed company, Compagnie Française des Pétroles (CFP), the following year, under the leadership of French industrialist Ernest Mercier, to develop its new Mesopotamian interests.

Sir Henry Deterding, a naturalized British citizen who headed Royal Dutch Shell, and served as a trusted agent of British secret intelligence in that capacity, had secured dominant control over the huge untapped oil reserves of the Mosul and Mesopotamia by promising France a share for its needs in neighboring French Syria. The San Remo agreement itself was the work of Sir John Cadman, then head of the Petroleum Imperial Policy Committee, later head of the British government's Anglo-Persian Oil Company. Cadman and Deterding privately shaped the terms of the San Remo accord. Not surprisingly, British state petroleum hegemony was greatly enhanced by it.

Under the San Remo petroleum agreement Britain accorded France 25 per cent of all petroleum extracted in Mesopotamia. France in return granted generous rights to the British oil companies to run an oil pipeline through French Syria to an oil port on the Mediterranean. The pipeline and everything related to it were to be exempt from French taxation. Cadman had calculated that the lack of substantial French oil capacity would ensure a virtual British monopoly of the emerging oil wealth of the entire Middle East. The San Remo agreement included a clause which allowed Britain to exclude any foreign concessions on its territories.

In addition, San Remo formalized an agreement whereby France would harmonize policy with Britain over oil relations with both Romania and Bolshevik Russia. The consequences of the latter agreement will shortly become clear. With France weakened economically by the war far more than Britain, San Remo appeared to be a coup by London, ensuring French support for a global oil dominion centered around the oil riches of the Arab Middle East of the old Ottoman Empire.

## CHURCHILL AND THE ARAB BUREAU

In March 1921, His Britannic Majesty's secretary of state for colonial affairs, Winston Churchill, convened some 40 top British experts on the Near East in Cairo to discuss the ultimate political divisions in the newly won territories of the region. Out of this gathering, attended by all the top British Arabists, including Churchill's close friend T.E. Lawrence, Sir Percy Cox, Gertrude Bell and others, the British Colonial Office Middle East Department was created, superseding, in effect, the 1916 Arab Bureau. Under the scheme agreed at Cairo, Mesopotamia was renamed Iraq and given to the son of Hashemite

Husain ibn Ali of Mecca, Feisal bin Husain. British Royal Air Force aircraft were permanently based in Iraq and its administration was placed under the effective control of Anglo-Persian Oil Company officials.

When the U.S. State Department registered an official protest on behalf of American Standard Oil companies eager to share the concessions in the Middle East, British Foreign Secretary Lord Curzon, on April 21, 1921, sent a curt reply to the British ambassador in Washington that no concessions were to be allowed American companies in the British Middle East.[6]

The San Remo accord ignited a fierce battle for world oil control between British and American interests, which raged through the 1920s and played a decisive part in shaping the form of U.S. and British diplomatic and trade relations with the new Bolshevik regime in the Soviet Union in the critical first years under Lenin, and later Stalin. Alarmed American oil and banking interests feared Britain was well on the way towards securing a global monopoly on oil at U.S. expense. Deterding's Royal Dutch Shell had an iron grip on the vast oil concessions of the Dutch East Indies, on Persia, Mesopotamia (Iraq) and most of the postwar Middle East.

Latin America now became the focus for a fierce battle between British and American interests into the 1920s.

## A BATTLE FOR CONTROL OF MEXICO

Shortly after the discovery in 1910 of huge petroleum reserves in the coastal Mexican town of Tampico on the Gulf of Mexico, U.S. President Wilson sent American troops into Mexico. The real objective was not the Mexican regime as such, but British interests behind that regime. In 1912, using as pretext a minor incident in which U.S. Marines were detained while in the Tampico port, President Wilson ordered the U.S. naval fleet to take Vera Cruz. US Marines landed under fire and seized the Mexican customs house, in an exchange in which 20 Americans and 200 Mexicans perished.

Their objective was to oust the regime of General Victoriano Huerta, which significantly had been placed in power and was financially backed by the Mexican Eagle Petroleum Company. The Mexican Eagle president, Weetman Pearson, later Lord Cowdray, was an English oil promoter who had been recruited to the British Intelligence Service, and who worked closely with Deterding and Shell in carving out Mexico's oil potential for British interests. Mexican Eagle had managed to gain concessions for half of Mexico's oil by the time of Wilson's invasion.

With clear expectations of a coming war with Germany, Britain decided tactfully to back away from Huerta's regime, and General Venustiano Carranza's government was immediately recognized as the legitimate one by President Wilson. Rockefeller's Standard Oil ran guns and money to Carranza including $100,000 in cash and large fuel credits. U.S. oil had taken Mexico from British oil. Tampico's wells at the time were the world's envy, with one well, Cerro Azul, pumping a record 200,000 barrels of oil per day.

When Carranza then proceeded to act to defend Mexican national economic interests rather than those of the American oil companies, he became the focus of an intense campaign in which, in 1916, Standard Oil financially backed the roving bandit, Pancho Villa, against Carranza.

General Pershing, just prior to the U.S. entry into the European war, was sent with troops into Mexico for a brief but unsuccessful mission. With the imminent U.S. entry on the side of Britain into the European war, Britain and America mutually decided to boycott Mexico under Carranza. Fortunately for Mexico, the exigencies of war left the country with something of a respite from the Anglo-American oil wars. Carranza remained president until 1920, when, following Versailles, he was assassinated.

But among the legacies left by Carranza was Mexico's first national constitution, approved in 1917, which contained a special paragraph, number 27, vesting the nation with 'direct ownership of all minerals, petroleum and all hydro-carbons—solid liquid or gaseous ...' The only ground on which non-Mexican nationals could obtain concessions to develop oil was to agree to the full sovereignty of Mexican law in their business affairs, without interference from foreign governments. Nonetheless, British and American oil interests continued a fierce behind-the-scenes battle for Mexico's oil through the 1920s, lasting until the late 1930s, when a decisive nationalization of all foreign oil holdings by the Cardenas government led the British and American oil majors to boycott Mexico for the next 40 years.

THE SECRET OF BRITISH OIL CONTROL

During the time between the discovery of major oilfields in 1910 and the mid 1920s, the British company Mexican Eagle Petroleum Ltd., under chairman Weetman Pearson (Lord Cowdray), was able to maintain a strong presence in Mexican oil exploitation, presenting itself as a counter to the demanding American Rockefeller oil companies.

Pearson worked for British secret intelligence, as did executives of all the other major British oil groups. He sold his Mexican Eagle interests in 1926 to Deterding's Royal Dutch Shell group. Pearson became Lord Cowdray, and his Mexican oil fortune was established in a protected trust which later, as the Pearson Group, was one of the most influential corporate groups in Britain. It owned the publishing enterprises of the London *Economist* and the *Financial Times,* and a significant share of the influential London–New York–Paris merchant bank, Lazard Freres.

In global pursuit of major oil reserves, the policies of the British Foreign Office, the secret intelligence services and British oil interests were intermeshed in a covert and highly effective manner, as no other countries' were at this time, with the possible exception of Bolshevik Russia.[7]

By the early 1920s, the British government controlled a formidable arsenal of apparently private companies which, in reality, served the direct interests of His Majesty's Government to dominate and ultimately control all the identified major regions believed to contain significant petroleum deposits. Four companies played an instrumental role, all of which were an integral part of British secret intelligence activities.

Royal Dutch Shell, despite its name, had passed into the secret control of parties who were proxies for the British government. Deterding, a Dutchman, first saw the potential of petroleum as a civil servant in Sumatra in the Dutch East Indies, and rose to become president of a small Dutch lamp oil company using Indonesian oil, the Royal Dutch Oil Company.

In 1897, Deterding had realized the crucial importance of his controlling the vast overseas terms of his trade, and formed a strategic alliance with a ship transport company. He merged his Royal Dutch Oil Co. with the London-based Shell Transport & Trading Co., founded by the shrewd English shipping magnate, Marcus Samuel, Lord Bearsted, the man who built the world's first oil transport tanker ship. The alliance between Deterding's Royal Dutch and Samuel's Shell Transport & Trading Co. created what went on to become the world's most powerful trust, not least because it enjoyed the covert backing of the British government. It soon rivaled the leading Rockefeller Standard Oil group, even within America, through California Oil

Fields Ltd and Roxana Petroleum Co. of Oklahoma, both wholly owned by Shell from abroad, but exempt from the U.S. antitrust laws which restricted Rockefeller's Standard inside the United States.

At the same time they had created the Anglo-Persian Oil Company to exploit for the exclusive interest of the British government the oil resources of Persia and the Middle East, the British authorities created another related company, little-known but intimately tied to the British Foreign Office and secret intelligence services worldwide in the quest for control of future oil discoveries. The company was called The d'Arcy Exploitation Company.

The fight for oil had assumed a markedly political character by the early 1920s, and Britain's d'Arcy Exploitation Company was in the midst of the politics. 'The agents of the d'Arcy Exploitation Company in Central America or West Africa, China or Bolivia, seem always first of all the agents of the British government,' noted one contemporary.[8]

The fourth and final entity of the British government's worldwide secret oil war at this time was a nominally Canadian company, headed by a Mr. Alves, called British Controlled Oilfields or BCO. BCO was also secretly owned by His Britannic Majesty's government, as were Shell and the others. Alves' mission was to secure new key oil provinces for Britain in Central and South America, countering the designs of the American Rockefeller companies.

Alves secured British recognition of the Tinoco government in Costa Rica in 1918, in return for which his BCO was rewarded with an oil concession covering 7 million acres, near to the Panama border and the important Canal Zone. The United States had refused to recognize Tinoco, and, when in 1921 a border dispute 'arose' between Panama and Costa Rica, America intervened, in what was dubbed the Central American 'toy war', on behalf of a new Costa Rican regime which immediately declared all previous concessions of the deposed Tinoco regime, most especially that with BCO, to be 'null and void.' American oil companies immediately got large new concessions, and the new Costa Rica regime found itself able to secure large new loans from New York banks on easy credit terms.

At that point, BCO moved south to Maracaibo in Venezuela, where, in 1922, prolific new wells had been discovered near the mouth of the Orinoco. Alves had secured the largest wells for his British Controlled Oilfields. Royal Dutch Shell was quick to follow, setting up its wholly-owned Venezuelan Oil Concessions Ltd., and Colon Development Co. Of course, Rockefeller's Standard Oil Company, through the

Standard Oil Company of Venezuela, was soon fighting for hegemony as well, in what was to become one of the most important petroleum countries in the world in the early 1920s.

The successes of the British, with their unique reliance on secret backing by their government, able to utilize British secret intelligence services worldwide, was considerable. In 1912, on the eve of the Great War, Britain commanded no more than 12 per cent of world oil production through British companies. By 1925, she controlled the major part of the world's future supplies of petroleum.

In an article in a British bank journal, *Sperling's Journal*, dated September 1919, Sir Edward Mackay Edgar reviewed the overall situation:

> I should say that two-thirds of the improved fields of Central and South America are in British hands ... The Alves group, whose holdings encircle practically two-thirds of the Caribbean Sea, is wholly British, working under arrangements which ensure that perpetual control of its undertakings shall remain in British hands ... Or take again that greatest of all oil organizations, the Shell group. It owns exclusively or controls interests in every important oil field in the world, including in the United States, Russia, Mexico, the Dutch East Indies, Rumania, Egypt, Venezuela, Trinidad, India, Ceylon, the Malay States, North and South China, Siam, the Straits Settlements, and the Philippines. We shall have to wait a few years before the full advantages of this situation shall begin to be reaped, but that that harvest eventually will be a great one, there can be no manner of doubt ... America before long will have to purchase from British companies, and to pay for, in dollar currency in progressively increasing proportion, the oil she cannot do without, and is no longer able to furnish from her own store.[9]

But in 1922, an unexpected shock forced a process which led some years later to a 'truce' in this Anglo-American conflict of the post-Versailles period. A threatening new combination coming out of the East forced Washington and London to forge a condominium of global power, in which has formed the strategic center of that power to the present day. We must go to Genoa to see how this development shaped events of global consequence.

Once again, it was Germany which crossed British policy design and forced a closer English collaboration with its Washington rival.

# 6
# The Anglo-Americans Close Ranks

## A CONFERENCE IN GENOA

On April 16, 1922, in Genoa's Villa de Alberti, the German delegation to the postwar international economics conference dropped a bomb whose shock waves reached across the Atlantic. It was a political bomb. German Foreign Minister Walther Rathenau announced to the assembled ministers of state, with the Russian Foreign Minister Chicherin present, that Germany and the Soviet Union had entered into a bilateral agreement, whereby Russia agreed to forgive its war reparations claims on Germany in return for a German agreement to sell industrial technology to the Soviet Union, among other things.

The Rapallo Treaty, named for the village near Genoa where the Germans and Soviets had finalized it, astonished the delegates at the Villa de Alberti. It produced an immediate panic reaction, especially among the British and French members present.

The Genoa conference had been called on British urging, in order to accomplish a number of British strategic objectives in the post-Versailles period of the early 1920s. It was meant to lay the basis for reestablishment of the pre-1914 London-centered international gold standard; and secondly, by inviting Bolshevik Russia (the pariah in the international community, since the new Bolshevik government had unilaterally repudiated all debts of the czarist government), the British intended to use the conference to reopen diplomatic relations with Soviet Russia. Significantly, the American government had been convinced not to participate at Genoa on any official basis, leaving the field even more open to British domination.

Britain's overture to Moscow was to be no small gesture. Renewed diplomatic relations were intended to open the door to lucrative trade deals which would allow Royal Dutch Shell and other British petroleum interests to control Russia's war-ravaged Baku oilfields. While secretly financing a White Russian counterrevolution beginning 1918, in concert with Colonial Secretary Winston Churchill, Shell's Deterding quietly went to France and bought up the prerevolutionary oil leases for the Russian Baku, anticipating the imminent collapse of an economically isolated and badly damaged Soviet regime.

This was the period of the notorious Lockhart Plot, in which Britain's Moscow envoy, Sir Robin Bruce Lockhart, together with Sidney Reilly, were tried in absentia and sentenced to death for the August 1918 attempt on Lenin's life. It was also the period of British and allied military landings at Archangel. British policy, under Churchill's Colonial Office, had been to back an exile government around the dubious figure of Boris Savinkoff, former minister of war under the ill-fated Kerensky regime, and at the time a morphine addict. With the backing of Churchill and the British government, Deterding had channeled large sums of money to a White Russian counterrevolution under the leadership of Generals Wrangel and Denikine, Admiral Kolchak and others, as late as 1920. Deterding had formed the Anglo-Causasian Company in anticipation of his taking the prize of Baku oil. At one point, an increasingly frustrated Deterding even funneled monies to create a Baku separatist movement which was to have honored Deterding's oil concessions.[1]

Four years of such covert and overt efforts at overthrowing the new Bolshevik regime had failed to yield results. By 1922, British had shifted their tactics, intending to intersect what London saw as a more pragmatic, though actually desperate, economic policy coming from Lenin's Moscow, through the 1921 New Economic Program.

## SINCLAIR AND THE AMERICAN BID

Determined as Deterding and the British were in 1922 to secure monopoly rights to develop and control the vast Russian oilfields, powerful American oil interests, including the Rockefeller Standard group, were equally determined. But by 1922, it appeared that conditions were ideal for the new British approach to Russia. Britain's chief apparent rival for Soviet oil concessions, the American Sinclair Petroleum Company of Harry Sinclair, was implicated in a conveniently timed scandal which had erupted in the United States over oil leases on the Wyoming Teapot Dome Naval Reserve.

Harry Sinclair, who portrayed himself as an Oklahoma oil 'independent,' in reality was a convenient 'middle man' for the Standard oil and banking interests to secure markets where a direct Standard bid might arouse suspicion—above all from Britain's powerful rival Shell group. In the early 1920s, Sinclair was not the 'maverick' self-made man he appeared. On the board of directors of his Sinclair Refining Company was Theodore Roosevelt Jr., son of the U.S. former president. Archibald Roosevelt, his brother, was vice president of Sinclair Oil. William Boyce Thompson, director of Rockefeller's Chase Bank in New York, the bank of Standard Oil, was also on Sinclair's board.

Harry Sinclair had met with Leonid Krassin, Soviet representative in London in the early 1920s. As a result of their talks, he, together with U.S. Senator Albert Fall and Archibald Roosevelt, went to Moscow, where they negotiated an agreement to obtain the concession to develop the prized Baku field, as well as rights to develop the oil deposits of the Sakhalin Island, and to form a 50–50 joint venture company with the Soviet government, to share equally in the profits from its oil sales worldwide. The Sinclair group agreed to invest a sum of not less than $115 million in the project, and to obtain a large loan in the United States for the Russian government. Moscow knew of Sinclair's close ties to President Harding and the Republican administration in Washington. A U.S. loan required U.S. diplomatic recognition of Russia, breaking the international isolation of the Soviet Union. Sinclair agreed, and Harding was persuaded to accord the Soviet government recognition.

But suddenly in Wyoming, reportedly with the covert encouragement of representatives of Deterding's rival Shell group, a scandal began to surface, implicating Sinclair, Fall, and even President Harding, involving the granting of lucrative oil leases from U.S. government property at Teapot Dome, Wyoming. In the subsequent media scandals and congressional inquiries, no mention was made of the remarkable coincidence that the Teapot Dome affair hit just as Sinclair and the United States had secured the prized Baku oil concession from right under the noses of Deterding and the British.[2]

Harding had been about to announce U.S. diplomatic and trade ties with Soviet Russia when the Teapot Dome affair, and Harry Sinclair's involvement, hit the front page of the *Wall Street Journal* on April 14, 1922. Within a year, Harding himself had died, under strange circumstances. The Coolidge presidency dropped Sinclair and the Baku project, and with it any plans to recognize Russia. There was more than a little suspicion that the skillful hand of British secret intelligence was active in blocking this American bid to dominate Russian oil development.

## GERMANY TRIES TO OUTFLANK THE BRITISH

This was the setting in which the Genoa conference was to take place, intended to become a victory for British interests in securing their grip on the enormous Soviet economic resources in the wake of the major setback for the American effort. But Rathenau and the Soviet foreign minister, Georgi W. Chicherin, had signed a comprehensive treaty in the midst of the weeks-long Genoa deliberations, without the prior knowledge of the British, French or American governments.

Rathenau's preferred option was by no means to deal with the Soviet Union. He had made repeated pleas and proposals to the British and other Allied governments, initially in his capacity as German economic reconstruction minister after Versailles, to allow the German economy to get back on its feet so that German export earnings could begin to pay the Versailles war reparations burden. Again and again, his pleas were rejected. Adding insult to injury, the British government in 1921 imposed a prohibitive 26 per cent tariff on all German imports, further obstructing German efforts to work out a realistic debt repayment process.

Faced with this Anglo-French fist under his nose, Rathenau, scion of a noted German engineering family and former chairman of the large AEG electrical company, determined to develop a strategy of allowing German industry to rebuild itself through development of heavy industry exports to Soviet Russia.

Since Versailles, deficit financing had been a necessary expedient of the German government, amid the ruins of the German postwar economy. The Reichsbank in effect printed money to cover the state deficits, creating a situation in which money supply expanded more rapidly than the productive output of Germany's economy during the early 1920s. The result was an inevitable inflation, but the alternative options appeared limited, short of national economic suicide.

As Rathenau well knew, the costs of the unsuccessful war itself had laid the seeds of an already dangerous inflation in the economy. The gold parity of the Reichsmark had fallen to half its prewar levels by 1919. Official statistics showed that the war had created a wholesale price inflation of 150 per cent, and black market prices were vastly higher. The war had been financed through the expedient of enormous state indebtedness to the German population. Unlike Britain, which had been able to finance its war costs from foreign sources, especially J.P. Morgan & Co. in New York, Germany had been blocked from these major credit markets.

Moreover, after the war the Allied victors had systematically stripped Germany of her most vital economic resources. All her valuable colonies, especially Tanganyika and South West Africa, were taken by Britain. The growing economic markets of the Ottoman Empire, opened through the expansion of the Baghdad Railway were gone. And Germany herself had lost her most valuable source of iron ore for her steel industry: Alsace-Lorraine and the east, including Silesia, with its rich mineral and agricultural resources. Germany had lost 75 per cent of her iron ore, 68 per cent of her zinc ore and 26 per cent of her coal as a consequence of Versailles. Alsatian textile industries and potash mines were gone. Her entire merchant fleet, a fifth of her river transport fleet, a quarter of her fishing fleet, 5,000 locomotives, 150,000 railroad cars and 5,000 motor trucks were taken by the Allied powers after Versailles. All was justified as part of an as yet undefined German war 'reparations' levy.

In May, 1921, the Allied Reparations Committee met and drew up what was called the London ultimatum, the 'final' payments plan demanded of Germany. It fixed Germany's reparations debt to the victorious Allies at the astronomical sum of 132 billion gold marks, an amount which even British reparations expert, John Maynard Keynes, said was more than three times the maximum that Germany could possibly pay. The reparations debt was to accumulate an annual 6 per cent interest charge. A 26 per cent duty on the declared value of all German exports was to be paid to the Allied reparations agent in Berlin. In addition, numerous onerous conditions were imposed, including several taxes as 'guarantee.' Payment-in-kind for any part of the reparation sum could be unilaterally demanded by the reparations commission.

The 'London ultimatum' was not merely an ultimatum in name. The terms were that unless the German parliament fully agreed to the unbelievable conditions set forth, within six days, Allied troops would occupy and control the Ruhr industrial heartland of Germany. Not astonishingly, the Reichstag approved the draconian ultimatum by a slim majority.[3]

The really alarming aspect of the Rapallo Treaty, for certain influential circles in London, was the implications of its provisions. A major infusion of German machinery and equipment, steel and other technology was to be sold to Russia for the rebuilding and expansion of her Baku oilfields.

In return, Germany established a network of jointly owned German–Soviet oil and gasoline distribution centers in Germany to market the Soviet oil under the firm DEROP, the Deutsch–Russische Petroleumgesellschaft. This had the added advantage of allowing Germany to get out from under the iron grip of British and American oil interests, which had had a total monopoly on German petroleum sales since Versailles. Rathenau never refused the London Ultimatum reparations demands. But he insisted on a practical means of realizing those demands.[4]

## MILITARY OCCUPATION OF THE RUHR

The response to Rapallo was not long in arriving. Within two days of its formal announcement, on April 18 at Genoa, the German delegation was presented with an Allied note of protest that Germany had negotiated the Russian accord 'behind the backs' of the Reparations Committee.

Then, on June 22, 1922, little more than two months after the Rapallo Treaty had been made public, Walther Rathenau was assassinated while leaving his home in the Berlin Grünewald. Two right-wing extremists, later identified as members of a pro-monarchist 'Organization C,' were charged with the murder, and it was portrayed as part of the growing wave of extremism and anti-Semitism. But reports circulated in Germany pointing to 'foreign interests,' and some said Britain, or British interests, stood behind the two hitmen. In any event, the most prominent statesman and architect of Rapallo was gone, and the nation was shaken to the roots. But the murder of Rathenau was to be only the beginning of a horror to which few nations before or since have been subjected.

Britain took care to distance herself publicly from the French revanchist policy of Poincaré's regime, but behind the scenes she had worked out a quid pro quo. France was to cede rights over the French territories in the Mosul, granted her during the secret Sykes–Picot accords of 1916, to the British. In return, as we noted in Chapter 3, Britain gave France its private assurance that Britain would do no more than offer verbal protest to a French military occupation of the Ruhr. It well suited British balance-of-power requirements that France should be the marcher lord to bring Germany into submission.[5]

All that was lacking for the Poincaré regime was a visible pretext. On December 26, 1922, at the scheduled year-end meeting of the Allied Reparations Committee in London, President Poincaré announced that Germany had violated the strict terms of the Versailles Treaty by failing to deliver to France the agreed volume of wood for telegraph poles, as well as a minor shortfall in coal deliveries.[6]

## THE REAL ORIGINS OF WEIMAR HYPERINFLATION

Following the murder of Rathenau, the gold mark rate by July 1922 plunged internationally to 493 Marks to the U.S. dollar, as confidence in political stability in Germany sank to a new post-Versailles low. The Reichsbank began dramatically expanding the money supply, in a frantic attempt to meet unpayable London reparations demands, while maintaining employment and a strong export industry domestically to service the reparations requirements imposed. By December, the mark had fallen to the alarming level of 7,592 to the dollar.

Then, on January 9, 1923, the Reparations Committee voted 3 to 1 (with Britain formally on record as opposing France, Belgium and the newly installed Mussolini government of Italy) that Germany was in default of her reparations payments. On January 11, Poincaré ordered the military forces of France, with token participation from Belgium and Italy, to march into Essen and other cities of the German industrial Ruhr to occupy it by force. England hypocritically denounced the occupation, though she had threatened precisely the same action in 1921.

In reaction, the German government called on its citizens to engage in universal passive resistence to the occupation. The government ordered all German officials, including Reichsbahn personnel, to refuse to take orders from the occupying authorities. Workers refused to work the steel mills and factories of the Ruhr. To support the families of striking miners and other workers, the government resorted to expanded printing of money. The area occupied was merely 100 kilometers long and some 50 kilometers wide, yet it contained 10 per cent of the entire German population, produced 80 per cent of Germany's coal, iron and steel and accounted for fully 70 per cent of its freight traffic.

The French occupation brought the industrial activity of Germany almost to a grinding halt. It took until the end of 1923 for French troops and engineers to bring production in the Ruhr to even a third of the former level of 1922. More than 150,000 Germans were deported from the Ruhr occupation zone, some 400 were killed and more than 2,000 wounded.

The economic strain of the German resistance was incalculable. The French occupation forces had cut off the Ruhr economically from the rest of the nation. Funds of German banks and Reichsbank branches, and inventories of factories and mines, were all seized. Germany ceased all reparations payments to France, Belgium and Italy for the duration of the resistance, but scrupulously maintained its payments and deliveries in kind to Britain.

Germany's currency became utterly ruined as a consequence. As we have noted, already by the end of 1922, when it became obvious that France's Poincaré government wanted to force a military occupation, the mark's value had begun to fall. By January, after the Ruhr occupation, the mark had dropped to 18,000 to the dollar. Attempts by the Reichsbank to defend the currency at all costs held the level somewhat until May, when all possibilities had been exhausted. By May the results of the Ruhr economic losses became so catastrophic that Berlin was forced to abandon efforts to save the currency.

From that point onward, the situation was totally out of control. By July, the mark had fallen exponentially to 353,000 to the dollar; by August, it had reached the unbelievable level of 4,620,000 to the dollar. The plunge continued until November 15, when it hit 4,200,000,000,000 to the dollar. No such phenomenon had ever before been experienced in the economic history of nations.

With some months' time lag, German wholesale prices increasingly began to reflect the collapse of the currency. From an index-level of 100 in July 1922, just after the Rathenau assassination, prices increased some thirty-fold by the onset of the Ruhr occupation at the end of January 1923, to 2,785. By July, prices had soared to the unbelievable level of 74,787 compared with the level of 100 a year earlier, by September to 23,949,000 and finally by November to 750,000,000,000. The savings of the entire population were destroyed. Living standards collapsed. While a few were able to build immense fortunes at the beginning, the vast majority sank into poverty. Government bonds, mortgages, bank deposits—all became worthless. The entire stable middle stratum of the country was pauperized.

By September 1923, the government, now under a coalition headed by Gustav Stresemann, ordered an end to the passive resistance. In November 1923, a formal agreement with France and the other occupying forces was signed. The hyperinflation had peaked. But this was only the softening up of Germany for what was to appear a welcome relief.

In October 1923, the U.S. secretary of state, Charles Evans Hughes, former chief counsel to Rockefeller's Standard Oil, recommended a new scheme to President Calvin Coolidge to continue the reparations pyramid of debt collection which had been shaken since the April 1922 Rapallo shock. Hughes won the appointment of a banker tied to the J.P. Morgan group, General Charles C. Dawes, a man whose prior career had been tainted with corruption and Republican Party payoff scandals in Illinois.

Dawes, as chairman of what came to be called the Dawes Committee, presented his plan to the Allied Reparations Committee on April 9, 1924. His plan was immediately seized by all parties, including the exhausted German government. France's Poincaré lost in the May elections, but a cabinet under Edouard Herriot immediately agreed to the Dawes reparations scheme. On September 1, the Dawes reparations plan formally began. The Dawes Plan was the first major indication of the growing Anglo-American agreement to consolidate and join forces in the post-Versailles period. London had wisely reckoned it better to let the Americans take center stage, while preserving its powerful influence on American policy.[7]

The Dawes Plan was the Anglo-American banking community's reassertion of full fiscal and financial control over Germany. It was vastly more effective than Poincaré's soldiers, but had required the military intervention and the attendant hyperinflation crisis to enable its enactment.

By November, 1923 a German banker, Hjalmar Schacht, had been named commissioner of the currency. Schacht, who had developed a close correspondence at this time with Montagu Norman, governor of the Bank of England, implemented the Rentenmark, in an attempt to stabilize the mark by a fiction of declared real estate backing. On November 20, the day the Rentenmark stabilization plan was made public, the Reichsbank president, Rudolf Havenstein, who had headed the Reichsbank since 1908, died, in the first of a remarkable series of such events. Stresemann and Finance Minister Rudolf Hilferding had repeatedly attempted to get the unwilling Havenstein to step down. It soon became clearer why.

On December 4, 1923 the Reichsbank board of governors voted their overwhelming choice that Karl Helfferich, the former Deutsche Bank director and architect of the Baghdad railway project before the war, be named successor to Havenstein. Stresemann and the government had other preferences. On December 18, 1923, his choice, and the friend of the Anglo-American Morgan interests, Hjalmar Schacht, was named president of the Reichsbank. The way was ready for the Dawes Plan to proceed. Helfferich died a few months later in a suspicious train accident.[8]

Under the Dawes Plan, Germany paid reparations for five years, until 1929. At the end of 1929, she owed more than at the beginning. It was a scheme of organized looting by the international banking community dominated by London and New York. Guarantees were made for reparations payments of special funds in Germany. An agent-general for reparations, S. Parker Gilbert, a J.P. Morgan partner and protégé of Owen D. Young, was installed in Berlin to collect the repayments for the Anglo-American banks. With their risk thus all but nil, the London and New York banks began a vastly profitable lending to Germany, money which was recycled back to the banks of New York and London in the form of reparations with commission and interest. It was a vast international credit pyramid at the top of which sat London and ultimately, the New York banks.

Between 1924 and 1931 Germany paid 10.5 billion marks in reparations, but borrowed 18.6 billion marks from abroad. German recovery after 1923, under the guiding hand of Montagu Norman and his Reichsbank colleague, Hjalmar Schacht, was all controlled by the borrowings from the Anglo-Americans. There were no more fears of any Rapallo initiatives upsetting the Anglo-American order—that is, until the pyramid collapsed in 1929, when the credit flowing from the New York and London banks into Germany to roll over the debt suddenly stopped.[9]

## THE ANGLO-AMERICAN RED LINE

By then, the Anglo-American power struggle for primacy in world finance and economic affairs had been resolved. The oil wars, which had shaken the world for more than a decade, were finally resolved in a 'ceasefire,' which resulted in the creation of an enormously powerful Anglo-American oil cartel, later dubbed the 'Seven Sisters.' The peace agreement was formalized in 1927, at Achnacarry, the Scottish castle of Shell's Sir Henri Deterding. John Cadman, representing the British government's Anglo-Persian Oil Co. (British Petroleum), and Walter Teagle, president of Rockefeller's Standard Oil of New Jersey (Exxon), gathered under the cover of a grouse shoot to conclude the most powerful economic cartel in modern history. The Seven Sisters were effectively one.

Their secret pact was formalized as the 'As Is' agreement of 1928, or the Achnacarry agreement. British and American oil majors agreed to accept the existing market divisions and shares, to set a secret world cartel price, and to end the destructive competition and price wars of the previous decade. The respective governments merely ratified this private accord the same year in what became the Red Line agreement. Since this time, with minor interruption, the Anglo-American grip over the world's oil reserves has been hegemonic. Threats to break that grip have been met with ruthless responses, as we shall later see.

Britain and a weakened France agreed in 1927 to let the Americans into the Middle East and revised the secret wartime accords to reflect this. A Red Line was drawn from the Dardanelles down through Palestine, to Yemen and up through the Persian Gulf; it encompassed Turkey, Syria, Lebanon, Saudi Arabia, Jordan, Iraq and Kuwait. Inside the line, the oil interests of the three countries worked out iron-clad divisions of territory which have largely held to this day. Inside Iraq, Anglo-Persian, the Royal Dutch Shell group, and the French Compagnie Française des Pétroles, which had been 'given' the old Deutsche Bank share of the Turkish Petroleum Gesellschaft from 1914, along with the Rockefeller group, gained 'concessions' from Iraq for exclusive exploitation for 75 years of Iraq's oil. Kuwait was given to Anglo-Persian and the American Mellon family's Gulf Oil.[10]

By 1932, all seven major companies in the Anglo-American sphere—Esso (Standard of N.J.), Mobil (Standard of N.Y.), Gulf Oil, Texaco, Standard of California (Chevron), as well as Royal Dutch Shell and Anglo-Persian Oil Co. (British Petroleum)—were part of the Achnacarry cartel.

The cartel then devised a strategy to deal with companies not in the cartel, so called 'outsiders.' According to the terms of their cartel agreement:

> It is recognized that it is desirable to convert uncontrolled outlets into the controlled class; in view of this, the purchase by the 'as is' members [i.e. Achnacarry cartel companies] of going distributing concerns outside 'as is' is to be recommended as tending to improve the stability of the markets.

The cartel was also prepared to deal with outsiders less compliant, as soon became clear.[11]

The sinews of the Anglo-American 'special relationship' had been definitively formed around the control of oil. The way was now clear for major new initiatives.

## DETERDING, MONTAGU NORMAN
## AND SCHACHT'S HITLER PROJECT

The unstable international monetary order imposed after Versailles by London and New York bankers on a defeated central Europe came to an abrupt, if predictable, end in 1929. Montagu Norman, then the world's most influential central banker as governor of the Bank of England, precipitated the crash of the Wall Street stock market in October 1929. Norman had asked the governor of the New York Federal Reserve Bank, George Harrison, to raise U.S. interest rate levels. Harrison complied, and the most dramatic financial and economic collapse in U.S. history ensued in the following months.

By early 1931, Montagu Norman and a small circle in the British establishment had plans to shift the political dynamic in central Europe in a most astonishing manner. At the time, Austria's largest banking institution was the Creditanstalt of Vienna. Closely tied to the Austrian branch of the house of Rothschild, the Creditanstalt had grown during the 1920s through an unhealthy process of merging smaller troubled banks. The largest such merger was forced onto Creditanstalt during the month of the October 1929 stock market crash, when it was asked by the authorities to take over the Vienna Bodenkreditanstalt, a real estate lender which itself had swallowed several other unhealthy banks in the previous years.

At the beginning of 1931, Creditanstalt appeared to the world to be one of the mightiest of world banks. In reality, it was one of the sickest. The draconian Versailles conditions imposed by Britain, France and the United States had dismantled the Austro-Hungarian Empire, isolating Austria's economy from the valuable economic ties and raw materials of Hungary and the lands of eastern Europe. Austria's industrial economy had never recovered from the devastation of the First World War. Industry had run-down plants, outmoded equipment and huge unredeemable war loans. The political circumstances in Austria in the 1920s had led major parts of insolvent Austrian industry to pass into the hands of the ever-larger Creditanstalt.

Thus, by early 1931, Austria in general, and the Vienna Creditanstalt in particular, were the weak links of an international credit chain which had been built under the unhealthy foundation set by the New York banking firm of J.P. Morgan, in concert with the Bank of England and the London banks. Creditanstalt was unable to generate sufficient capital for its activities from the depressed Austrian economy and had become largely dependent on very short-term borrowings from

London and New York to finance its activities. The Bank of England itself was actually a significant lender to Creditanstalt.

In March 1931, the French government and French Foreign Minister Briand declared themselves in determined opposition to announced negotiations between Berlin and Vienna for the forming of an Austro-German trade and customs union, a belated attempt to counter a growing world economic depression that had begun in America some months earlier. France reportedly ordered its banks to cut short-term credit lines to Creditanstalt, in a bid to bring pressure to bear on the Austrian government. What ensued that May, as rumors of a run on the deposits of Creditanstalt broke in the Vienna press, was a credit crisis which shook all of Europe. The Austrian National Bank, and ultimately the Austrian state, were forced to come to the rescue of the Creditanstalt, in what became the largest bank failure in history. Subsequent examination revealed that the crisis need never have reached such dramatic dimensions. It was intended to do so by certain powerful London and New York financiers who were preparing a dramatic shift in European geopolitics.[12] By the end of the 1920s, influential circles in Britain and the United States had decided to back a radical course for Germany.

J.P. Morgan bankers had already proved to themselves the usefulness of radical top-down political solutions to ensure repayment of bank loans, when they gave foreign credit to the fascist regime of Italian strongman Benito Mussolini. In November 1925, Italian Finance Minister Volpi di Misurata announced that the Mussolini government had reached an agreement on repaying the Versailles war debts of Italy to Britain and the United States. One week later, J.P. Morgan & Co., financial agents of the Mussolini government in the United States, announced a crucial $100 million loan to Italy to 'stabilize the lira.'

In reality, Morgan had decided to stabilize Mussolini's fascist regime. On the urging of J.P. Morgan & Co. and Montagu Norman, governor of the Bank of England, Volpi di Misurata established in 1926 a single Italian central bank, the Bank of Italy, to control national monetary policy and further ensure repayment of foreign debts. Mussolini had shown himself to be the ideal strongman to discipline Italian labor unions, drive down wages and enforce sufficient austerity to guarantee foreign bank lending, or so thought Morgan's people in New York.

The man who controlled U.S. monetary policy at the time, former Morgan banker Benjamin Strong, an intimate personal friend and collaborator of Britain's Montagu Norman, met with Volpi and the Bank of Italy governor, Bonaldo Stringher, to confirm the final details of the Italian 'stabilization' program. From Poland to Romania during the 1920s, the same combination of powerful persons—J.P. Morgan & Co., Montagu Norman and the New York Federal Reserve—organized effective economic control over most countries of Continental Europe, under the pretext of the establishment of 'creditworthy' national policies—an informal precursor of the role of the International Monetary Fund in the 1980s. The New York banks were the source of the significant short-term capital for this lending, and the Bank of England, together with the British Foreign Office establishment, provided the political experience to impose the policy.[13]

The most concentrated efforts of this Anglo-Saxon circle were focused on Germany during the 1920s. Following the successful imposition of Hjalmar Schacht as president of the Reichsbank in 1923, and Schacht's implementation of the draconian Dawes Plan of war reparations repayment, drafted by Morgan & Co., the German economy during the 1920s became dependent on short-term loans from London and New York banks and their collaborators in Paris. For the banks, these German short-term credits were the most lucrative in the entire world financial markets of the day. For many of Germany's banks, including the fourth-largest, Darmstädter und Nationalbank Kommandit-Gesellschaft (Danat), dependence on short-term New York and London capital borrowings had become substantial, and at punitively high interest rates. The Weimar hyperinflation had largely destroyed the capital and reserves of major German banks during the early part of the decade. Thus the expansion of German bank lending during the late 1920s was by banks with a precariously small capital base in the event of loan default or other crises. Germany stood unique among major European industrial countries by the time of the 1929–30 New York stock market collapse. She owed international bank creditors an estimated 16 billion Reichsmarks in such short-term debts.

This unsound banking structure required only a small push to topple it in its entirety. The push came from the New York Federal Reserve and the Bank of England, which, in a series of moves in 1929, raised their interest rates following more than two years of unprecedented stock market speculation as they pursued ever lower interest rates. The predictable crash in the New York stock market and the London market led to a massive withdrawal of U.S. and British banking funds from Germany and Austria. By May 13, 1931, the fuse was ready for the torch.

On that day, the large Vienna Creditanstalt collapsed. The French had decided to 'punish' Austria for entering into customs union talks with Germany by imposing currency sanctions. Creditanstalt was a Rothschild bank with heavy ties to French banking. As French funds were recalled from Austria, this toppled the fragile Creditanstalt, the largest Austrian bank, which had large interests in some 70 per cent of Austria's industry. To attempt to stop the run on the Creditanstalt, Austrian banks called in all funds they had in German banks. Creditanstalt was the weak link which started the domino collapse of banking throughout central Europe.

The ensuing banking crisis, economic depression and the related tragic developments in Austria and Germany were dictated virtually to the letter by Montagu Norman of the Bank of England, the governor of the New York Federal Reserve, George Harrison, and the house of Morgan and friends in Wall Street. A decision had been made to cut all credits to Germany, though even a minimal roll-over of nominally small sums would probably have stopped the crisis from erupting out of control at this early stage.

Instead, capital began to flow out of Germany in ever greater amounts. On the demand of Montagu Norman and George Harrison, a new Reichsbank President, Hans Luther, dutifully abstained from doing anything to stop the collapse of the large German banks. The immediate consequence of the Creditanstalt collapse in Vienna was the related failure of the Danat-Bank of Germany. The Danat-Bank, heavily dependent on foreign credits, lost almost 100 million Reichsmarks of deposits that May. The next month, Danat lost 848 million Reichsmarks, or 40 per cent of all the deposits it held, while Dresdner Bank lost 10 per cent and even Deutsche Bank lost 8 per cent of its deposits. By late June, Bankers Trust, a Morgan bank, cut the credit line to Deutsche Bank.

Harrison demanded that Reichsbank head Hans Luther impose rigorous credit austerity and tightening in the German capital markets, claiming that this was the only way to stop the flight of foreign capital. What it ensured was the overall collapse of the German banking system and industry into the worst depression imaginable.

Montagu Norman backed Harrison, and the governor of the Bank of France joined them in blaming Germany for the crisis. Desperate last-minute efforts by the Brüning government to persuade Luther to seek an emergency stabilization credit from other central banks to contain the national banking crisis were, as a result, refused by Luther. When he finally capitulated and asked Montagu Norman for help, Norman slammed the door in his face. Germany as a consequence no longer effectively had any lender of last resort.

By July 1931, some two months after the collapse of the Vienna Creditanstalt had initiated the flight of capital out of Germany, the Basle *Nationalzeitung* reported that the Danat-Bank was 'in difficulties,' which was sufficient in the electric climate to trigger a full panic run on that bank. The bank's chairman, Goldschmidt, later charged that the Reichsbank had selectively precipitated his bank's failure with discriminatory credit rationing. The ensuing banking crisis and collapse of industry created in Germany in the winter of 1931–32 what was said to be 'the hardest winter in one hundred years.' It was the breeding ground for radical political alternatives.

In March 1930, some months before the credit cutoff against Germany was imposed by the Anglo-American bankers, Reichsbank president Hjalmar Schacht surprised the government by handing in his resignation. The actual issue he resigned over was the offer of an emergency stabilization credit of 500 million Reichsmarks, which the Berlin government had been offered by the Swedish industrialist and financier, Ivar Kreuger, the famous Swedish 'match king.' Kreuger and his American bankers, Lee Higginson & Co., were major lenders to Germany and other countries that had been cut off by the London and New York banks. But Kreuger's loan offer of early 1930 had explosive and unacceptable political consequences for the long-term strategy of Montagu Norman's friends. German Finance Minister Rudolf Hilferding urged Schacht, who, under the terms of the Dawes reparations plan, had to approve all foreign loans, to accept the Kreuger loan. Schacht refused and on March 6 handed Reichspresident von Hindenburg his resignation. Schacht had other duties to tend to.

Kreuger himself was found dead some months later, in early 1932, in his Paris hotel room. Official autopsy registered the death as suicide, but detailed inquiry by Swedish researchers decades later made a conclusive case that Kreuger had been murdered. The persons who stood to gain most from Kreuger's death were in London and New York, though the actual details will likely remain buried along with Kreuger. With Kreuger's death ended also Germany's hope for relief. She was totally cut off from international credit.[14]

For his part, Schacht was anything but idle after his resignation from the Reichsbank. He devoted his full energies to organizing financial support for the man he and his close friend, Bank of England governor Norman, agreed was the man for Germany's crisis.

Since 1926 Schacht had secretly been a backer of the radical National Socialist German workers' Party (NSDAP) or Nazi party of Adolf Hitler. After resigning his Reichsbank post, Schacht acted as a key liaison between powerful, but skeptical, German industrial leaders, the so-called 'Schlotbarone' of the Ruhr, and foreign financial leaders, especially Britain's Lord Norman.

British policy at this juncture was to create the 'Hitler Project,' knowing fully what its ultimate geopolitical and military direction would be. As Colonel David Stirling, the founder of Britain's elite Special Air Services, related in a private discussion almost half a century later, 'The greatest mistake we British did was to think we could play the German Empire against the Russian Empire, and have them bleed one another to death.'

The British support for the Hitler option reached to the very highest levels. It included Britain's prime minister, Neville Chamberlain, the man infamous for the 1938 Munich appeasement which set Hitler's armies marching to Sudetenland in the east. Philip Kerr (later Lord Lothian), of the Cecil Rhodes Round Table group which we met earlier, was a close adviser to Neville Chamberlain. Lothian backed the Hitler project as part of the infamous Cliveden set in Brirish circles, as did Lord Beaverbrook, the most influential British press magnate of the day, who controlled the mass-circulation *Daily Express* and *Evening Standard*. But perhaps the most influential backer of Hitler's movement at this time in Britain was the Prince of Wales, who became Edward VIII in early 1936, until his abdication at the end of the same year.

Certain influential American establishment figures were hardly ignorant of what the Hitler movement was about. Leading Wall Street and U.S. State Department circles had been informed from an early stage. Even before the ill-fated 1923 Munich 'beer hall putsch,' a U.S. State Department official stationed in Munich as part of the Versailles occupation of Germany, Robert Murphy, later a central figure in the postwar Bilderberg group, personally met the young Hitler through General Erich Ludendorff. Murphy, who had served under Allen Dulles in Berne during the First World War, gathering intelligence on the German Reich, was in Munich with another influential U.S. government official, Truman Smith, assigned to U.S. Army intelligence occupying Germany.

In his memoirs, Smith later recalled his arrival in Munich in late 1922:

I talked at length about National Socialism with the Munich Consul, Mr. Robert Murphy (later a very distinguished American Ambassador), General Erich Ludendorff, Crown Prince Rupert of Bavaria and Alfred Rosenberg. The latter later became the political philosopher of the Nazi party. On this visit I also saw much of Ernst F.S. ('Putzi') Hanfstaengl, of the well-known Munich art family. 'Putzi' was a Harvard graduate and later became Hitler's foreign press chief ... My interview with Hitler lasted some hours. The diary I kept in Munich indicates I was deeply impressed by his personality and thought it likely that he would play an important part in German politics.

In his November 1922 report to his superiors in Washington, Smith filed the following recommendation regarding his evaluation of the tiny Hitler group. Speaking of Hitler, Smith said:

His basic aim is the overthrow of Marxism ... and the winning of labor to the nationalist ideals of state and property ... The clash of party interests has ... demonstrated the impossibility of Germany's rescue from her present difficulties through democracy. His movement aims at the establishment of a national dictatorship through non-parliamentary means. Once achieved, he demands that the reparations demands be reduced to a possible figure, but that done, the sum agreed on to be paid to the last Pfennig, as a matter of national honor. To accomplish this the dictator must introduce universal reparations service and enforce it with the whole force of the state. His power during the period of fulfillment cannot be hampered by any legislature or popular assembly ...

To ensure that his colleagues in Washington's Division of Military Intelligence got the point, Smith added his personal evaluation of Hitler: 'In private conversation he disclosed himself as a forceful and logical speaker, which, when tempered with a fanatical earnestness, makes a very deep impression on a neutral listener.'[15]

In late autumn of 1931, a man arrived at London's Liverpool Street railway station from Germany. His name was Alfred Rosenberg. Rosenberg met with the editor in chief of the influential London *Times*, Geoffrey Dawson. *The Times* gave Hitler's movement invaluable positive international publicity in the coming months. But the most important meeting Rosenberg had during this first England visit in 1931 was with Montagu Norman, governor of the Bank of England, and arguably the most influential figure of the day in world finance. Norman had three hatreds, according to his trusted personal secretary—the French, the Catholics and the Jews. Norman and Rosenberg found no difficulty in their talks together. The introduction to Norman had come through Hjalmar Schacht. From their first meeting in 1924, Schacht and Norman developed a friendship which lasted until Norman's death in 1945.

Rosenberg concluded his fateful London visit with a meeting with a leading person of the London Schroeder Bank, which was affiliated with J.H. Schroeder Bank in New York and with the Cologne-based private bank, J.H. Stein of Baron Kurt von Schroeder. The man whom Rosenberg met from Schroeder Bank in London was F.C. Tiarks, who was also a member of the Bank of England directorate and a close friend of Montagu Norman.

As Baron von Schroeder and Hjalmar Schacht went to leading German industrial and financial figures to secure support for the NSDAP after 1931, the first question of nervous and skeptical industrialists was, 'How does international finance, and especially Montagu Norman, regard the prospect of a German government under Hitler?' Was Norman prepared to come in with financial credit for Germany in such an event? The reality is that at this critical juncture, when Hitler's NSDAP had little more than 6 million votes in the 1930 elections, the international backing of Montagu Norman, Tiarks and friends in London was decisive.

On January 4, 1932, at the Cologne villa of Baron Kurt von Schroeder, Adolf Hitler, von Papen and the Cologne banker, von Schroeder, secretly arranged financing of Hitler's NSDAP, at that time de facto bankrupt with huge debts, until the planned seizure of power by Hitler. Another meeting between Hitler and Franz von Papen took place on January 4, 1933, at von Schroeder's Cologne villa, at which the plan was finalized to topple the weak government of Schleicher and build a right-wing coalition. On January 30, 1933, Adolf Hitler became chancellor of the Reich.

The final London visit of Alfred Rosenberg was in May 1933, this time as one of the inner figures in the new Hitler government. He went directly to the country home in Buckhurst Park in Ascot of Sir Henri Deterding, the head of Royal Dutch Shell and arguably the world's most influential businessman. According to English press accounts, the two had a warm and eventful discussion. Rosenberg had first met Deterding during his 1931 London trip. Royal Dutch Shell had intimate contact with, and provided support for the German NSDAP. Though the details were kept secret, reliable British reports of the day were that Deterding had provided substantial financial support to the Hitler project in its critical early phases.

While Norman and the Bank of England had adamantly refused to advance a pfennig of credit to Germany at the critical period in 1931 (thus precipitating the banking and unemployment crisis which made desperate alternatives such as Hitler even thinkable to leading circles in Germany), as soon as Hitler had consolidated power, in early 1933, the same Montagu Norman moved with indecent haste to reward the Hitler government with vital Bank of England credit. Norman made a special visit to Berlin in May 1934 to arrange further secret financial stabilization for the new regime. Hitler had responded by making Norman's dear friend Schacht his minister of economics as well as president of the Reichsbank. The latter post Schacht held until 1939.[16]

# 7
# Oil and the New World Order of Bretton Woods

In 1945, after six years of a war spanning the entire globe, which had left more than 55 million dead in its wake, the world had changed in many significant ways. However, for vast regions of the world, most especially for eastern Europe and the less developed regions in the southern hemisphere, 1945 merely marked a transition to a new form of chronic war—most often, economic.

In 1919, following the Versailles peace conference, the British Empire was at its largest extent, its dominion covering one quarter the entire surface of the world, the empire 'upon which the sun never set.' A mere 30 years later, by 1949, the British Empire was disintegrating in every region as demands for colonial independence were made against the oppressive mother country. The British Empire was in the throes of the largest upheaval of perhaps any empire in history.

Following the mutiny of the Indian Royal Navy in February 1946, the postwar British government of Labour Prime Minister Clement Attlee appointed Viscount Mountbatten of Burma to be the last Viceroy of India, with the task of arranging the fastest possible withdrawal of British forces and government administration. Mountbatten's partition of the vast Indian subcontinent into a bizarre quilt of East and West Pakistan, with predominantly Muslim populations, separated by India, was completed by August 15, 1947, five months after his arrival in India.

Within a few short years, Britain ceded formal colonial control over large parts of her empire in Africa, the Pacific and the Mediterranean. It was not out of beneficence or a sudden burning passion for the principle of self-determination of subject peoples, but rather from driving necessity, which dictated a reshaped form of postwar dominion in the late 1940s and early 1950s.

As a consequence of the war, the trading mechanisms of the empire, which had formed the foundation of British financial power, were shattered. Vast overseas investments had long since been sold to pay war costs. The British national debt had soared to unheard-of heights. Domestically, Britain's plant and equipment were decaying and worn out, even the electricity supply was no longer reliable; housing stock was dilapidated, the population exhausted. By the end of the war, British export trade had withered to a mere 31 per cent of its prewar (1938) level.

Britain was utterly dependent on the postwar support of the United States. For its part, the United States, or rather, the internationalist elements of the 'East Coast establishment' as it was becoming known, realized that if America were to dominate the postwar world, it needed the vast worldwide expertise and cooperation of London. The long-discussed new concept of empire, first introduced in the years before the First World War by Lord Lothian, Lord Milner, Cecil Rhodes and the Round Table circle, as we mentioned earlier, was rapidly becoming reality. Britain after 1945 would exert global influence indirectly, through developing and deepening a 'special relationship' with the United States.

The seeds of this special relationship had been carefully planted following Versailles, with the simultaneous establishment of the Royal Institute of International Affairs and the New York Council on Foreign Relations as conduits of strategic policy debate.

During the war a new element was added. While England and the United States agreed to a full integration of military command, the still fledgling U.S. intelligence operations, under the Office of Strategic Services (OSS), worked principally out of a London command center in joint cooperation with the British Special Operations Executive (SOE). The emergence of the postwar American Central Intelligence Agency and the entire array of U.S. covert government institutions evolved directly out of these wartime British ties. The consequences for later American policy were to be as enormous as they were tragic.

A significant turning point in redirecting American energies and policy in the immediate postwar period was the intervention by the British into the American domestic debate. In a supremely calculated move, Winston Churchill came to Fulton in Missouri, President Truman's home state, to deliver his famous 'Iron Curtain' speech on March 5, 1946. What are generally not discussed are the policy gains for the postwar British position secured by Churchill's calculated rhetoric. Granted, Stalin was indeed violating the letter and the spirit of various wartime agreements made with Churchill and Roosevelt. But Churchill's aim at Fulton was to manipulate the naive and inexperienced American president into a renewed Anglo-American special relationship.

Shortly after Churchill's extraordinary visit, during which he deliberately lost $75 in playing a game of poker with Truman, the former prime minister had turned events to the distinct advantage of Britain. The prototype of the CIA was established on the wartime network of the London-trained OSS. American defense policy was based on joint U.S.–British sharing of intelligence and military defense secrets. Truman began to purge his administration of any anti-British elements, most notably agriculture secretary and Anglophobe, Henry Wallace. U.S. and British intelligence agencies resumed close collaboration in many key areas.

## THE DOLLAR STANDARD, BIG OIL AND THE NEW YORK BANKS

Anglo-American petroleum interests emerged from the Second World War in a position of enormously increased power. In the final agreement for a postwar 'New World Order' in monetary and economic affairs, hammered out between British and American negotiators in 1944 at Bretton Woods, New Hampshire, Anglo-American hegemony over world petroleum played a central role in the thinking of Lord Keynes and his American counterpart, Harry Dexter White, assistant U.S. Treasury secretary.

The Bretton Woods system was to be built around the 'three pillars' of the International Monetary Fund, whose member-country contributions would constitute an emergency reserve available in times of balance-of-payments distress; the World Bank, which would grant loans to member governments for large public projects; and the General Agreement on Tariffs and Trade (GATT), designed to create a managed agenda of 'free trade.'

But there were certain clauses skillfully designed by Lord Keynes and his American counterparts to ensure a postwar Anglo-American hegemony over world monetary and trade affairs. First, de facto voting control was given to the United States and Britain within the IMF and the World Bank. Second, Bretton Woods created what was called a gold exchange system. Under this system, each member country's national currency was pegged to the U.S. dollar. The U.S. dollar was in turn set at an official rate of $35 per fine ounce of gold, the rate set by President Roosevelt in 1934, during the depths of the Great Depression, and before a world war.

Because the New York Federal Reserve Bank had accumulated the bulk of the world's official gold reserves during the war, and because the dollar emerged from the ravages of the war as the world's strongest currency, backed by what was unquestionably the world's strongest economy, few were in a position to argue with what amounted to a postwar U.S. dollar standard.

Among those least inclined to complain about the terms of the Bretton Woods monetary order were the large American petroleum companies, the Rockefeller companies of the Standard Oil group, together with the Pittsburgh Mellon family's Gulf Oil. They had secured a major stake in concessions for oil in the Middle East, above all in Saudi Arabia. Partly through the clever diplomacy of President Roosevelt, and the bungling of Britain's Winston Churchill, Saudi Arabia slipped from the British grip during the war. Saudi King Abdul Aziz gained an unprecedented lend–lease agreement in 1943 from Roosevelt, a gesture intended to ensure Saudi goodwill to American oil interests after the war.

Roosevelt acted on the advice of Harold Ickes, then petroleum coordinator for national defense, and the State Department, which in December 1942 had noted, 'It is our strong belief that the development of Saudi Arabian petroleum resources should be viewed in the light of the broad national interest.' This was the first time American national security had been officially linked with the fate of the desert kingdom on the Persian Gulf, more than 10,000 miles from its shores. It was not to be the last time. State Department planners realized that the implications were that U.S. foreign policy, at least in key areas, might become more imperial, along British lines of controlling strategic interests in lands far from its shores, as the pillar of its postwar power.[1]

But in the first years after the end of the Second World War, few other Americans realized the implications. They were far too preoccupied with returning to normal life after depression and war.

## THE MARSHALL PLAN FORMS A POSTWAR OIL HEGEMONY

Little attention has been paid to the role of oil in the postwar European Recovery Program (ERP), better known as the Marshall Plan, named after its architect, Secretary of State George C. Marshall. From its inception in 1947, the largest single expenditure by ERP recipient countries in Western Europe was to use Marshall Plan dollars to purchase oil, oil supplied primarily by American oil companies.

According to official records of the State Department, more than 10 per cent of all U.S. Marshall aid went to buy American oil.[2]

By the end of the war, the U.S. oil industry had become every bit as international as its British counterpart. Its main resources were in Venezuela, the Middle East and other far away places. After the war, 'Big Oil,' as the five U.S. companies were called—Standard Oil of New Jersey (Exxon), Socony-Vacuum Oil (Mobil), Standard Oil of California (Chevron), Texaco, and Gulf Oil—moved to take decisive control of Europe's postwar petroleum markets.

The ravages of war had severely hurt European dependence on coal as the primary energy source. Germany had lost her eastern coal reserves and coal output in the war-torn west was only 40 per cent of prewar levels. British coal output was 20 per cent below the level of 1938. The oil of eastern Europe fell behind what Churchill called the Iron Curtain, inaccessible to the West. In 1947, half of all western Europe's oil was being supplied by the five American companies.

The American oil majors did not hesitate to take advantage of this remarkable opportunity. Despite some congressional inquiry and mid-level bureaucratic protest at the obvious misuse of Marshall Plan funds, Big Oil forced Europe to pay a dear price, a very dear price. They more than doubled the price they charged European customers between 1945 and 1948, going from $1.05 per barrel to $2.22 per barrel. Though the oil was supplied from the inexpensive Middle East reserves of the U.S. companies, the freight rates were calculated in a deliberately complex formula, tied to freight rates from the Caribbean to Europe, a far higher cost.

Even within European markets, there were staggering cost differences. Greece was forced to pay $8.30 per ton for fuel oil, the same fuel oil for which Britain paid only $3.95 per ton. Further, the U.S. companies, with support of the Washington government, refused to allow Marshall Plan dollars to be used to build indigenous European refining capacity, further tightening the stranglehold of American Big Oil on postwar Europe.[3]

As the two major British oil companies, Anglo-Persian and Shell, recovered their capacities, the American five were forced to expand to seven companies, parceling out the oil markets of postwar Europe and the rest of the world. By the 1950s, the position of the Anglo-American oil companies appeared unassailable. They controlled incredibly cheap Middle Eastern supplies and captive markets in Europe, Asia, Latin America and North America.

The price of petroleum seemed a constant of daily life during the 1950s. The companies reaped enormous profit from their dollar sales of oil to the new world market. The automobile and its associated industries had become the single largest component of the American economy. U.S. tax dollars poured billions into construction of a national modern highway infrastructure under the Eisenhower National Defense Highway Act, using the pretext that fast motorways were required to flee cities in the event of Soviet nuclear war. The railroad infrastructure was neglected and allowed to decay, to the advantage of the far less energy-efficient motor transport. This was the time when a secretary of defense, Wilson, former chairman of a major Detroit automobile corporation, could say without flinching, 'What's good for General Motors is good for America.' He should have added, good too for Exxon, Texaco and the oil majors. Oil had become the most important commodity to fuel the economy.

## THE POWER OF THE NEW YORK BANKS TIED TO U.S. OIL

A little-noted consequence of this extraordinary global market grab by the major American oil companies following the Second World War was the parallel rise to international dominance of the New York banking groups tied to oil. Since the period of the Dawes reparations loans and related lending of the 1920s, New York banks had increasingly oriented their business towards the international arena and away from domestic finance. As U.S. petroleum companies became an ever larger element in international oil supply during the Second World War, the New York banks benefited from the capital inflows of the world oil trade. To preserve this advantage, the powerful New York banks exerted influence to modify the original Bretton Woods scheme devised by Keynes and Dexter White.

During the early 1950s, a wave of little-noted New York bank mergers contributed to increasing the already enormous political and financial influence the banks exerted over domestic U.S. policy. In 1955, Rockefeller's Chase National Bank merged with the Bank of Manhattan and the Bronx County Trust to create the Chase Manhattan Bank. The National City Bank of New York, also, like Chase, closely tied to the international operations of the Standard Oil group, acquired the First National Bank of New York to form the First National City Bank, later Citibank Corp. Bankers' Trust took over the Public Bank & Trust, Title Guarantee & Trust and several other regional banks to form another powerful group, while the Chemical

Bank & Trust merged with the Corn Exchange Bank and the New York Trust Co. to form New York's third largest bank group, Chemical Bank New York Trust, also tied to Standard Oil. J.P. Morgan & Co. merged in the same period with Guaranty Trust Co. to form Morgan Guaranty Trust Co., the fifth largest bank.

The net effect of this postwar cartelisation of American banking and financial power into the tiny handful of banks in New York, which were strongly oriented towards the fortunes of the international petroleum markets and policy, had enormous consequence for the following three decades of American financial history, overshadowing all other policy influences in U.S. and international policy, with the possible exception of the Vietnam war deficit financing.

The New York banks had traditionally been oriented towards international business, but they now held disproportionate power over world finance, as never before. Their power resembled that of the old London imperial banking groups such as Midland Bank, Barclays, and the like. By 1961, the deposits concentrated into the five largest New York banks were fully 75 per cent of all bank deposits of the entire metropolitan region, America's largest economic region.[4]

The membership of the increasingly influentiual New York Council on Foreign Relations (CFR) during the 1950s, also reflected this concentration of financial and economic power. The CFR chairman was the Wall Street lawyer John J. McCloy, also chairman of Chase Bank and a former lawyer for the Rockefeller Standard Oil interests.

While most Americans only dimly realized the ominous implications of the concentration of economic and financial power into a small number of hands in New York banks, corporations and related law firms during the early postwar years in the 1950s, the point was not lost on their British cousins in the City of London. American society was increasingly being reshaped along the lines of the British 'informal empire,' with finance, raw materials control, and control of international terms of trade as its underpinning, rather than the traditional American foundation of technological and industrial progress.

## MOHAMMED MOSSADEGH TAKES ON ANGLO-AMERICAN OIL

While Britain during the 1950s appeared to be losing her most extensive attributes of empire, she held tenaciously to a reordered set of colonial priorities. Rather than stake everything on maintaining the extensive formal empire reaching to India, she regrouped around the far more profitable empire of world oil and strategic raw material control, with the assistance of the United States. Thus Egypt and the Suez Canal, through which the bulk of Middle East oil flowed into Europe, became a strategic priority, as did maintenance of British interests in the oil-producing Middle East Gulf states, especially Iran, where the British government, through its Anglo-Iranian Oil Company, retained a stranglehold on the country's political and economic fortunes, despite the pressures of world war.

Since its efforts (described earlier) to gain a monopoly of Persian oil rights at the time of William Knox d'Arcy, in 1901–02, Britain had fought like a tiger to control what became of Iran's oil minerals. During the Second World War, Britain played an especially perfidious role, persuading Stalin's Russia to join forces in invading Iran on the flimsy pretext that the presence of a handful of German engineers in the neutral territory constituted a *casus belli*. A month after British and Russian forces occupied Iran in August 1941, the Shah abdicated in favor of his son, Mohammed Reza Pahlevi, who was disposed under the circumstances to accomodate the Anglo-Russian occupation.

The British occupation forces, later complemented by a smaller American contingent, sat idly by while their wartime 'ally' Russia requisitioned most food supplies from the northern zone of Iran occupied by the Soviet army. Tens of thousands of Iranians died of hunger while 100,000 Russian and 70,000 British and Indian troops were given priority in supplies. Typhoid and typhus became epidemic. Diversion of supplies along the Iranian railroad to carry Anglo-American lend-lease goods to Russia during the winter of 1944–45 killed thousands more for want of heating oil in the bitter winter. British policy during the entire period was systematic humiliation of nationalist Iranian elements and the government, while encouraging the most superstitious and feudal reaction inside the country.

In a desperate bid to seek help from a third party, the Iranian government asked for American aid, and in 1942 an American military officer, General M. Norman Schwarzkopf (father of the commander of the U.S. forces in the 1990–91 Operation Desert Storm), went to Iran, where he trained a national police force during a six-year period, until 1948. Schwarzkopf and his Iranian army contacts were later to prove crucial in the toppling of Iran's nationalist Premier Mossadegh in August 1953.

Despite the solemn declaration of the wartime Tehran conference regarding the restoration of postwar Iranian sovereignty, signed by Stalin, Churchill and Roosevelt, Russia demanded an extensive exclusive oil concession in the northern part of Iran bordering Azerbaijan, while Britain demanded further concession for the government-linked Royal Dutch Shell. In the midst of this blatant foreign blackmail from what amounted to occupation forces on Iranian territory, in December 1944 the Iranian nationalist leader, Dr. Mohammed Mossadegh, introduced a bill in the Iranian parliament which would prohibit oil negotiations with foreign countries.

Mossadegh cited a November 2, 1944, *Times* of London editorial which proposed a postwar partition of Iran among the three powers, Britain, Russia and the United States. The resolution passed, but it explicitly left for a later debate the resolution of the Anglo-Iranian Oil Company concession in southern Iran, the old d'Arcy concession from 1901.

By 1948, following a bitter fight that included taking the case before the new United Nations, Iran had finally succeeded in forcing a withdrawal of foreign troops from her soil. But the country and its economy were still under the effective control of the British government through the Anglo-Iranian Oil Company. Iran's southern region contained the richest oil province then known in the entire world, and it was controlled under the exclusive concession given decades earlier to the British. Since 1919, British administrative officials had de facto run the administration of the country to secure this vital monopoly. Niceties of Iranian sovereignty were pushed to one side.

But following the end of the Second World War, with the anticolonial movement emerging from India across Africa into Asia, Iran would no longer tolerate such an abrogation of its national sovereignty. In late 1947, the government of Iran proposed that the Anglo-Iranian Oil Co. should increase the ridiculously low revenue share Anglo-Iranian allowed the government of Iran for the world's most profitable oil exploitation.

Iran cited the case of Venezuela, where the American Standard Oil companies had agreed on a 50–50 split with the government of Venezuela. Iran noted that had she had such terms, instead of getting a paltry $36 million per year for draining its precious natural resource, it would have accrued $100 million, at that time a significant sum. As it was, Iran calculated that Anglo-Iranian and the British were de facto paying total royalties of a mere 8 per cent of their net profit. Britain held exclusive concession over a vast area comprising 100,000 square miles, on which it was refusing to engage in significant new exploration. Iran had calculated that in 1948 on its production of 23 million tons of Iranian oil, the Anglo-Iranian Oil Co. made a profit of $320,000,000, while paying Iran a royalty of $36,000,000. The government of Iran suggested in light of the data presented, that the original concession be renegotiated with the principle of justice and fairness in mind.[5]

This suggestion was not greeted with joy in London. BBC radio began broadcasting faked news accounts designed to embarrass the Iranian government, claiming that Foreign Minister Esfandiari had agreed to humiliating concessions to British Foreign Minister Ernest Bevin for amending Iran's constitution. That was only the initial response.

The talks about altering the Anglo-Iranian agreement dragged on through 1949 without significant concession from the British side. Their strategy was to stall and delay, while working always to weaken the Iranian government. But in Iranian parliamentary elections towards the end of 1949, Dr. Mossadegh and his small National Front party campaigned on the issue of the oil negotiation. The National Front won six seats in the new parliament, and by December Mossadegh was named head of a parliamentary commission on the oil issue. Iran had asked for a 50–50 split of the profits as well as for Iranian participation in the management of Anglo-Iranian Oil Co. As one government after another fell over the contentious issue, British refusal to meet Iran even half way continued until April 1951, when Mohammed Mossadegh was made prime minister. Contrary to subsequent propaganda from various circles in Washington and London, Mossadegh was not a proxy for the Tudeh communists or Russia or any wild extremist, but a passionate patriot of Iran and a staunch enemy of Soviet Russia, whatever other faults he may have had.

On March 15, the Iranian Parliament, the Majlis, had voted to accept the Mossadegh commission's recommendation and to nationalize, with fair compensation, the Anglo-Iranian Oil Company. The final nationalization plan was approved by the Majlis the day before Mossadegh was asked to form his government, on April 28, 1951.

In British eyes, Iran had committed the unforgivable sin. It had effectively acted to assert national interest over British interests. Britain promptly threatened retaliation and within days British naval forces arrived near Abadan. Here the hypocrisy of the British came to light. Previously, the British Foreign Office had refused to intervene into negotiations between Anglo-Iranian and Iran, claiming it would not interfere in the affairs of a 'private company,' despite the fact that

53 per cent of Anglo-Iranian was held by His Majesty's Government. Now, with Anglo-Iranian nationalized by Iran,

> the British government not only intervened in the negotiation between Iran and the company but also backed up its demands by dispatching units of the Royal Navy to Iranian waters, and threatened the occupation of Abadan by paratroopers for the ostensible reason of protecting British interests.

Abadan was the site of the world's largest oil refinery, part of Anglo-Iranian Oil Co.[6]

In all the 28 months of Mossadegh's premiership, the British labored under one overwhelming obstacle. Iran was fully within her legal rights to nationalize a company on her territory so long as she offered just compensation, which Mossadegh's government had done. Moreover, Iran would guarantee to Britain the same level of oil supply she had enjoyed before nationalization, as well as offering to continue to employ British nationals in Anglo-Iranian.

By September 1951, Britain had declared full economic sanctions against Iran, including an embargo against Iranian oil shipments as well as a freeze on all Iranian assets in British banks abroad. British warships were stationed just outside Iranian coastal waters and land and air forces were dispatched to Basrah in British-controlled Iraq, close to the Abadan refinery complex. The British embargo was joined by all the major Anglo-American oil companies. Economic strangulation was London and Washington's response to assertions of national sovereignty from developing states which interfered with their vital assets. British secret intelligence bribed informants within the Iranian central bank, Bank Melli, and other parts of the government, to gain a minute-by-minute reading of the exact effect of their economic sanctions on the country.

Prospective buyers of nationalized Iranian oil were warned by the Anglo-American oil companies that they would face legal action on the grounds that a compensation agreement had not yet been signed between Anglo-Iranian Oil Co. and Iran. This tortuous legal argument covered a self-fulfilling strategy. The company and the British refused to sign any compensation agreement. Meanwhile, as month rolled into month, the bite of the embargo on Iran's fragile economy took hold and the economic troubles besetting Mossadegh's regime multiplied. The major source of the country's export earnings, oil revenues, plummeted from $400 million in 1950 to less than $2 million between July 1951 and the fall of Mossadegh in August 1953.

Mossadegh went to the United States in person that September to address the UN Security Council, which timidly voted to defer the matter, whereupon Mossadegh went to Washington in a vain effort to enlist American help for his country's position. The major political blunder made by Mossadegh was his lack of appreciation of the iron-clad cartel relationship of Anglo-American interests around the vital issue of strategic petroleum control. U.S. 'mediator' W. Averill Harriman had gone to Iran, accompanied by a delegation packed with people tied to Big Oil interests, including State Department economist Walter Levy. Harriman recommended that Iran accept the British 'offer.' When Mossadegh went to Washington, the only suggestion he heard from the State Department was to appoint Royal Dutch Shell as Iran's management company.

When the British insisted the case be brought before the World Court for arbitration, Mossadegh, himself educated in law in Belgium and Switzerland, argued his country's case successfully, and the Court, on July 22, 1952, denied Britain jurisdiction, referring the matter back to Iran's internal jurisdiction.

Commenting on the situation in December 1952, journalist Ned Russell of the *New York Herald-Tribune* noted accurately that there were few, if any, leaders of small nations with Mossadegh's courage, who, watching their country suffer under a massive financial and economic blockade imposed by Britain, and now the United States, would say to Truman and Churchill, 'No.' Russell noted that Churchill's ploy was to 'pit the United States and Britain together against Dr. Mossadegh.'

By 1953, Anglo-American intelligence had its response ready. In May of that year, the new U.S. President, Dwight Eisenhower, turned down Mossadegh's request for economic aid, on advice of his secretary of state, John Foster Dulles, and the CIA chief, Allen Dulles. On August 10, CIA director Allen Dulles met with the US ambassador to Tehran, Loy Henderson, and the Shah's sister in Switzerland. At the same time, in August, 1953, after a five-year absence, Gen. Norman Schwarzkopf, Sr. arrived in Tehran to see 'old friends.' He was close to the Shah and to key army generals he had earlier trained, who were being promised power in the event of a successful coup against Mossadegh.

With the aid of royalist elements in the Iranian armed forces, British and American intelligence staged a coup and forced Mossadegh's arrest, his influence severely undermined by two years of unrelenting Anglo-American economic warfare against the country, combined with subversion of key support for the government. Britain's Secret Intelligence Services had convinced the CIA's Allen Dulles and his brother, Secretary of State John Foster Dulles, who then convinced Eisenhower, that the overthrow of Mossadegh was indispensable.

The CIA, under code name Operation AJAX, cooperated fully with British SIS in the overthrow of Mohammed Mossadegh in August 1953. The young Reza Shah Pahlevi was backed by the Anglo-Americans as opposition to Mossadegh. The Shah returned, and economic sanctions were lifted. Anglo-American oil interests had prevailed and had shown what they were prepared to do in the postwar era to anyone who tried to challenge their mandate. Ironically, those same Anglo-American interests would turn on the Shah himself some 25 years later.[7]

The U.S.–Soviet cold war period in the immediate postwar years provided a marvelous opportunity to British and American intelligence services. Any significant opposition which stood in the way of major policy initiatives could conveniently be painted with a red brush as communist or 'communist-leaning.' Nowhere was this easier to apply than against little-known leaders of developing or newly independent former colonial nations. This was the tactic used by London and by Washington all too often during the postwar decades. As a consequence, Mohammed Mossadegh was to become known in Western accounts as an irresponsible wild radical who was working with communists against vital Western strategic security.

## ITALY ATTEMPTS INDEPENDENCE IN OIL AND DEVELOPMENT

One European company expressed interest in purchasing oil from Mossadegh's nationalized oil supply. This was in Italy. More specifically, it was an individual—Enrico Mattei, the founder of a new Italian state enterprise, who would later cause severe headaches for the Anglo-American oil cartel.

Enrico Mattei had *Entschlossenheit* (determination) in the classical Prussian meaning of the term. He was the leader of the largest noncommunist resistance organization in Italy during the Second World War. When Alcide de Gasperi formed his Christian Democratic government in 1945, he named Mattei as head in the north Italian region of a moribund entity created two decades earlier called Azienda Generale Italiana Petroli, or AGIP.

Despite the fact that Italy had switched sides in 1943, two years of Allied fighting and bombing, following more than two decades of Mussolini's fascism, had left the country in ruins. In 1945, Italy's gross national product was only at the level of 1911, and had fallen in real terms by 40 per cent from the level of 1938. A large increase in population, despite war losses, came as a result of repatriation from lost colonies. Starvation threatened, and the standard of living was alarmingly low.

In this situation, Enrico Mattei set out to create indigenous energy resources to begin the reconstruction of Italy's postwar economy. Despite a mandate to prepare AGIP for privatization as rapidly as possible, Mattei set about finding oil and gas. This he did with an aggressive exploration effort under the Po Plain in the north of Italy, with a series of increasingly significant discoveries, first in 1946 near Caviaga, then a major find south of Cremona at Cortemaggiore in 1949, where not only natural gas but also the first oil in Italy was found. Mattei was given carte blanche to build his enterprise after these finds, having become overall head of AGIP.

Efforts by the jealous American oil majors to co-opt this new rival in the Italian energy market were resisted. Mattei was a staunch Italian nationalist, determined to build the economy of the nation as a self-sufficient country. The drain on the precious dollar reserves of Italy to pay for oil imports from the American and British oil majors was the largest problem in Italy's postwar balance-of-payments deficit. Mattei tackled this problem with a boldness which cut across awesome obstacles. A 2,500-mile long network of gas pipelines was constructed, to bring the natural gas from Cortemaggiore into the industrial cities of Milan and Turin. The revenues from the new gas finds were used to finance the expansion of the industrial infrastructure of AGIP across Italy's industrial north.

It was Mattei, referring to the ruthless cartelization of world oil markets, who coined the term *Sette Sorelle* or Seven Sisters, to refer to the seven Anglo-American companies who ruled the world of oil in the 1950s. Mattei was determined that Italy should not be subjugated to the power of these seven, whom he accurately accused of pursuing a worldwide policy of limiting production to maintain the highest prices for their holdings, and selling their crude to oil-poor Europe at prices rigged to match the high cost of production in the United States. Mattei set out to secure maximum production and supply at the lowest price possible. Needless to say, he soon came into bitter conflict with those seven powerful companies and their friends in government.

In February 1953, Mattei successfully lobbied for a new law which created a central semiautonomous state energy holding, Ente Natzionale Idrocarburi, or ENI, as it came to be known. ENI, with Mattei as its founding president, subsumed AGIP for oil and gas refining, as well as the pipeline subsidiary SNAM, and was soon to develop a tanker fleet and a network of gasoline stations across Italy, surpassing those of Esso and Shell in quality and customer service, the first to incorporate modern restaurants and other conveniences. Using the same development formula he had applied in AGIP, Mattei used the proceeds from ENI to invest in the construction of oil refineries, a giant chemicals plant, a synthetic rubber plant using ENI natural gas as feedstock, a heavy engineering subsidiary which constructed all the ENI refineries and related infrastructure, as well as acquisition of an oil tanker fleet to haul ENI crude oil from abroad, independently of the Anglo-American shipping monopoly.

By 1958, total proceeds from ENI's Italian natural gas sales alone topped the considerable sum of $75,000,000 yearly. This was money saved—otherwise precious Italian dollar reserves would have had to be spent for imported oil and coal. Perhaps no single individual accomplished more in the 15 years after the war to develop industry in Italy.[8]

As early as 1954, the U.S. Embassy in Rome had become visibly alarmed at the activities of Enrico Mattei. 'For the first time in the economic history of Italy,' stated an American Embassy memorandum to Washington, 'a government-owned entity has found itself in the unique position of being financially solvent, capably led, and responsible to no one other than its leader.'[9]

## MATTEI'S BOLD DEVELOPMENT INITIATIVE

But if Mattei's efforts to secure energy independence within Italy had irritated the Seven Sisters and the Anglo-American interests behind them, his growing efforts to secure independent supplies of crude oil from abroad turned that annoyance into a rabid hatred of the Italian industrialist—most notably, when the Anglo-Americans learned what kind of contracts Mattei was willing to sign, especially with developing countries.

When the Shah of Iran was restored after the fall of Mossadegh, with the active backing of British and American intelligence, he did not move to completely undo the work of his defeated prime minister. The National Iranian Oil Company was to remain a state entity with control over all subsurface oil and gas reserves. But by April 1954, less than a year after the coup, the Anglo-American companies, joined by their 'little sister,' France's state-owned CFP, entered into negotiations with the government of Iran and NIOC to secure a 25-year participation agreement for exploitation of oil on 100,000 square miles of Iranian territory.

Anglo-Iranian Oil, which that same year changed its name to British Petroleum, was given the lion's share of its old d'Arcy concession, or 40 per cent. Royal Dutch Shell got the second largest, 14 per cent, giving the British companies the majority or 54 per cent of Iran's output from the area. The American majors, together with a handful of selected 'independents' which were part of the old Standard Rockefeller group, divided 40 per cent of the oil between them. France's CFP got 6 per cent. Mattei approached the Seven Sisters to discuss a small ENI participation in the Iran concession, and was given what he later called a 'humiliating' rejection by the Anglo-Americans.

Not to be thwarted, in 1955, a year before Britain's own humiliation at Suez, Mattei entered into successful negotiations with Egypt's new nationalist leader, Gamal Abdel Nasser. ENI secured a share of the concession to develop the oil of Egypt's Sinai peninsula, which by 1961 was to grow into a considerable volume of some 2.5 million tons per year of crude oil, the vast bulk of which was then refined in ENI refineries to fill the rapidly expanding demand in Italy for petroleum, all without having to be paid for in scarce U.S. dollars.

But Mattei's real challenge to the Anglo-American major oil companies came in Iran in 1957. Mattei began negotiations with the Shah in the spring of 1957 for an unprecedented arrangement. Under the terms of the deal, the National Iranian Oil Company would get 75 per cent of total profits, ENI 25 per cent, in a new joint venture, Société Irano-Italiènne des Pétroles (SIRIP), which had a 25-year exclusive right to explore and develop some 8,800 square miles of promising petroleum prospects in the non-allocated regions of Iran. A senior British official stated at the time, 'The Italians are determined somehow or another to muscle in on Middle East oil.'

The view of Washington and London was much the same as that of the Seven Sisters. Mattei's revolutionary initiatives, if allowed to go unchecked, would upset the entire global world oil order. The standard agreement with developing countries from the major U.S.

and UK companies was a 50–50 split of the crude oil, with ample margin for manipulation of downstream profits built in. If Mattei were 'let into the club' of the Sisters, they feared that Belgian and German and other companies would also demand their rightful share of oil possibilities. So the U.S. and British governments officially protested to the Shah's government against the pending deal with Mattei.

But to no immediate avail. In August 1957, Mattei and the Iranians had secured their revolutionary agreement. Speaking about the potential of his new contract, Mattei declared his view that 'the Middle East should now be industrial Europe's Middle West,' signalling his intention of using the oil agreement as a first step towards the European building of significant industrial and technological infrastructure in the Middle East.

By March 1961 the first ENI oil tanker, *Cortemaggiore*, landed at the Italian port of Bari, with the first fruits of the new Iranian partnership, 18,000 tons of crude oil from the Persian Gulf. Mattei had pioneered some of the first successful underwater oil explorations in his SIRIP joint venture.

Inside Italy itself, Mattei continued to exert pressure on the Seven Sisters companies through a policy of progressive price reductions at the gasoline pump for consumers, as well as by persuading the Italian government to reduce the severely high excise tax on gasoline. As a direct result of this policy, in which the Anglo-American companies were forced reluctantly to acquiesce, gasoline prices in Italy dropped 25 per cent between 1959 and 1961, a factor which is credited with significantly aiding Italy's first real postwar economic revival.

Outside Italy, Mattei continued an active foreign policy of seeking out those regions which had been deliberately neglected by the Anglo-Americans as 'too small' to warrant attention. ENI and Mattei personally went to newly independent countries of Africa and Asia, and discussed prospects unlike any then being offered to these forgotten former colonies.

Mattei would build local oil refineries in the given country, which would then be owned by the country. This broke with the ironclad Seven Sisters control of the vastly more lucrative refining end of the business. The supplier country would no longer be merely a primitive raw material source, but would begin to develop the basis of modern indigenous industry from the proceeds of its mineral wealth. In return, ENI would get a guaranteed return on its capital invested in the country; it would secure the exclusive engineering and construction contracts for the refining facilities, as well as being the exclusive worldwide marketer for the oil.

But it was in October 1960 that Enrico Mattei blew the fuses inside the White House and 10 Downing Street, as well as in the headquarters of the Seven Sisters. Italy's leading anticommunist resistance leader, life-long Christian Democrat, Enrico Mattei, was in Moscow. Once again, Moscow and the vast Russian petroleum resources became the focus of European negotiations, as in the 1920s at Rapallo. And, once again, the Anglo-Americans stood dead opposed to the success of the negotiations.

Since 1958, ENI had contracted to buy a small volume of crude oil from the Soviet Union, fewer than 1 million tons annually. But word leaked out in the West that a far more ambitious undertaking was being discussed in Moscow between Mattei and Soviet Foreign Trade Minister Patolitschev. On October 11, 1958 Mattei signed an agreement whereby, in exchange for guaranteed delivery of 2.4 million tons of Soviet oil annually, over a five-year period, ENI would ensure a significantly expanded Soviet oil export capability into the West. The oil would not be paid in cash, but rather in kind, in the form of deliveries of large-diameter oil pipe. This would enable construction of a huge pipeline network bringing Soviet oil from the Volga–Urals into Czechoslovakia, Poland and Hungary. When complete, that pipeline network would bring some 15 million tons annually of Soviet crude oil into eastern Europe, where it was to be exchanged for industrial goods and food products for the USSR. At that time, the USSR had a desperate need for large-diameter oil pipe, and lacked the capacity to produce it in the necessary volume and quality.

ENI secured the support of the Italian government and the state-owned Finsider Group was commissioned to build a new steelworks in Taranto with a capacity to deliver 2 million tons of large-diameter pipe annually. The Taranto plant was rushed into completion, and began to produce pipe for the Soviet market by September 1962.

Italy was able to buy crude oil from the Soviet Union at a price of $1.00 per barrel f.o.b. the Black Sea, compared with a cost in Kuwait of $1.59 per barrel plus an added $0.69 per barrel for shipping costs, and in the United States in the early 1960s, for oil of comparable quality, of $2.75 per barrel. With the added boost of new jobs in the Italian steel and chemicals sector, few in Italy were alarmed at charges in certain parts of the American and British press that Mattei was a 'crypto-communist,' or at the very least had become a 'fellow traveler' with Moscow.[10]

One month after the Finsider pipe works began rolling steel for Soviet pipelines, on October 27, 1962, under circumstances which to the present day stir speculation and charges of deliberate sabotage, the private airplane carrying Enrico Mattei crashed after taking off from Sicily en route to Milan, killing all three on board.

Mattei was 56 years old, at the peak of his powers. The Rome CIA station chief at that time, Thomas Karamessines, left Rome soon afterwards without explanation. He was later instrumental in the Chilean coup against Salvador Allende. Perhaps it is merely a coincidence, but CIA chief John McCone, at the time of Mattei's suspicious death, held more than $1 million in shares in Standard Oil of California (Chevron). A detailed report dated 28 October, 1962, from Karamessines on the Mattei assassination has never been made public by the U.S. government, which cites 'matters concerning national security' as reason for its refusal.

Before his death, Mattei had managed to secure the construction of Italy's first nuclear power test reactor, and had created a new subsidiary of ENI, called ENEL, a state electricity utility to work in the development of the country's electric grid with ambitious plans for nuclear energy well in view. Furthermore, in addition to his agreements with Iran, Egypt and the Soviet Union for oil supply, he had signed similar developmental agreements with Morocco, Sudan, Tanzania, Ghana, India and Argentina.

In noting Mattei's death, the London *Economist*, the weekly of the British financial establishment, founded to open the way for repeal of the Corn Laws in the 1840s, and owned by the trust of Royal Dutch Shell's Lord Cowdray, made the following editorial comment:

> Just how great or how sinister a man Enrico Mattei was will long remain the subject of passionate debate: put him somewhere between [Royal Dutch Shell's] Deterding and Kreuger [Ivar Kreuger, Swedish financier who died in 1931 also under suspicious circumstances]. But it is difficult to think of any other man in world oil or in Italy, the areas where Mattei cast the longest shadow, whose abrupt subtraction from the scene might make as much difference to either.

The *New York Times* called him 'the most important individual in Italy,' who more than any other individual had been responsible for Italy's postwar 'Italian economic miracle.'[11]

At the time of his death, Mattei had been preparing for a trip to meet with the president of the United States, John F. Kennedy, who was then pressing the U.S. oil companies to reach some form of détente with Mattei. The agenda of that Kennedy–Mattei talk was not to be realized. One can only speculate at the possibilities. Instead, in little more than a year, Kennedy himself was assassinated, the trail of blood also leading to the door of U.S. intelligence, through a complex web of organized crime cutouts.

# 8

# A Sterling Crisis and the Adenauer–De Gaulle Threat

## CONTINENTAL EUROPE EMERGES FROM THE RUBBLE OF WAR

By the end of the 1950s the world began to look promising for the first time in more than almost three decades, at least for a majority of western Europeans, as well as for aspiring nations of what in those days was still called the 'developing sector' of the southern hemisphere.

In 1957, a new form of economic cooperation, the European Economic Community, with France, West Germany and Italy at the center, was formed with the signing of the Treaty of Rome. In January 1959, according to terms of that treaty, the European Economic Community was born. The Federal Republic of Germany had begun recovery from the ravages of war, on its way to rebuilding Europe's strongest industrial capacities. In France, General Charles de Gaulle returned to power in 1958 and began a vigorous program, under the guidance of an emergency restructuring plan drafted by his economic adviser, Jacques Rueff, to build modern infrastructure and expand France's devastated industrial and agricultural economy, and restore the nation's fiscal stability. By the late 1950s, Italy was enjoying the fruits of an economic prosperity largely the consequence of the initiatives set into motion by ENI's Enrico Mattei.

In fact, in the first two decades following the end of the Second World War, the noncommunist economies of Europe and many developing sector-countries experienced an unprecedented industrial and agriculture growth. Continental European manufacturing industry was expanding at a healthy 5 per cent annual rate by the early 1960s. The total volume of world trade, which had been stagnant for the decade after 1938, had increased by some 250 per cent in relative terms between 1948 and 1963, and with no end to the growth in sight. By 1957, for the first time ever, world trade in manufactured goods exceeded that in primary goods—food and raw materials.

What drove this expansion was the rapidly growing trade of the European Common Market. In 1953, the countries comprising the

Common Market counted for 19 per cent of world export trade; by 1960, they had surpassed U.S. exports, both in relative and absolute terms, at 26 per cent of total world exports and some $30 billion.

Western European investment in new steel plants, highway and electricity infrastructure and port modernization, for cities such as Hamburg, Rotterdam and other major terminals, together created the foundations for an impressive expansion of the west European economy's productivity. Measured in terms of output per man-hour of the industrial labor force, labor productivity in western Continental Europe from the 1950s into the 1960s was growing at a healthy rate of nearly 7 per cent per annum, fully one-and-a-half times more rapidly than in the United States in the same period.[1]

In the course of this dramatic industrial and trade growth in Continental Europe, European trade relations with the developing sector also expanded significantly beginning in the late 1950s, leading to a more rapid industrial growth in many developing nations than at any time during the century. Indicative of the process was the growth of the developing sector's share of world manufacturing production, which grew from 6.5 per cent of an expanding total output in 1953 to almost 9 per cent by 1963—an increase of 50 per cent in relative terms over the decade, a far greater increase in absolute terms of output.[2]

When de Gaulle was brought back to power in France in 1958, this gave a strong new political voice to the economically expanding European continent. De Gaulle, a seasoned military and political figure, had no illusions about the ultimate designs of the British in Europe, and increasingly regarded American postwar designs as dangerously similar to those of the British. On assuming the presidency in 1958, de Gaulle began a series of fruitless exchanges with President Eisenhower, proposing a fundamental reform of the NATO structure in order to allow a French 'veto' on the use of nuclear weapons, among other things. In September 1959, General de Gaulle expressed his concerns in a letter to the American president:

> In the course of two world wars, America was France's ally, and France has not forgotten what she owes to American help. But neither has she forgotten that during the First World War, that help came only after three long years of struggle which nearly proved mortal for her, and that during the Second she had already been crushed before you intervened ... I know as you yourself know, what a nation is, with its geography, its interests, its political system, its public opinion, its passions, its fears, its errors. It can

help another, but it cannot identify itself with another. That is why, although remaining faithful to our alliance, I cannot accept France's integration into NATO.[3]

As Washington turned a deaf ear to France's proposals, de Gaulle initiated an independent French nuclear *force de frappe* and announced it was withdrawing its Mediterranean naval fleet from the NATO command. In 1960, France successfully tested its first atomic bomb in the Sahara. De Gaulle was articulating a new independent voice for the emerging postwar Continental Europe.

One of the first steps de Gaulle took after assuming the presidency of France in 1958 was to invite German Chancellor Konrad Adenauer to meet with him at de Gaulle's private retreat in Colombey-les-deux-Eglises in September 1958. It was the beginning not only of an historic political rapprochement between the two former wartime antagonists, but also of a close personal friendship between the two seasoned statesmen. The process culminated some five years later on January 22, 1963, when de Gaulle and Adenauer signed the 'Treaty Between the French Republic and the Federal Republic of Germany,' outlining a process of close heads-of-state cooperation, combined with various forms of economic and industrial policy coordination.

The de Gaulle–Adenauer accords sent alarm bells ringing in both Washington and London. Continental Europe, under the leadership of de Gaulle, Adenauer and Italy's Aldo Moro, was becoming far too independent in every respect for the comfort of some. Nor did it pass unnoticed in London that the very day after the historic signing of the Franco-German treaty, France's government announced she would veto British application to enter the European Common Market, a veto exercised by de Gaulle out of the years of deep distrust for British motives regarding a strong independent Continental Europe.

## ANGLO-AMERICAN GRAND DESIGNS AGAINST EUROPE

Early in 1962, the policy circles influencing the Washington administration of John Kennedy had formulated their alternative to the assertion of European independence represented by the growing collaboration between Germany under Adenauer and France under Charles de Gaulle. A group of policy advisers, including the ever influential John J. McCloy, who had been Truman's high commissioner for Germany from 1949 to 1952, White House National Security Adviser McGeorge Bundy, Treasury Secretary Douglas Dillon, Under

Secretary of State George Ball and the CIA's Robert Bowie, formulated a counter to the Franco-German notion of a strong independent Europe with what they termed their 'Atlanticist Grand Design.'

With effusive rhetoric supporting the Europe of Jean Monnet, the essence of the Washington policy was that the new Common Market open itself to American imports and be firmly locked into a NATO military alliance in which British and American voices dominated. Washington's plan also demanded support for British membership of the six-nation Common Market, a move which, as noted, de Gaulle for very good reasons adamantly opposed.

By the time of the January 1963 de Gaulle–Adenauer meeting, Washington's opposition policy was in full force, in coordination with that of Britain. Kennedy's State Department made no secret of its extreme displeasure over the France–Germany accord. The U.S. Embassy in Bonn had been instructed to exert maximum pressure on select members of both the Christian Democrats of Adenauer, the liberal FDP of Erich Mende, and the opposition Social Democrats. Two days before the first formal reading of the Franco-German Treaty in the German Bundestag, on April 24, 1963, Ludwig Erhard, a firm opponent of de Gaulle and an outspoken Atlanticist who favored British entry into the Common Market, was elected Adenauer's successor. The culmination of Adenauer's life's work, ratification of the Franco-German treaty, was stolen from him by Anglo-American interests at the last moment.

After this, the content of the Franco-German accord, though formally ratified, amounted to a lifeless piece of paper. Chancellor Erhard presided ineffectively over a divided party. By July 1964, de Gaulle himself, when asked by press on the progress of the Franco-German accord, painted a grim picture of the state of German–French relations. 'One could not say,' declared de Gaulle with bitterness over his relations with Adenauer's successor, 'that Germany and France have yet agreed to make policy together, and one could not dispute that this results from the fact that Bonn has not believed, up to now, that this policy should be European and independent.'

For the moment, the influential London and Washington circles had blocked the danger of a powerful bloc of Continental European policy that was independent of Anglo-American Atlantic designs. The weakest European link, postwar 'occupied' Germany, had for the moment been broken. Britain's basic nineteenth-century 'balance-of-power' strategy against Continental Europe had again been maintained, as in the years before 1914. This time, Britain had reestablished 'balance' through the surrogate arm of the U.S. State Department. Now it remained for the Anglo-Americans to deal with de Gaulle directly. But that was to prove no easy affair. [4]

## 1957: AMERICA AT THE TURNING POINT

While Washington had initially encouraged the creation of a European Common Market, in order to provide a more efficient market for American industrial and capital exports, the last thing certain circles in the Anglo-American establishment wanted was a politically and economically independent Continental Europe. This problem took on a sinister new twist when, beginning in late 1957, the United States underwent the first phase of a deep, persisting postwar economic recession, with resulting industrial stagnation and growing unemployment—a recession which lasted into the mid 1960s.

The fundamental causes for the recession were not difficult to foresee, had anyone seriously sought them. The vast amount of investment into industrial plant and equipment, which had lifted the U.S. economy out of the 1930s depression, had taken place almost two decades earlier, during the wartime industrial buildup of 1939–43. By 1957, plant and equipment, as well as labor-force skill levels, needed to be rejuvenated with more modern resources. The United States in the late 1950s faced the demand of a huge reinvestment into its productive labor force, education system and technology base, if she were to continue to be the world's leading industrial economy. But, sadly for the United States and the rest of the world, leading U.S. policy circles ensured that precisely the wrong policy alternative dominated Washington in the wake of the 1957 recession.

A debate took place within U.S. policy circles over how to respond to the crisis. The New York Council on Foreign Relations, the Rockefeller Brothers Fund, and others drafted policy options. An ambitious young Harvard professor named Henry Kissinger became an appendage of the Rockefeller group at this time.

The issue was what to do about the deeper implications of the U.S. recession. The natural demand of industry and farmers for cheap credit and technological progress and capital investment was overshadowed by the powerful combination of the liberal East Coast establishment. As we noted earlier, by the end of the 1950s New York banks had merged into enormously powerful concentrations of financial power and were looking far beyond American shores for sources of their profits.

A decisive voice in this debate was the chairman of the New York Council on Foreign Relations, John J. McCloy. McCloy personally brought Kissinger down from Harvard in the late 1950s, to shape the policy options being readied for the nation by the 'Wise Men' of McCloy's Council on Foreign Relations. McCloy, a Wall Street lawyer, was at the time chairman of the Chase Manhattan Bank. Chase Manhattan, as we have noted earlier, was the bank of 'Big Oil.' The large U.S. oil multinationals and their New York bankers viewed the entire world market as their domain in the 1950s, not the narrow confines of the United States. Saudi Arabia, in a certain sense, was more 'strategic' for them than Texas. As we shall see, this difference was to become crucial.

The post-1957 U.S. policy debate was tilted to the advantage of the international banks of Lower Manhattan and Wall Street, through the influential national television and newspaper media which they controlled. Their control of then-emerging network television, centered in New York, where it enjoyed intimate links with the big international banks of McCloy and friends, and their control over select news media such as the *New York Times*, were central to the success of these New York interests in promoting policies which went directly counter to the best interests of the nation and its citizens at this critical turn. It was in this period that these interests were popularly identified as the liberal East Coast establishment.

## 'THAT '58 CHEVY'

The Iowa farmer or the skilled machinist in Cincinnati had little idea of what was at stake at the end of the 1950s, the last days of the Eisenhower presidency. But by that time, the large, internationally oriented New York banks had already begun preparing to abandon U.S. investment for greener pastures abroad.

Henry Ford once stated that he would gladly pay the highest wages in industry, sell the world's cheapest car, and in the process become the world's richest man—all by using the most modern technology. Unfortunately, by the early 1960s most influential voices in the U.S. policy establishment had forgotten Ford's lesson. They were too obsessed with making a 'quick buck' by the typical merchant's game of 'buy cheap, sell dear.' By the end of the 1950s, the U.S. establishment had walked away from investment in rebuilding American cities, from educating a more skilled labor force and from investing in more modern factory production and improving the national economy.

Instead, their dollars flowed out of the United States to grab up, 'on the cheap,' already-operating industrial companies in western Europe, South America or the emerging economies of Asia. At Ford Motor Company itself, Robert McNamara, an accountant, had taken over corporate control by the end of the 1950s.

Increasingly, after the 1957 crisis, large U.S. industries and banks began to follow the 'British model' of industrial policy. Systematic cheating on product quality became the fashion of the day. Milton Friedman and other economists preferred to call this 'monetarism,' but it was nothing other than the wholesale infestation of Britain's post-1846 'buy cheap, sell dear' methods into America's productive base. Pride in workmanship and commitment to industrial progress began to give way to the corporate financial 'bottom line,' a goal calculated every three months for corporate stockholders.

The average American needed to look no further than his family automobile to see how it worked. After 1957, rather than making the required change to more modern plant and equipment to increase its technological productivity, Detroit began manipulating instead. By 1958, the amount of steel used in a General Motors Chevrolet was cut to half that of the 1956 model. Needless to say, highway death rates soared as one result. The domestic steel industry also reflected this big drop. U.S. blast furnaces poured out 19 million tons of steel for automotive use in 1955, but by 1958 this had fallen to 10 million tons. By the early 1960s, 'what's good for General Motors' was becoming bad for America and for the world.

And the American worker paid a lot more for that 1958 Chevy. Slick Madison Avenue advertising, ever-larger tail fins and chrome trim served to hide the reality. U.S. industry had been persuaded to commit systematic suicide, cheating the customer to make up for falling profits. But, like the drunk falling from a 20-story window, who imagines at first that he is enjoying the free flight, most Americans would not realize the real implications of this 1960s 'post-industrial' drift for another ten or twenty years.

## THE DOLLAR WARS OF THE 1960s

With higher interest rates to be earned abroad by buying up operating western European companies on the cheap, New York bankers began to turn their back on the United States. Europe was suffering a huge shortage of capital because of the war and the collapse of industry. As a result, Europe was forced to pay excessively high interest rates to attract the only 'international' currency then available—U.S. dollars from the large New York banks.

For their part, Chase Manhattan, Citibank and the others took the chance to make windfall profits in Europe, often doubling what their money would have earned if they had invested in municipal bonds to rebuild U.S. sewage systems, bridges or housing stock. The problem was that Washington, fearful of alienating the powerful New York financial community, refused to address this vital problem in any serious way. The money fled U.S. shores for higher profits abroad.

By early 1957, for the first time since the Second World War, funds began to flow out of the United States in amounts greater than those coming in. During the period 1957 to 1965, U.S. annual net capital export into western Europe mushroomed from less than $25 billion to more than $47 billion, a staggering sum at the time.

But if it were only American dollars which were leaving U.S. shores, that would have been one problem. The added problem was that U.S. gold reserves also began what became, increasingly after 1958, a continuous and at times precipitous decline. The breakdown of the postwar Bretton Woods monetary system was rapidly approaching, but American policy makers refused to take heed. They were listening to the voices of the New York banks, the big oil companies and the large American corporations, which were beginning, after the 1957 recession, to turn to cheap labor production outside the United States to improve their profit margins.

By the end of the 1950s, what had been the overwhelming advantage of the postwar Bretton Woods system, the United States dollar as the world's reserve currency, had turned into a liability—with a vengeance. As western Europe began to achieve independent industrial stature again, with far higher rates of productivity than the aging U.S. economy, this only dramatized the growing weakness of the U.S. economic position by the time of President Kennedy's inauguration in early 1961.

When the American negotiators at Bretton Woods set down their terms for the postwar international monetary order in 1944, they established it on a basis which contained a fatal flaw. Bretton Woods established a 'gold exchange standard' under which all member countries of the new International Monetary Fund agreed to fix the value of their currency, not directly to gold, but directly to the U.S. dollar, which in turn had fixed its value to a fixed weight of gold—$35 per fine ounce.

This $35 per ounce was the price at which the dollar had been fixed ever since Roosevelt set it in 1934, during the depths of the Great Depression. The ratio of the dollar to gold had not been altered in more than a quarter century, despite an intervening world war and the dramatic postwar developments in the world economy.

As long as the United States remained the only strong economic power in the Western world, these fundamental flaws could be ignored. In the decade after the war, Europe urgently needed dollars to finance reconstruction and the purchase of American and British oil for its economic recovery. The U.S. also held the vast bulk of world gold reserves. But by the beginning of the 1960s, as Europe began to grow at rates outpacing that of the United States, it was becoming clear to many that something had to change in the fixed Bretton Woods arrangement.

But Washington, under the growing influence of the powerful New York banking community, refused to play by the very rules it had imposed on its allies in 1944. New York banks began to invest abroad in new sources of higher profits. The failure of Washington effectively to challenge this vast outflow of vital investment capital, under both Eisenhower and his Democratic successor, Kennedy, was at the center of a problem which turned the decade of the 1960s into a succession of ever worsening international monetary crises.

What New York's international bankers were not eager to advertise was the fact that they were earning huge profits by walking away from investing in America's future. Between 1962 and 1965, U.S. corporations in western Europe earned between 12 and 14 per cent return, according to a January 1967 presidential report to Congress. The same dollar investment in U.S. industry earned less than half of that!

The banks quietly lobbied Washington to keep their game going. They kept their dollars in Europe rather than repatriating the profits to invest in American development. This was the beginning of what came to be known as the Eurodollar market. It was to be the cancer which, by the late 1970s, threatened to destroy its entire host—the world monetary system.

It would, of course, have been far better for the nation, and also for the rest of the world, had the U.S. Congress and the White House insisted on tax and credit policies to channel those billions, at fair rates of return, into new U.S. plant and equipment, advanced technologies, transportation infrastructure, modernization of the rotting rail system, and developing the untapped industrial market potential of the Third World for U.S. industrial exports. More sensible for the nation perhaps, but not for the power of certain influential New York banks.

If a given national economy produces the same volume of saleable goods under the same technological basis over a period of, say, ten years, and prints double the volume of its domestic currency for that same volume of goods as at the beginning of the decade, the 'consumer' notes the effect as a significant price inflation. He pays two dollars in 1960 for a loaf of bread which cost him only one dollar in 1950. But when this effect was spread around the entire world economy by virtue of the dominant position of the U.S. dollar, the inflated reality could be masked for a bit longer. The results, however, were every bit as destructive.

In his first days in office, under guidance from his advisers, President Lyndon Baines Johnson, a small-town Texas politician with little knowledge of international politics, let alone monetary policy, reversed the earlier decision of John Kennedy. President Johnson was led to believe that a full-scale military war in southeast Asia would solve many problems of the stagnant U.S. economy and show the world that America was still resolute.

## THE VIETNAM OPTION IS TAKEN

Volumes have been written since the tragic Vietnam war about the reasons and causes for it. But, on one level, it was clear that a significant faction of the American defense industry and New York finance had encouraged the decision of Washington to go to war, despite its absurd military justification and a divisive domestic reaction, because the military buildup offered their interests a politically saleable excuse to revive a massive diversion of U.S. industry into the production of defense goods. More and more during the 1960s, the heart of the U.S. economy was being transformed into a kind of military economy, in which the cold war against communist danger was used to justify tens of billions of dollars of spending. The military spending became the backup for the global economic interests of the New York financial and oil interests, another echo of nineteenth-century British Empire, dressed in the garb of twentieth-century anticommunism.

The Vietnam war strategy was deliberately designed by Defense Secretary Robert McNamara, National Security Adviser McGeorge Bundy, with Pentagon planners and key advisers around Lyndon Johnson, to be a 'no-win war' from the onset, in order to ensure a prolonged buildup of this defense component of the economy. The American voter, Washington reasoned, would accept large costs for a new war against an alleged 'godless encroachment of communism' in Vietnam, despite the gaping U.S. budget deficits, if this produced local jobs in defense plants.

Under the Bretton Woods rules, by inflating the dollar through huge spending deficits at home, Washington, in effect, could force Europe and other trading partners to 'swallow' this U.S. war cost in the form of cheapened dollars. So long as the United States refused to devalue the dollar against gold to reflect the deterioration of U.S. economic performance since 1944, Europe had to pay the cost by accepting dollars at the same ratio as it had some 20 years before.

To finance the enormous deficits of his Great Society program and the Vietnam buildup during the 1960s, Johnson, fearful of losing votes if he raised taxes, simply printed dollars, by selling more U.S. Treasury bonds to finance the deficits. In the early 1960s, the U.S. federal budget deficit averaged approximately $3 billion annually. It hit an alarming $9 billion in 1967 as the war costs soared, and by 1968 it reached a staggering $25 billion.

The European central banks began to accumulate large dollar accounts during this period, which they used as official reserves, the so-called Eurodollar accumulation abroad. Ironically, Washington in 1961 had requested that U.S. allies in Europe and Japan, the Group of Ten countries, should ease the drain on U.S. gold reserves by retaining their growing U.S. dollar reserves instead of redeeming the dollars for U.S. gold, as mandated under Bretton Woods.

The European central banks earned interest on these dollars by investing in U.S. government treasury bonds. The net effect was that the European central banks thereby 'financed' the huge U.S. deficits of the 1960s Vietnam debacle. American futurist Herman Kahn reportedly exclaimed to a friend, when told how this deficit financing operated, 'We've pulled off the biggest ripoff in history! We've run rings around the British Empire.' But it was not so obvious who was running rings around whom at this time. The City of London was preparing a comeback with expatriate American dollars, as we shall soon see.

Obviously the economic status of European economies such as Germany and France was different in 1964 from what it had been in 1944, when Bretton Woods was drafted. But U.S. policy circles refused to listen to European protestations, especially those from de Gaulle's France, because they reasoned that a devaluation of the dollar would cut the power of the 'omnipotent' New York banks in the world capital markets. Washington had imitated the disastrous example of England from the period before the 1914 war.

Earlier, when New York bankers first began to funnel large funds out of the United States to speculate in western Europe or Latin America, President Kennedy attempted to spark a renewed American technological optimism and encourage greater investment in new technologies by announcing the Apollo moon-shot program and the creation of NASA. A significant majority in America in 1962 still believed that the country should 'produce its way out' of the crisis.

But on November 22, 1963, John F. Kennedy was assassinated in Dallas, Texas. New Orleans Judge Jim Garrison, at the time involved in investigating leads to the assassination in his capacity as New Orleans district attorney, years later continued to insist that the murder had been carried out by the CIA, with the aid of select organized crime figures, including Carlos Marcello. Kennedy had among other things been on the verge of pulling out from Vietnam, after talks with the former general Douglas A. MacArthur days before his murder, a policy shift confirmed by his close friend and adviser Arthur Schlesinger.

The reasons for the assassination of John F. Kennedy have been a subject of much speculation. But what is clear is that the young president was moving on a variety of strategic fronts to establish his own mold for US policy, in a direction which, in issue after issue, began to run at odds with the powerful financial and political interests controlling the liberal East Coast establishment.

In May 1961, more than two years before his fateful motorcade tour along Dealy Plaza in Dallas, Kennedy went to Paris and met with Gen. de Gaulle. In his book *Memoirs of Hope*, de Gaulle gives a telling personal assessment of the American president. Kennedy had presented de Gaulle with the American argument for backing the dictatorship of Ngo Dinh Diem in South Vietnam and for installing an American expeditionary corps under cover of economic aid to the southeast Asian country. Kennedy had argued to de Gaulle that this was essential to build a bulwark against Soviet expansion in Indochina. 'But instead of giving him the approval he wanted, I told the President that he was taking the wrong road,' de Gaulle writes.

'You will find,' de Gaulle told Kennedy, 'that intervention in this area will be an endless entanglement.' De Gaulle went on to elaborate his reasons. 'Kennedy listened to me.' De Gaulle concludes his impressions: 'Kennedy left Paris. I had been dealing with a man whose age, and whose justifiable ambition inspired immense hopes.

He seemed to me to be on the point of taking off into the heights, like some great bird.' For his part, on his return to Washington, Kennedy was to say in a 'Report to the American People' on June 6 that he had found General de Gaulle a 'wise counsellor for the future and an informative guide to the history that he had helped to make ... I could not have more confidence in any man.'

It seems that certain powerful interests in the Anglo-American world were less than enthusiastic over the prospects of such confidence between the French president and his young American counterpart becoming a full-fledged change in direction for United States foreign policy. Lyndon B. Johnson, who became president on November 22, 1963, could never be accused of inspiring similar hopes. As President, Johnson never dared defy the powerful Wall Street interests.[5]

LBJ soon escalated Vietnam from a CIA 'technical advisory,' into a full-scale military conflict, pouring tens of billions of dollars and 500,000 uniformed men into a self-defeating war in southeast Asia. The war kept Wall Street bond markets busy financing a record level of U.S. Treasury debt, while select defense-related U.S. companies kept their profits flowing from the Asian campaign. The persisting U.S. economic stagnation, which worried the politician Johnson, was seemingly 'solved' by the boom in war spending, so that he secured a landslide victory over Republican Barry Goldwater in 1964. But he bought his 'victory' at a staggering cost.

## THE BEGINNINGS OF AMERICA'S INTERNAL ROT

Faced with the need to address America's growing urban decay, on August 20, 1964, President Johnson signed the Equal Opportunities Act. In signing it, he boasted, with characteristic bravado, 'Today, for the first time in the history of the human race, a great nation is able and willing to make a commitment to eradicate poverty among its people.' The War on Poverty and LBJ's Great Society program, as he called it, hardly eradicated poverty. But it provided an additional excuse for one of the largest increases of deficit spending and financial looting in modern history, a deficit in effect financed by surplus European dollars.

Millions of the nation's youth were herded into colleges during the mid 1960s as a form of 'hidden unemployment,' with the university student population rising from less than 4 million in 1960 to almost 10 million in 1975. It was the excuse for Wall Street to float additional billions of dollars of state-guaranteed public bonds for university construction. Investment in expansion of the real industrial economy was being shifted into this 'post-industrial' or 'service economy,' in a path similar to that traveled by Britain on its road to ruin late in the previous century. Social Security and welfare spending increased, as entire sections of the population were thrown onto a permanent human scrap heap of unemployment.

The NASA space program reached a spending peak of $6 billion in 1966, and was sharply cut by Johnson every year after. The technology push in American universities began to stagnate and then decline, with students instead being encouraged to pursue careers in 'social relations' or Zen meditation. University education, once the heart of the American dream, was transformed during the 1960s into low-quality mass production, as standards were deliberately lowered.

Investment in transport, electric power installations, water supplies and other necessary infrastructure began a steady deterioration as a portion of the total economy. If you don't care about producing industrial goods anymore, the New York bankers reasoned, why invest more in roads or bridges to carry them to market?

In order to sell this policy of de facto disinvestment in the economy of the United States during the 1960s, the more far-sighted of the Anglo-American establishment realized they must alter the traditional American commitment to scientific and industrial progress.

With the Vietnam War and the unleashing of the drugs and sex 'flower power' counterculture of Aldous Huxley and Timothy Leary, this is what a part of the Anglo-American liberal establishment set out to do. Under a top-secret CIA research project, code-named MK-Ultra, British and American scientists began carrying out experiments using psychedelic and other mind-altering drugs. By the mid 1960s, this project resulted in what was known as the Hippie movement, sometimes referred to as the launching of New Age Thinking, or the 'Age of Aquarius.' Its heroes were rock and drug advocates such as the Rolling Stones and Jim Morrison, and author and LSD victim Ken Kesey. Mystical irrationality was rapidly replacing faith in scientific progress for millions of young Americans.[6]

Government commitments to scientific and industrial development were cut, as the Johnson administration embraced Wall Street's 'post-industrial' policy. A new, young elite, preoccupied with personal pleasure and cynical about national purpose, began to emerge from American college campuses, starting with Harvard, Princeton, and the other so-called elite universities. They had 'turned on, tuned in, and dropped out,' as Harvard professor Timothy Leary expressed it.

To transform thinking in America's corporations and industry, managers were also treated to a new form of training, run by outside psychologists from the National Training Laboratories, kown as 'T-group sessions,' or 'sensitivity training.' The effect of this was to dull the wits and help prepare the population to accept the coming shocks. People were so preoccupied with being more sensitive and more understanding of each other's defects that they failed to see that the nation was losing its sense of purpose.

In 1968, the same year that Senator Robert Kennedy was killed in Los Angeles by a 'lone assassin' as he threatened to win the Democratic convention, civil rights leader Dr. Martin Luther King was also assassinated outside his Memphis motel room. Few realized the strategic circumstances around King's murder. He had come to Memphis to lend his powerful support to a black municipal workers' strike in a drive to unionize the non-union south. In the new era of 'runaway plants' following the 1957 recession, the southern United States was to be simply another 'cheap labor' haven for industrial production. This would work only so long as trade unions, which dominated the industrial centers of Detroit, Pittsburgh, Chicago and New York, were kept out of the 'New south.'

While the big factories fled to the cheap non-union-labor areas of the south, or to developing countries, slums, drug addiction and unemployment grew on an epidemic scale in the northern industrial cities. Wall Street's policy of disinvestments in established U.S. industry began to show real effects. Skilled white blue-collar workers in northern cities were pitted against increasingly desperate unskilled black and hispanic workers for a shrinking number of jobs. Riots were deliberately incited in industrial cities like Newark, Boston, Oakland and Philadelphia by government-backed 'insurgents', such as Tom Hayden. The goal of this operation was to break the power of established industrial trade unions in the northern cities by labeling them racist. These domestic insurgents were nurtured by the Ford Foundation's Grey Areas program, the model for President Johnson's War on Poverty.

Johnson's War on Poverty was a government-financed operation, aimed to exploit the economic decay created by the Anglo-American establishment's policies. The goal was to break resistance to what were about to be new levels of wage-gouging of the American population. The financial establishment was preparing to impose on the United States nineteenth-century British colonial-style looting. And manipulated 'race war' was to be their weapon.

The newly created U.S. Office of Economic Opportunity weakened the political voice of traditional American labor and the influential urban constituency machines. The targeted white blue-collar industrial operatives, only a decade earlier hailed as the lifeblood of American industry, were suddenly labeled 'reactionary' and 'racist' by the powerful liberal media. These workers were mostly fearful and confused as they saw their entire social fabric collapsing in the wake of the disinvestment policy of the powerful banks.

Harvard Dean McGeorge Bundy had run the Vietnam War as Kennedy's, and later as Johnson's White House national security adviser. By 1966 Bundy had gone to New York to turn the United States into a new 'Vietnam,' as head of the influential Ford Foundation. Black was pitted against white, unemployed against employed, in this new Great Society, while Wall Street bankers benefited from slashed union wages and cuts in infrastructure investment, or funneled investment overseas to cheap labor havens in Asia or South America. This writer had direct personal experience of this sad chapter in American history.

## STERLING, THE WEAK LINK, BREAKS

By the early 1960s, de Gaulle's independent policy initiatives were not the only major problem facing the financial interests governing New York and the City of London. In 1959, the external liabilities of the United States still approximated the total value of her official gold reserves, some $20 billion for both. By 1967, the year the sterling crisis threatened to break the entire Bretton Woods fabric, the U.S. total of external liquid liabilities had soared to $36 billion, while her gold reserves had plummeted to only $12 billion, one third the liability sum.

As U.S. short-term liabilities abroad began to exceed her gold stock, certain astute financial institutions reckoned, quite correctly, that something sooner or later had to break. In his first State of the Union Address to Congress in January 1961, President Kennedy noted that,

> since 1958 the gap between the dollars we spend or invest abroad and the dollars returned to us has substantially widened. This overall deficit in our balance of payments increased by nearly $11 billion in the last three years, and holders of dollars abroad

converted them to gold in such a quantity as to cause a total outflow of nearly $5 billion of gold from our reserve.

There are indications that President Kennedy seriously tried to tackle the growing dollar drain. Shortly before his death, in a message to Congress of July 18, 1963, Kennedy had proposed redressing the growing U.S. balance-of-payments problem through a series of measures aimed at increasing U.S. manufactures' exports and through a controversial Interest Equalization Tax. The aim was to impose a tax of up to 15 per cent on American capital invested abroad, in order to encourage domestic investment of American capital, rather than foreign.

Kennedy was not to live to see through his version of the Interest Equalization Tax legislation. When it was finally passed in September, 1964, certain powerful New York and London financial interests had inserted a seemingly innocent amendment, which exempted one country from the effects of the new tax—Canada, a key part of the British Commonwealth! Montreal and Toronto thereby became the vehicle for an enormous loophole which ensured that the U.S. dollar outflow continued, mediated through London-controlled financial institutions. It was one of the more skillful financial coups of British history.

In addition, bank loans made by foreign branches of American banks to foreign residents were exempt from the new U.S. tax. American banks scrambled to establish branches in London and other appropriate centers. Once again, the City of London had maneuvered to become a centerpiece of world finance and banking through development of the vast new 'Eurodollar' banking and lending market, with its center in London.[7]

London's sagging fortunes began once more to brighten as the former 'world's banker' began to corner the market in expatriate U.S. dollars. The Bank of England and London's Sir Siegmund Warburg, with the assistance of his friends in Washington, especially Undersecretary of State George Ball, had cleverly lured the dollars into what was to become the largest concentration of dollar credit outside of the United States itself—the London Eurodollar market, by the 1970s an estimated $1.3 trillion pool of 'hot money,' all of it 'offshore,' that is, beyong the control of any nation or central bank. New York banks and Wall Street brokerage houses set up offices in London to manage the blossoming new Eurodollar casino, away from the prying eyes of the U.S. tax authorities. U.S. banks obtained cheap funds from the Eurodollar market as well as from the large multinational corporations. During the early 1960s, Washington willingly allowed the floodgates to be opened wide to a flight of the dollar from American shores into the new 'hot money' Eurodollar market.

Buyers of these new Eurodollar bonds, called Eurobonds, were anonymous persons, cynically called 'Belgian dentists' by the London, Swiss and New York bankers running this new game. These Eurobonds were 'bearer' bonds, i.e. buyers' names were not registered anywhere, so they became a favorite for so-called Swiss investors seeking to evade taxes, or even for drug kingpins wanting to launder illegal profits. What better than to hold your black earnings in Eurodollar bonds, with interest paid by General Motors?

As an astute Italian analyst of this Eurodollar process, Marcello De Cecco, noted, 'the Eurodollar market was the most important financial phenomenon of the 1960's, for it was here that the financial earthquake of the early 1970's originated.'[8]

But in contrast to the benefits to London's international financial stature, due to the Canadian loophole and the resulting deposits of American dollars in select London-based banks, the industrial economy of Great Britain by the mid 1960s was a rotting mess and getting worse.

Confidence in Britain's pound sterling, the second 'pillar' of the original postwar Bretton Woods system after the American dollar, was eroding rapidly. Britain's external trade balance and general economic situation had been precarious for some time, with rising official commitments abroad to maintain vestiges of empire, a rotting industrial base and woefully inadequate reserves. When the Labour Party took office in October 1964 the crisis had become more or less chronic.

After the war, under Bretton Woods, Britain, through her sterling bloc ties with colonies and former colonies, had been able to make the pound sterling a strong currency, in many parts of the world regarded the equal of the dollar as a stable reserve currency. Member countries in the British Commonwealth were required, among other 'courtesies,' to deposit their national gold and foreign exchange reserves in London and to maintain sterling balances in City of London banks. Britain's quota share in the IMF was second only to that of the United States. Therefore the pound was disproportionately important to the stability of the Bretton Woods dollar order in the 1960s, despite the clearly depleted condition of her economy.

During the 1960s, Britain, like America, was a net exporter of financial funds to the rest of the world, despite the fact that her technologically stagnant industrial base created increasing trade deficits. Continental European economies, through growth of trade within the new Common Market and their productive advantages from strong investment in technology, grew vigorously.

Thus Britain's deficiencies and her lack of new technological investment grew ever larger by comparison. The powerful financial interests of the City of London again preferred to focus single-mindedly on drawing the world's financial flows into London banks by maintaining the highest interest rates of any major industrial nation throughout the mid 1960s. Industry went into a slump, unable to borrow for essential technological innovations.

By 1967, the British position was becoming alarming. Despite several large emergency borrowings from the IMF to help stabilize the pound, British foreign debts continued to grow, rising another $2 billion, or some 20 per cent, in that year alone. In January 1967, de Gaulle's principal economic adviser, Jacques Rueff, came to London to deliver a proposal for raising the official price of gold held by the leading industrial nations. The United States and Britain refused to hear such arguments, which would have meant a de facto devaluation of their currencies.

Throughout 1967, Bank of England gold reserves were falling, as foreign creditors, sensing an obvious imminent devaluation of the weakening pound, scrambled to redeem paper for gold, which they calculated must rise in value. By June 1967, de Gaulle's government announced that France had withdrawn from the American-instigated 'gold pool.' In 1961, under Washington pressure, the central banks of ten leading industrial countries had created the Group of Ten, as it became known. In addition to the United States, Britain, France, Germany and Italy, the group included Holland, Belgium, Sweden, Canada and Japan. The Group of Ten had agreed in 1961 to pool reserves in a special fund, the gold pool, to be administered in London by the Bank of England. Under the arrangement, temporary remedy at best, as events revealed, the U.S. central bank contributed only half the costs of continuing to maintain the world price of gold at the artificially low $35 per ounce price of 1934. The other nine, plus Switzerland, had agreed to pay the second half of such 'emergency' interventions, on the understanding that the situation would be temporary.

But the 'emergency' had become chronic by 1967, as Washington refused to bring its war-spending deficits under control and sterling continued to weaken along with the collapsing British economy. De Gaulle withdrew from the gold pool, not wanting to lose further French central bank gold reserves to the bottomless pit of interventions. The American and British financial press, led by the London *Economist*, began a heightened attack against French policy.

But de Gaulle made one tactical blunder in the process. On January 31, 1967, a new law came into effect in France which allowed unlimited convertibility for the French franc. At the time, with French industrial growth among the strongest in Europe, and the franc, backed by strong gold reserves, one of the strongest currencies, convertibility was seen as a confirmation of France's successful economic policy since de Gaulle took office in 1958. But it was soon to become the Achilles' heel which finished de Gaulle's France at the hands of Anglo-American financial interests.

French Prime Minister Georges Pompidou, in a public speech in February 1967, reaffirmed French adherence to a gold-backed monetary system as the only way to avoid international manipulations, adding that the 'international monetary system is functioning poorly because it gives advantages to countries with a reserve currency [i.e., the United States]: these countries can afford inflation without paying for it.' In effect, the Johnson administration and the Federal Reserve simply printed dollars and sent them abroad in place of its gold.

The lines were becoming sharper through 1967 as France's central bank determined to exchange its dollar and sterling reserves for gold, leaving the voluntary 1961 gold pool arrangement. Other central banks followed. The situation assumed near panic dimensions, as some 80 tons of gold were sold on the London market toward the end of the year in an unheard-of period of five days, in an unsuccessful effort to stop the speculative attack. Fear grew that the entire Bretton Woods edifice was about to fall apart at its weakest link, the pound sterling.

Financial speculators by the second half of 1967 were selling pounds and buying dollars or other currencies which they then used to buy commercial gold in all possible markets from Frankfurt to Pretoria, sparking a steep rise in the market price of gold, in contrast to the $35 per ounce official U.S. dollar price. The sterling crisis indirectly focused attention on the growing vulnerability at the core of the international monetary system, the U.S. dollar itself.

By November 18, 1967, the British Labour government of Harold Wilson bowed to the inevitable, despite strong pressure from Washington, and announced a 14 per cent devaluation of sterling from $2.80 down to $2.40 per pound, the first devaluation since 1949. The sterling crisis abated, but the dollar crisis was only just beginning.

Once sterling had been devalued, speculative pressures immediately turned to the U.S. dollar. International holders of dollars went to the gold discount window at the New York Federal Reserve and demanded their rightful gold in exchange. The market price of gold began an even steeper rise as a result, despite efforts of the U.S. Federal Reserve to dump its gold reserves onto the market to stop the rise. Washington, under the sway of the powerful dollar-based New York banks, adamantly refused to budge from the $35 per ounce official valuation of gold. But the withdrawal of France, one of the largest holders of gold, from the Group of Ten gold pool, had intensified Washington's problem. By the end of the year, Washington's official gold stock had declined another $1 billion to only $12 billion.

## DE GAULLE IS TOPPLED

The crisis gathered momentum into 1968, and between March 8 and March 15 of that year, the gold pool in London had to provide nearly 1,000 tons to hold the gold price. The weighing-room floor at the Bank of England, loaded with gold, almost collapsed under the weight. U.S. Air Force planes had been commandeered to rush gold in from the U.S. reserve at Fort Knox. On March 15, the U.S. requested a two-week closing of the London gold market.

By April, 1968, a special meeting of the Group of Ten was convened in Stockholm, at Washington's request. U.S. officials planned to unveil yet another scheme, creation of a new 'paper gold' substitute through the IMF, so-called Special Drawing Rights (SDRs), in an effort to postpone the day of reckoning still further.

At the Stockholm gathering, designed to set the stage for official IMF adoption of the Washington SDR scheme at the upcoming IMF meeting the following month, France defiantly blocked unanimous agreement, with France's minister Michel Debré reasserting traditional French policy on a return to the original rules of Bretton Woods. De Gaulle's adviser Rueff had repeatedly proposed a 'shock' devaluation of the U.S. dollar of 100 per cent against gold, which would have been elegantly simple, would have doubled official U.S. gold reserves in dollar terms and would have been sufficient to allow the United States to convert the approximately $10 billion of foreign-held dollars, while still maintaining the value of its gold reserves as before. This would have been far more rational and painless in human terms than what ensued. But, tragically, it was not to result.[9]

Within days of the French refusal to back Washington's SDR dollar bailout scheme, France itself was the target of the most serious political destabilization of the postwar period. Beginning with leftist students at the University of Strasbourg, soon all of France was brought to a chaotic halt as students rioted and struck across the country. In coordination with the political unrest (which, interestingly, the French Communist Party attempted to calm down), U.S. and British investment houses started a panic run on the French franc, which gained momentum as it was touted loudly in the Anglo-American financial media.

The May 1968 student riots in France, were the result of the vested London and New York financial interests in the one G-10 nation which continued to defy their mandate. Taking advantage of the new French law allowing full currency convertibility, these financial houses began to cash in francs for gold, draining the French gold reserves by almost 30 per cent by the end of 1968, and bringing about a full-blown crisis in the franc.

Sadly, the Anglo-American counterattack succeeded. Within a year, de Gaulle was out of office and France's voice was severely weakened. One of his last meetings while still president, in February 1969, was with the British Ambassador to France, Christopher Soames. Once again, the general told Soames, in a broad review of French postwar policy, that Europe must be independent and that her independent stance had been profoundly compromised by the 'pro-American' sentiments of many European countries, most especially of Britain.[10]

One other country openly daring to defy the powerful financial interests of London and New York at this time was the largest gold-producing country in the West, the Republic of South Africa. During the early part of 1968, South Africa refused to sell its newly-mined gold for pounds or dollars at the official price of $35 per ounce. France and South Africa had been holding talks to form a new gold basis for reforming the Bretton Woods monetary order. This provoked a U.S.-led central bank boycott of South Africa, a move again repeated by the same interests almost exactly 20 years later, in the mid 1980s.

But, despite the apparent decline of the French 'threat,' Washington and London's success was to prove a Pyrrhic victory.

# 9
# Running the World Economy in Reverse: Who Made the 1970s Oil Shocks?

## NIXON PULLS THE PLUG

By the end of President Richard Nixon's first year in office, 1969, the U.S. economy had again gone into recession. By 1970, in order to combat the downturn, U.S. interest rates had been sharply lowered. As a consequence, speculative 'hot money' began once again to leave the dollar in record amounts; higher short-term profits were sought in Europe and elsewhere.

One result of the by now almost decade-long American refusal to devalue the dollar, and her reluctance to take serious action to control the huge unregulated Eurodollar market, was an increasingly unstable short-term currency speculation. As most of the world's bankers well knew, King Canute could pretend to hold the waves back for only so long.

As a result of Nixon's expansionary domestic U.S. monetary policy in 1970, the capital inflows of the previous year were reversed, and the United States incurred a net capital outflow of $6.5 billion. But the U.S. recession persisted. As interest rates continued to drop into 1971 and the money supply to expand, these outflows reached huge dimensions, totaling $20 billion. Furthermore, in May 1971 the United States recorded its first monthly trade deficit, triggering a virtually international panic sell-off of the U.S. dollar. The situation was indeed becoming desperate.

By 1971, U.S. official gold reserves represented less than a quarter of her official liabilities: theoretically, if all foreign dollar holders demanded gold instead, Washington would have been unable to comply without taking drastic measures.[1]

The Wall Street establishment persuaded President Nixon to abandon fruitless efforts to hold the dollar against a flood of international demand to redeem dollars for gold. But, unfortunately,

Wall Street did not want the required dollar devaluation against gold, which had been intensely sought for almost a decade.

On August 15, 1971, Nixon took the advice of a close circle of key advisers that included his chief budget adviser, George Shultz, and a policy group then at the Treasury Department, including Paul Volcker and Jack F. Bennett, who later went on to become a director of Exxon. That quiet, sunny August day, in a move which rocked the world, the president of the United States announced formal suspension of dollar convertibility into gold, effectively putting the world fully onto a dollar standard with no gold backing, thereby unilaterally ripping apart the central provision of the 1944 Bretton Woods system. No longer could foreign holders of U.S. dollars redeem their paper for U.S. gold reserves.

Nixon's unilateral action was reaffirmed in protracted international talks that December in Washington between the leading European governments, Japan, and a few others, which resulted in a poor compromise known as the Smithsonian agreement. With an exaggeration which exceeded even that of his predecessor, Lyndon Johnson, Nixon announced after the Smithsonian talks that they were 'the conclusion of the most significant monetary agreement in the history of the world.' The United States had formally devalued the dollar a mere 8 per cent against gold, placing gold at $38 per fine ounce instead of the long-standing $35—hardly the 100 per cent devaluation being asked for by her allies. The agreement also officially permitted a band of currency-value fluctuation of 2.25 per cent, instead of the original 1 per cent of the IMF Bretton Woods rules.

By declaring to world dollar holders that their paper would no longer be redeemed for gold, Nixon 'pulled the plug' on the world economy, setting into motion a series of events which was to rock the world as never before. Within weeks, confidence in the Smithsonian agreement had begun to collapse. De Gaulle's defiance of Washington in April 1968 on the issue of gold and adherence to the rules of Bretton Woods had not been sufficient to force through the badly needed reordering of the international monetary system, but it had sufficiently poisoned the well of Washington's ill-conceived IMF Special Drawing Rights scheme to obscure the problems of the dollar. The suspension of gold redemption and the resulting international 'floating exchange rates' of the early 1970s solved nothing. It only bought some time.

An eminently workable solution would have been for the United States to set the dollar to a more realistic level. From France, de Gaulle's former economic adviser, Jacques Rueff, continued to plead for a $70 per ounce gold price, instead of the $35 level the U.S. unsuccessfully defended. This, Rueff argued, would calm world speculation and allow the U.S. to redeem her destabilizing Eurodollar balances abroad, without plunging the domestic U.S. economy into severe chaos. If done properly, this could have given a tremendous spur to U.S. industry, since its exports would have cost less in foreign currency. American industrial interests would again have predominated over financial voices in U.S. policy circles. But reason did not prevail. The Wall Street rationale was that the power of their financial domain must be untouched, even if this was at the expense of economic production or American national prosperity.

Gold itself has little intrinsic value. It has certain industrial uses. But historically, because of its scarcity, it has served as a standard of value against which different nations have fixed the terms of their trade and therefore their currencies. When Nixon decided no longer to honor U.S. currency obligations in gold, he opened the floodgates to a worldwide Las Vegas speculation binge of a dimension never before experienced in history. Instead of calibrating long-term economic affairs to fixed standards of exchange, after August 1971 world trade was simply another arena of speculation about the direction in which various currencies would fluctuate.

The real architects of the Nixon strategy were in the influential City of London merchant banks. Sir Siegmund Warburg, Edmond de Rothschild, Jocelyn Hambro and others saw a golden opportunity in Nixon's dissolution of the Bretton Woods gold standard that summer of 1971. London was once again to become a major center of world finance, and again on 'borrowed money,' this time American Eurodollars.

After August 1971, the dominant U.S. policy under the White House national security adviser, Henry A. Kissinger, was to control, not to develop, economies throughout the world. U.S. policy officials began proudly calling themselves 'neo-Malthusians.' Population reduction in developing nations, rather than technology transfer and industrial growth strategies, became the dominating priority during the 1970s, yet another throwback to nineteenth-century British colonial thinking. How this transformation took place we shall soon see.

The ineffective basis of the Smithsonian agreement led to further deterioration into 1972, as massive capital flows again left the dollar for Japan and Europe, until February 12, 1973, when Nixon finally announced a second devaluation of the dollar, of 10 per cent against gold, pricing gold where it remains to this day for the Federal Reserve, at $42.22 per ounce.

At this point all the major world currencies began a process of what was called the 'managed float.' Between February and March 1973, the value of the U.S. dollar against the German Deutschmark dropped another 40 per cent. Permanent instability had been introduced into world monetary affairs in a way not seen since the early 1930s, but this time strategists in New York, Washington and the City of London were preparing an unexpected surprise to regain the upper hand and recover from the devastating loss of the monetary pillar of their system.

## AN UNUSUAL MEETING AT SALTSJÖBADEN

The design behind Nixon's August 15, 1971, dollar strategy did not emerge until October 1973, more than two years later, and even then, few persons other than a handful of insiders grasped the connection. The August 1971 demonetization of the dollar was used by the London–New York financial establishment to buy precious time, while policy insiders prepared a bold new monetarist design, a 'paradigm shift' as some preferred to term it. Certain influential voices in the Anglo-American financial establishment had devised a strategy to create again a strong dollar, and once again to increase their relative political power in the world, just when it appeared they were in a decisive rout.

In May 1973, with the dramatic fall of the dollar still vivid, a group of 84 of the world's top financial and political insiders met at Saltsjöbaden, Sweden, the secluded island resort of the Swedish Wallenberg banking family. This gathering of Prince Bernhard's Bilderberg group heard an American participant, Walter Levy, outline a 'scenario' for an imminent 400 per cent increase in OPEC petroleum revenues. The purpose of the secret Saltsjöbaden meeting was not to prevent the expected oil price shock, but rather to plan how to manage the about-to-be-created flood of oil dollars, a process U.S. Secretary of State Kissinger later called 'recycling the petrodollar flows.'

The American speaker to the Bilderberg on Atlantic–Japanese energy policy, was clear enough. After stating the prospect that future world oil needs would be supplied by a small number of Middle East producing countries, the speaker declared, prophetically: 'The cost of these oil imports would rise tremendously, with difficult implications

January 8, 1973

BILDERBERG MEETINGS

Names of Americans Proposed For Participation

In The Salsjobaden Conference, May 10-13, 1973

(There will be room for 20 Americans at Salsjobaden, not including the
authors of the papers and me. There are ten Steering Committee Members.
This makes only ten places free.)

The following individuals have been proposed by one person or another --
including in two cases themselves. In considering possible participants
we must remember the importance of having some younger people and some
women. It is also desirable to have one or two persons connected with
the press and one labor leader if possible.

U.S. Government - Executive Branch

Henry Kissinger (Alternate: Under Secretary of State Rush)
George Schultz (Alternate: Donald Rumsfeld; Ambassador Eberle)
James Akins (Energy Expert in White House and State Department)

U.S. Government - Congressional

Senator John Tower (Alternates: Senators Brook, Percy and Scott)
Senator Jackson (Alternates: Senators Mondale or Proxmire)
Congressman John Culver

Journalism                              Others

Donald Cook          Graham Allison        Richard Holbrooke
Osborn Elliott       Robert Anderson       Robert Hunter
Katherine Graham     Robert Bowie          General G. A. Lincoln
Andrew Heiskell      Harvey Brooks         Dean Robison of Bowdoin
Max Frankel          Zbig Brzezinski          College
Flora Lewis          William Bundy         Robert Schaetzel
Tom Wicker           Miriam Camps          Carroll Wilson.
                     Patricia Harris
                     Stanley Hoffman

*Figure 4*   Memo of January 8, 1973, from U.S. Bilderberg official Robert D.
Murphy, containing the United States' proposed list of May 1973 participants,
including Henry Kissinger. The memo is amongst Murphy's papers at the
Hoover Institute.

for the balance of payments of consuming countries. Serious problems
would be caused by unprecedented foreign exchange accumulations
of countries such as Saudi Arabia and Abu Dhabi.' The speaker added,
'A complete change was underway in the political, strategic and
power relationships between the oil producing, importing and home
countries of international oil companies and national oil companies
of producing and importing countries.' He then projected an OPEC
Middle East oil revenue rise, which would translate into just over 400
per cent, the same level Kissinger was soon to demand of the Shah.

... ........ ....... ... ...p......... .. ...........g ........ ...... ....ppr... ....
if they did not cooperate, this responsibility would lead them to competitive
bidding and finally into a clash.

The task of improving relations between energy importing countries should
begin with consultations between Europe, the US and Japan. These three
regions, which represented about 60 per cent of world energy consumption,
accounted for an even greater proportion of world energy trade in energy products, as
they absorbed 80 per cent of world energy exports.

Two other reasons for cooperation were bound up with the world respon-
sibilities of these countries. First, an energy crisis or an increase in energy costs
could irremediably jeopardize the economic expansion of developing countries
which had no resources of their own. Secondly, the misuse or inadequate
control of the financial resources of the oil producing countries could completely
disorganize and undermine the world monetary system.

B. *General principles and limits of cooperation:* The European Community had
already made it known unofficially that it favored energy cooperation with the
US and Japan, primarily to eliminate futile outbidding between the importer

years, oil would provide the mainstay of the world's energy supplies. Because
of the size of known reserves and the lead time for developing new resources,
our growing needs would be supplied mainly by huge increases of imports from
the Middle East.

The cost of these oil imports would rise tremendously, with difficult implications for the balance of payments of consuming countries. Serious problems
would be caused by unprecedented foreign exchange accumulations of countries such as Saudi Arabia and Abu Dhabi.

A complete change was underway in the political, economic, strategic and
power relationships between the oil producing, importing and home countries
of international oil companies and the national oil companies of producing and
importing countries.

An energy policy for the oil importing countries was an urgent necessity. It
could not be limited to the Atlantic nations, but had to include Japan, the
Free World's second strongest economic power and one of its largest oil im-

*Figure 5*   Two excerpts from the confidential protocol of the May 1973 meeting
of the Bilderberg group at Saltsjöbaden, Sweden. Note that there was discussion
about the danger that 'inadequate control of the financial resources of the oil
producing countries could completely disorganize and undermine the world
monetary system.' The second excerpt speaks of 'huge increases of imports
from the Middle East. The cost of these imports would rise tremendously.'
Figures given later in the discussion show a projected price rise for OPEC oil
of some 400 per cent.

Present at Saltsjöbaden that May were Robert O. Anderson of
Atlantic Richfield Oil Co.; Lord Greenhill, chairman of British
Petroleum; Sir Eric Roll of S.G. Warburg, creator of Eurobonds; George
Ball of Lehman Brothers investment bank, and the man who some
ten years earlier, as assistant secretary of state, told his banker friend

*Figure 6* Cover page of the confidential protocol of the 1973 Bilderberg meeting at Saltsjöbaden. The page bears the stamp of the Paris bookseller from whom the minutes were bought by the author.

## LIST OF PARTICIPANTS

CHAIRMAN:
H.R.H. THE PRINCE OF THE NETHERLANDS

HONORARY SECRETARY GENERAL FOR EUROPE:
ERNST H. VAN DER BEUGEL

HONORARY SECRETARY GENERAL FOR THE UNITED STATES:
JOSEPH E. JOHNSON

HONORARY TREASURER:
C. FRITS KARSTEN

| | |
|---|---|
| AGNELLI, GIOVANNI | ITALY |
| ANDERSON, ROBERT O. | UNITED STATES |
| BALL, GEORGE W. | UNITED STATES |
| BAUMGARTNER, WILFRID S. | FRANCE |
| BENNETT, SIR FREDERIC | UNITED KINGDOM |
| BEYAZIT, SELAHATTIN | TURKEY |
| BIRGI, M. NURI | TURKEY |
| BJØL, ERLING | DENMARK |
| BJÖRGERD, ANDERS | SWEDEN |
| BOITEUX, MARCEL | FRANCE |
| BREUEL, BIRGIT | GERMANY |
| BRZEZINSKI, ZBIGNIEW | UNITED STATES |
| BUNDY, WILLIAM P. | UNITED STATES |
| CITTADINI CESI, IL MARCHESE | ITALY |
| COLLADO, EMILIO G. | UNITED STATES |
| DEAN, ARTHUR H. | UNITED STATES |
| DRAKE, SIR ERIC | UNITED KINGDOM |
| DUCCI, ROBERTO | ITALY |
| GIROTTI, RAFFAELE | ITALY |

*Figure 7*   Partial list of official attendees at the 1973 Bilderberg meeting. It includes ARCO head Robert O. Anderson, Zbigniew Brzezinski and George Ball.

Siegmund Warburg to develop London's Eurodollar market; David Rockefeller of Chase Manhattan Bank; Zbigniew Brzezinski, the man soon to be President Carter's national security adviser; Italy's Gianni Agnelli and Germany's Otto Wolff von Amerongen, among others. Henry Kissinger was a regular participant at the Bilderberg gatherings.[2]

The Bilderberg annual meetings were initiated, in the utmost secrecy, in May 1954 by an Anglophile group which included George Ball, David Rockefeller, Dr. Joseph Retinger, Holland's Prince Bernhard and George C. McGhee (then of the U.S. State Department and later a senior executive of Mobil Oil). Named for the place of their first gathering, the Hotel de Bilderberg near Arnheim, the annual Bilderberg meetings gathered top elites of Europe and America for secret deliberations and policy discussion. Consensus was then 'shaped' in subsequent press comments and media coverage, but never with reference to the secret Bilderberg talks themselves. This Bilderberg process has been one of the most effective vehicles of postwar Anglo-American policy shaping.

What the powerful men grouped around Bilderberg had evidently decided that May was to launch a colossal assault against industrial growth in the world, in order to tilt the balance of power back to the advantage of Anglo-American financial interests and the dollar. In order to do this, they determined to use their most prized weapon— control of the world's oil flows. Bilderberg policy was to trigger a global oil embargo, in order to force a dramatic increase in world oil prices. Since 1945, world oil had by international custom been priced in dollars, since American oil companies dominated the postwar market. A sudden sharp increase in the world price of oil, therefore, meant an equally dramatic increase in world demand for U.S. dollars to pay for that necessary oil.

Never in history had such a small circle of interests, centered in London and New York, controlled so much of the entire world's economic destiny. The Anglo-American financial establishment had resolved to use their oil power in a manner no one could have imagined possible. The very outrageousness of their scheme was to their advantage, they clearly reckoned.

## DR. KISSINGER'S YOM KIPPUR OIL SHOCK

On October 6, 1973, Egypt and Syria invaded Israel, igniting what became known as the Yom Kippur War. Contrary to popular impression, the 'Yom Kippur' War was not the simple result of miscalculation, blunder or an Arab decision to launch a military strike against the state of Israel. The entire constellation of events surrounding the outbreak of the October War was secretly orchestrated by Washington and London, using the powerful secret diplomatic channels developed by Nixon's national security adviser, Henry

Kissinger. Kissinger effectively controlled the Israeli policy response through his intimate relation with Israel's Washington ambassador, Simcha Dinitz. In addition, Kissinger cultivated channels to the Egyptian and Syrian side. His method was simply to misrepresent to each party the critical elements of the other, ensuring the war and its subsequent Arab oil embargo.

U.S. intelligence reports, including intercepted communications from Arab officials confirming the buildup for war, were firmly suppressed by Kissinger, who was by then Nixon's intelligence 'czar.' The war and its aftermath, Kissinger's infamous 'shuttle diplomacy,' were scripted in Washington along the precise lines of the Bilderberg deliberations in Saltsjöbaden the previous May, some six months before the outbreak of the war. Arab oil-producing nations were to be the scapegoats for the coming rage of the world, while the Anglo-American interests responsible stood quietly in the background.[3]

In mid October 1973, the German government of Chancellor Willy Brandt told the U.S. ambassador to Bonn that Germany was neutral in the Middle East conflict, and would not permit the United States to resupply Israel from German military bases. With an ominous foreshadowing of similar exchanges which would occur some 17 years later, Nixon, on October 30, 1973, sent Chancellor Brandt a sharply worded protest note, most probably drafted by Kissinger:

> We recognize that the Europeans are more dependent upon Arab oil than we, but we disagree that your vulnerability is decreased by disassociating yourselves from us on a matter of this importance ... You note that this crisis was not a case of common responsibility for the Alliance, and that military supplies for Israel were for purposes which are not part of Alliance responsibility. I do not believe we can draw such a fine line ...[4]

Washington would not permit Germany to declare its neutrality in the Middle East conflict. But, significantly, Britain was allowed to clearly state its neutrality, thus avoiding the impact of the Arab oil embargo. Once again, London had skillfully maneuvered itself around an international crisis that it had been instrumental in precipitating. One enormous consequence of the ensuing 400 per cent rise in OPEC oil prices was that investments of hundreds of millions of dollars by British Petroleum, Royal Dutch Shell and other Anglo-American petroleum concerns in the risky North Sea could produce oil at a profit. It is a curious fact of the time that the profitability of these new North Sea oilfields was not at all secure until after the OPEC price rises. Of course, this might only have been a fortuitous coincidence.

By October 16, the Organization of Petroleum Exporting Countries, following a meeting on oil prices in Vienna, had raised their price by a staggering 70 per cent, from $3.01 to $5.11 per barrel. That same day, the members of the Arab OPEC countries, citing the U.S. support for Israel in the Middle East war, declared an embargo on all oil sales to the United States and the Netherlands—Rotterdam being the major oil port of western Europe.

Saudi Arabia, Kuwait, Iraq, Libya, Abu Dhabi, Qatar and Algeria announced on October 17, 1973, that they would cut their production below the September level by 5 per cent for October and an additional 5 per cent per month, 'until Israeli withdrawal is completed from the whole Arab territories occupied in June 1967 and the legal rights of the Palestinian people are restored.' The world's first 'oil shock,' or as the Japanese termed it, 'Oil Shokku' was underway.

Significantly, the oil crisis hit full force in late 1973, just as the president of the United States was becoming personally embroiled in what came to be called the 'Watergate affair,' leaving Henry Kissinger as de facto president, running U.S. policy during the crisis.

When the Nixon White House sent a senior official to the U.S. Treasury in 1974 in order to devise a strategy to force OPEC into lowering the oil price, he was bluntly turned away. In a memo, the official stated, 'It was the banking leaders who swept aside this advice and pressed for a "recycling" program to accommodate to higher oil prices. This was the fatal decision ...'

The U.S. Treasury, under Jack Bennett, the man who had helped steer Nixon's fateful August 1971 dollar policy, had established a secret accord with the Saudi Arabian Monetary Agency, SAMA, finalized in a February 1975 memo from U.S. Assistant Treasury Secretary Jack F. Bennett to Secretary of State Kissinger. Under the terms of the agreement, a sizeable part of the huge new Saudi oil revenue windfall was to be invested in financing the U.S. government deficits. A young Wall Street investment banker with the leading London-based Eurobond firm of White Weld & Co., David Mulford, was sent to Saudi Arabia to become the principal 'investment adviser' to SAMA; he was to guide the Saudi petrodollar investments to the correct banks, naturally in London and New York. The Bilderberg scheme was operating just as planned.[5]

Kissinger, as Nixon's all-powerful national security adviser already firmly in control of all U.S. intelligence estimates, secured control of

U.S. foreign policy as well, persuading Nixon to name him secretary of state in the weeks just prior to the outbreak of the October Yom Kippur War. Indicative of his central role in events, Kissinger retained both titles, as head of the White House National Security Council and as secretary of state, something no other individual has ever done, before or since. No other single person during the last months of the Nixon presidency wielded as much absolute power as did Henry Kissinger. To add insult to injury, Kissinger was given the 1973 Nobel Peace Prize.

Following a meeting in Teheran on January 1, 1974, a second price increase of more than 100 per cent brought OPEC benchmark oil prices to $11.65. This was done on the surprising demand of the Shah of Iran, who had been secretly put up to it by Henry Kissinger. Only months earlier, the Shah had opposed the OPEC increase to $3.01 for fear that this would force Western exporters to charge more for the industrial equipment the Shah sought to import for Iran's ambitious industrialization. The support of Washington and the West for Israel in the October War had fed OPEC anger at the meetings. Even Kissinger's own State Department had not been informed of his secret machinations with the Shah.[6]

From 1949 until the end of 1970, Middle East crude oil prices had averaged approximately $1.90 per barrel. They had risen to $3.01 in early 1973, at the time of the fateful Saltsjöbaden meeting of the Bilderberg group, which discussed an imminent 400 per cent future rise in OPEC's price. By January 1974, that 400 per cent increase was a fait accompli.

## THE ECONOMIC IMPACT OF THE OIL SHOCK

The social impact of the oil embargo on the United States in late 1973 could be described as panic. Throughout 1972 and early 1973, the large multinational oil companies, led by Exxon, had pursued a curious policy of creating a short supply of domestic crude oil. They were allowed to do this under an unusual series of decisions made by President Nixon on the advice of his aides. When the embargo hit in November 1973, therefore, the impact could not have been more dramatic. At the time, the White House was responsible for controlling U.S. oil imports under the provisions of a 1959 U.S. trade agreements act.

In January 1973, Nixon had appointed Treasury Secretary George Shultz to be assistant to the president for economic affairs as well. In this post, Shultz oversaw White House oil import policy. His deputy treasury secretary, William E. Simon, a former Wall Street bond trader, was made chairman of the important Oil Policy Committee, which determined U.S. oil import supply in the critical months leading up to the October embargo.

In February 1973, Nixon was persuaded to set up a special 'energy triumvirate,' which included Shultz, White House aide John Ehrlichman, and National Security Adviser Henry Kissinger, to be known as the White House Special Energy Committee. The scene was quietly being set for the Bilderberg plan, though almost no one in Washington or elsewhere realized the fact. By October 1973, U.S. stocks of domestic crude oil were already at alarmingly low levels. The OPEC embargo triggered panic buying of gasoline among the public, calls for rationing, endless gas lines and a sharp economic recession.[7]

The most severe impact of the oil crisis was on the United States' largest city, New York. In December 1974, nine of the world's most powerful bankers, led by David Rockefeller's Chase Manhattan, Citibank, and the London–New York investment bank, Lazard Freres, told New York Mayor Abraham Beame, an old-line machine politician, that unless he turned over control of the city's huge pension funds to a committee of the banks, the Municipal Assistance Corporation, the banks and their influential friends in the media would ensure the financial ruin of the city. Not surprisingly, the overpowered mayor capitulated and New York City was forced to slash spending for roadways, bridges, hospitals and schools in order to service their bank debt, and to lay off tens of thousands of city workers. The nation's greatest city had begun its descent into a scrap heap. Felix Rohatyn of Lazard Freres became head of the new bankers' collection agency, dubbed 'Big MAC' by the press.

In western Europe, the shock of the oil price rise and the embargo on supplies was equally dramatic. From Britain to the Continent, country after country felt the effects of the worst economic crisis since the 1930s. Bankruptcies and unemployment across Europe rose to alarming levels.

Germany's government imposed an emergency ban on Sunday driving, in a desperate effort to save imported oil costs. By June 1974, the effects of the oil crisis had contributed to the dramatic collapse of Germany's Herstatt-Bank and a crisis in the Deutschmark as a result. As Germany's imported oil costs increased by a staggering 17 billion Deutschmarks in 1974, with half a million people reckoned to be unemployed due to the effects of the oil crisis, inflation levels reached an alarming 8 per cent. The shock effects of a sudden 400 per cent increase in the price of Germany's basic energy feedstock were devastating to industry, transport, and agriculture. Key industries such as steel, shipbuilding and chemicals went into a deep crisis.

Willy Brandt's government was effectively defeated by the domestic impact of the oil crisis, as much as by the revelations of the Stasi affair against his close adviser, Günther Guillaume. By May 1974, Brandt had offered his resignation to Federal President Heinemann, who then appointed Helmut Schmidt as chancellor. Most of the governments of Europe fell during this period, victims of the consequences of the oil crisis on their economies.

But for the less developed economies of the world, the impact of an overnight price increase of 400 per cent in their primary energy source was staggering. The vast majority of the world's less developed economies, without significant domestic oil resources, were suddenly confronted with an unexpected and unpayable 400 per cent increase in the cost of energy imports, to say nothing of the cost of chemicals and fertilizers derived from petroleum. During this time, commentators began speaking of 'triage,' the wartime idea of survival of the fittest, and introduced the vocabulary of 'Third World' and 'Fourth World' (the non-OPEC countries).

India in 1973 had a positive balance of trade, a healthy situation for a developing economy. But by 1974, India had total foreign exchange reserves of $629 millions with which to pay—in dollars—an annual oil import bill of almost double that, or $1,241 million. Sudan, Pakistan, the Philippines, Thailand and country after country throughout Africa and Latin America were faced in 1974 with gaping deficits in their balance of payments. According to the IMF, developing countries in 1974 incurred a total trade deficit of $35 billion, a colossal sum in that day, and, not surprisingly, a deficit four times as large as in 1973—precisely in proportion to the oil price increase. Following the several years of strong industrial and trade growth of the early 1970s, the severe drop in industrial activity throughout the world economy in 1974–75 was greater than any such decline since the war.

But while Kissinger's 1973 oil shock had a devastating impact on world industrial growth, it had an enormous benefit for certain established interests—the major New York and London banks, and the Seven Sisters oil multinationals of the United States and Britain. By 1974, Exxon had overtaken General Motors as the largest American corporation in gross revenues. Her sisters, including Mobil, Texaco, Chevron and Gulf, were not far behind.

The bulk of the OPEC dollar revenues, Kissinger's 'recycled petrodollars,' was deposited with the leading banks of London and New York, the banks which dealt in dollars as well as international oil trade. Chase Manhattan, Citibank, Manufacturers Hanover, Bank of America, Barclays, Lloyds, Midland Bank—all enjoyed the windfall profits of the oil crisis. We shall later see how they recycled their petrodollars during the 1970s, and how this set the stage for the great debt crisis of the 1980s.[8]

## TAKING THE 'BLOOM OFF THE NUCLEAR ROSE'

One principal concern of the authors of the 400 per cent oil price increase was how to ensure that their drastic action would not drive the world to accelerate an already strong trend towards the construction of a far more efficient and ultimately less expensive alternative energy source—nuclear electricity generation.

Kissinger's former dean at Harvard, and his boss when Kissinger briefly served as a consultant to John Kennedy's National Security Council, was McGeorge Bundy. Bundy left the White House in 1966 in order to play a critical role in shaping the domestic policy of the United States as president of the largest private foundation, the Ford Foundation. By December 1971, Bundy had established a major new project for the foundation, the Energy Policy Project, under the direction of S. David Freeman, and with an impressive $4 million checkbook and a three-year time limit. Bundy's Ford study, titled 'A Time to Choose: America's Energy Future,' was released in the midst of the debate during the 1974 oil crisis. It was to shape the public debate in the critical time of the oil crisis.

For the first time in American establishment circles, the fraudulent thesis was proclaimed that 'Energy growth and economic growth can be uncoupled; they are not Siamese twins.' Freeman's study advocated bizarre and demonstrably inefficient 'alternative' energy sources such as wind power, solar reflectors and burning recycled waste. The Ford report made a strong attack on nuclear energy, arguing that the technologies involved could theoretically be used to make nuclear bombs. 'The fuel itself or one of the byproducts, plutonium, can be used directly or processed into the material for nuclear bombs or explosive devices,' the report asserted.

The Ford study correctly noted that the principal competitor to the hegemony of petroleum in the future was nuclear energy, warning against the 'very rapidity with which nuclear power is spreading in all parts of the world and by development of new nuclear technologies, most notably the fast breeder reactors and the centrifuge method of enriching uranium.' The framework of the U.S. financial establishment's antinuclear 'green' assault had been defined by Bundy's project.[9]

By the early 1970s, nuclear technology had clearly established itself as the preferred future choice for efficient electricity generation, vastly more efficient (and environmentally friendly) than either oil or coal. At the time of the oil shock, the European Community was already well into a major nuclear development program. As of 1975, the plans of member governments called for the completion of between 160 and 200 new nuclear plants across Continental Europe by 1985.

In 1975, the Schmidt government in Germany, reacting rationally to the implications of the 1974 oil shock, passed a program which called for an added 42 gigawatts of German nuclear plant capacity, to produce a total of approximately 45 per cent of German total electricity demand by 1985, a program exceeded in the EC only by France's, which projected 45 gigawatts of new nuclear capacity by 1985. In the fall of 1975, Italy's industry minister, Carlo Donat Cattin, instructed Italy's nuclear companies, ENEL and CNEN, to draw up plans for the construction of some 20 nuclear plants for completion by the early 1980s. Even Spain, just then emerging from four decades of Franco's rule, had a program calling for the construction of 20 nuclear plants by 1983. A typical 1 gigawatt nuclear facility is generally sufficient to supply all the electricity requirements for a modern industrial city of 1 million people.

The rapidly growing nuclear industries of Europe, especially France and Germany, were beginning for the first time to emerge as competent rivals to American domination of the nuclear export market by the time of the 1974 oil crisis. France had secured a Letter of Intent from the Shah of Iran, as had Germany's KWU, to build a total of four nuclear reactors in Iran, while France had signed with Pakistan's Bhutto government to create a modern nuclear infrastructure in that country. Negotiations between the German government and Brazil also reached a successful conclusion in February 1976, for cooperation in the peaceful uses of nuclear energy. This included German construction of eight nuclear reactors as well as facilities for reprocessing and enriching uranium reactor fuel. German and French nuclear companies, with the full support of their governments, entered in this period into negotiations with select developing sector countries, fully in the spirit of Eisenhower's 1953 Atoms for Peace declaration. Clearly, the Anglo-American energy grip, based on their tight control of the world's major energy source, petroleum, was threatened if these quite feasible programs went ahead.

In the postwar period, nuclear energy represented precisely the same technological improvement over oil which oil had represented over coal when Lord Fisher and Winston Churchill argued at the end of the nineteenth century that Britain's navy should convert to oil from coal. The major difference in the 1970s was that Britain and her cousins in the United States were firmly in control of world oil supplies. World nuclear technology threatened to open unbounded energy possibilities, especially if plans for commercial nuclear fast breeder reactors were realized, as well as for thermonuclear fusion.

In the immediate aftermath of the 1974 oil shock, two organizations were established within the nuclear industry, both, significantly enough, based in London. In early 1975, an informal semisecret group was established, the Nuclear Suppliers' Group, or 'London Club,' as it was known. The group included Britain, the United States and Canada, together with France, Germany, Japan and the USSR. This was an initial Anglo-American effort to secure self-restraint on nuclear export. This group was complemented in May 1975 by the formation of another secretive organization, the London 'Uranium Institute,' which brought together the world's major suppliers of uranium. This was dominated by the traditional British territories, including Canada, Australia, South Africa and the United Kingdom. These 'inside' organizations were necessary, but by no means sufficient, for the Anglo-American interests to contain the nuclear 'threat' of the early 1970s. As one prominent antinuclear American from the Aspen Institute put it, 'We must take the bloom off the "nuclear rose."' And take it off they did.

## DEVELOPING THE ANGLO-AMERICAN GREEN AGENDA

It was no accident that, following the oil shock recession of 1974–75, a growing part of the population of western Europe, especially in Germany, began talking for the first time in the postwar period about 'limits to growth,' or threats to the environment, and began to question their faith in the principle of industrial growth and technological progress. Very few people realized the extent to which their new 'opinions' were being carefully manipulated from the top by a network established by the same Anglo-American finance and industry circles that lay behind the Saltsjöbaden oil strategy.

Beginning in the 1970s, an awesome propaganda offensive was launched from select Anglo-American think tanks and journals, intended to shape a new 'limits to growth' agenda, which would ensure the 'success' of the dramatic oil shock strategy. The American oilman present at the May 1973 Saltsjöbaden meeting of the Bilderberg group, Robert O. Anderson, was a central figure in the implementation of the ensuing Anglo-American ecology agenda. It was to become one of the most successful frauds in history.

Anderson and his Atlantic Richfield Oil Co. funneled millions of dollars through their Atlantic Richfield Foundation into select organizations to target nuclear energy. One of the prime beneficiaries of Anderson's largesse was a group called Friends of the Earth, which was organized in this time with a $200,000 grant from Anderson. One of the earliest actions of Anderson's Friends of the Earth was an assault on the German nuclear industry, through such antinuclear actions as the anti-Brockdorf demonstrations in 1976, led by Friends of the Earth leader Holger Strohm. The director of Friends of the Earth in France, Brice Lalonde, was the Paris partner of the Rockefeller family law firm Coudert Brothers, and became Mitterrand's environment minister in 1989. It was Friends of the Earth which was used to block a major Japanese–Australian uranium supply agreement. In November 1974, Japanese Prime Minister Tanaka went to Canberra to meet Australian Prime Minister Gough Whitlam. The two made a commitment, potentially worth billions of dollars, for Australia to supply Japan's needs for future uranium ore and enter a joint project to develop uranium enrichment technology. British uranium mining giant Rio Tinto Zinc secretly deployed Friends of the Earth in Australia to mobilize opposition to the pending Japanese agreement, resulting some months later in the fall of Whitlam's government. Friends of the Earth had 'friends' in very high places in London and Washington.

But Robert O. Anderson's major vehicle for spreading the new 'limits to growth' ideology among American and European establishment circles was his Aspen Institute for Humanistic Studies. With Anderson as chairman and Atlantic Richfield head Thornton Bradshaw as vice-chairman, the Aspen Institute in the early 1970s was a major financial conduit for the creation of the establishment's new antinuclear agenda.

Among the better-known trustees of Aspen at this time was World Bank president and the man who ran the Vietnam war, Robert S. McNamara. Other carefully selected Aspen trustees included Lord Bullock of Oxford University, Richard Gardner, an Anglophile American economist who was later U.S. ambassador to Italy, Wall Street banker Russell Peterson of Lehman Brothers Kuhn Loeb Inc., as well as Exxon board member Jack G. Clarke, Gulf Oil's Jerry McAfee and Mobil Oil director George C. McGhee, the former State Department official who was present in 1954 at the founding meeting of the Bilderberg group. Also involved with Anderson's Aspen in this early period was Marion Countess Doenhoff, the Hamburg publisher of *Die Zeit*, as well as former Chase Manhattan Bank chairman and high commissioner to Germany, John J. McCloy.

Robert O. Anderson brought in Joseph Slater from McGeorge Bundy's Ford Foundation to serve as Aspen's president. It was indeed a close-knit family in the Anglo-American establishment of the early 1970s. The initial project Slater launched at Aspen was the preparation of an international organizational offensive against industrial growth and especially nuclear energy, using the auspices (and the money) of the United Nations. Slater secured support of Sweden's UN ambassador, Sverker Aastrom, who, in the face of strenuous objections from developing countries, steered a proposal through the United Nations for an international conference on the environment.

From the outset, the June 1972 Stockholm UN Conference on the Environment was run by operatives of Anderson's Aspen Institute. Aspen board member Maurice Strong, a Canadian oilman from Petro-Canada, chaired the Stockholm conference. Aspen also provided financing to create an international zero-growth network under UN auspices, the International Institute for Environment and Development, whose board included Robert O. Anderson, Robert McNamara, Strong and British Labour Party's Roy Jenkins. The new organization immediately produced a book, *Only One Earth*, by Rockefeller University associate Rene Dubos and British Malthusian Barbara Ward (Lady Jackson). The International Chambers of Commerce were persuaded at this time to sponsor Maurice Strong and other Aspen figures in seminars targeting international businessmen on the emerging new environmentalist ideology.

The 1972 Stockholm conference created the necessary international organizational and publicity infrastructure, so that by the time of the Kissinger oil shock of 1973–74, a massive antinuclear propaganda offensive could be launched, with the added assistance of millions of dollars readily available from the oil-linked channels of the Atlantic Richfield Company, the Rockefeller Brothers' Fund and other such elite Anglo-American establishment circles. Among the groups which were funded by these people at the time were organizations including the ultra-elitist World Wildlife Fund, then chaired by the Bilderberg's Prince Bernhard and later by Royal Dutch Shell's John Loudon.[10]

Indicative of the financial establishment's overwhelming influence in the American and British media is the fact that during this period no public outcry was heard about the probable conflict of interest involved in Robert O. Anderson's well-financed antinuclear offensive, and the fact that his Atlantic Richfield Oil Co. was one of the major beneficiaries from the 1974 price increase of oil. Anderson's ARCO had invested tens of millions of dollars in high-risk oil infrastructure in Alaska's Prudhoe Bay and Britain's North Sea, together with Exxon, British Petroleum, Shell and the other Seven Sisters.

Had the 1974 oil crisis not raised the market price of oil to $11.65 per barrel or thereabouts, Anderson's investments in the North Sea and Alaska, as well as those of British Petroleum, Exxon and the others, would have brought financial ruin. To ensure a friendly press voice in Britain, Anderson at this time purchased the London *Observer*. Virtually no one asked if Anderson and his influential friends might have known in advance that Kissinger would create the conditions for a 400 per cent oil price rise.[11]

So as not to leave any zero-growth stone unturned, Robert O. Anderson also contributed significant funds to a project initiated by the Rockefeller family at the Rockefeller's estate at Bellagio, Italy, with Aurelio Peccei and Alexander King. In 1972, this Club of Rome, and the U.S. Association of the Club of Rome, gave widespread publicity to their publication of a scientifically fraudulent computer simulation prepared by Dennis Meadows and Jay Forrester, titled 'Limits to Growth.' Meadows and Forrester added modern computer graphics to the discredited essay of Malthus, insisting that the world would soon perish for lack of adequate energy, food and other resources. As did Malthus, they chose to ignore the impact of technological progress on improving the human condition. Their message was one of unmitigated gloom and cultural pessimism.

One of the most targeted countries for this new Anglo-American antinuclear offensive was Germany. While France's nuclear program was equally if not more ambitious, Germany was deemed an area where Anglo-American intelligence assets had greater likelihood of success, given their history in the postwar occupation of the Federal Republic. Almost as soon as the ink had dried on the Schmidt government's 1975 nuclear development program, an offensive was launched.

A key operative in this new project was a young woman with a German mother and an American stepfather, who had lived in the United States until 1970, working for U.S. Senator Hubert Humphrey, among other things. Petra K. Kelly had developed close ties in her U.S. years with one of the principal new Anglo-American antinuclear organizations created by McGeorge Bundy's Ford Foundation, the Natural Resources Defense Council. The Natural Resources Defense Council included Barbara Ward (Lady Jackson) and Laurance Rockefeller among its board members at the time. In Germany, Kelly began organizing legal assaults against the construction of the German nuclear program during the mid 1970s, resulting in costly delays and eventual large cuts in the entire German nuclear plan.

## POPULATION CONTROL BECOMES A U.S. NATIONAL SECURITY ISSUE

In 1798 an obscure English clergyman, Thomas Malthus, professor of political economy in the employ of the British East India Company's East India College at Haileybury, was given instant fame by his English sponsors for his 'Essay on the Principle of Population.' The essay itself was a scientific fraud, plagiarized largely from a Venetian attack on the positive population theory of American Benjamin Franklin.

The Venetian attack on Franklin's essay had been written by Gianmaria Ortes in 1774. Malthus' adaptation of Ortes' 'theory' was refined with a facade of mathematical legitimacy which he called the 'law of geometric progression,' which held that human populations invariably expanded geometrically, while the means of subsistence were arithmetically limited, or linear. The flaw in Malthus' argument, as demonstrated irrefutably by the spectacular growth of civilization, technology and agriculture productivity since 1798, was Malthus' deliberate ignoring of the contribution of advances in science and technology to dramatically improving such factors as crop yields, labor productivity and the like.[12]

By the mid-1970s, as an indication of the effectiveness of the new propaganda onslaught from the Anglo-American establishment, American government officials were openly boasting in public press conferences that they were committed 'neo-Malthusians,' something for which they would have been laughed out of office a mere decade or so earlier. But nowhere did the new embrace of British Malthusian economics in the United States show itself more brutally than in Kissinger's National Security Council.

On April 24, 1974, in the midst of the oil crisis, the White House national security adviser, Henry Alfred Kissinger, issued National Security Council Study Memorandum 200 (NSSM 200), on the subject of 'Implications of Worldwide Population Growth for U.S. Security and Overseas Interests.' It was directed to all cabinet secretaries, the military Joint Chiefs of Staff as well as the CIA and other key agencies. On October 16, 1975, on Kissinger's urging, President Gerald Ford issued a memorandum confirming the need for 'U.S. leadership in world population matters,' based on the contents of the classified NSSM 200 document. The document made Malthusianism, for the first time in American history, an explicit item of security policy of the government of the United States. More bitterly ironic was the fact that it was initiated by a German-born Jew. Even during the Nazi years, government officials in Germany were more guarded about officially espousing such goals.

NSSM 200 argued that population expansion in select developing countries which also contain key strategic resources necessary to the U.S. economy posed potential U.S. 'national security threats.' The study warned that, under pressure from expanding domestic populations, countries with essential raw materials will tend to demand higher prices and better terms of trade for their exports to the United States. In this context, NSSM 200 identified a target list of 13 countries singled out as 'strategic targets' for U.S. efforts at population control. The list, which was drawn up in 1974, is instructive. No doubt, as with other major decisions of Kissinger, the selection of countries was made after close consultation with the British Foreign Office.

Kissinger explicitly stated in the memorandum, 'how much more efficient expenditures for population control might be than [would be funds for] raising production through direct investments in additional irrigation and power projects and factories.' British nineteenth-century imperialism could have expressed it no better. By the mid-1970s, the government of the United States, with this secret policy declaration, had committed itself to an agenda which would contribute to its own economic demise, as well as bringing untold famine, misery and unnecessary death throughout the developing sector. The 13 target countries named by Kissinger's study were Brazil, Pakistan, India, Bangladesh, Egypt, Nigeria, Mexico, Indonesia, the Philippines, Thailand, Turkey, Ethiopia and Colombia.[13]

# 10

# Europe, Japan and a
# Response to the Oil Shock

## THE PETRODOLLAR MONETARY ORDER
## DEVASTATES THE DEVELOPING WORLD

Despite the enormous economic and financial shocks on the world economy, resulting from the 1974 oil price inflation, by late 1975 certain parts of the world had begun to resume industrial development, as though they had sustained a stunning blow, recovered and continued on their path. The 1974 oil shock had secured certain of the objectives of the Anglo-American Bilderberg group, but by no means had the global parameters of industrial development yet been decisively altered to their satisfaction. Their continuing strategic domination was still mortally threatened.

The world's output of steel, as well as the total ton-miles of the world shipping trade, provide a striking measure of the health of the world's economic progress. Beginning in the early 1950s, as the world started to rebuild from the destruction of the Second World War, world crude steel production, measured in metric tons of crude steel produced, made a steady upward climb. Steel, to this day, is one of the best single measures against which to judge the overall industrial progress of a nation's economy. Unlike the all-too-fashionable gross national product, which measures price levels regardless of whether an activity is productive or non-productive, whether, for example, it involves construction of infrastructure or spending on a gambling casino in Las Vegas, output of steel, measured in tons, cannot be manipulated. Steel, moreover, is essential—for transport, for building, for infrastructure of all kinds.

The Western world, including the developing sector, steadily increased its steel output from less than 175 million metric tons in 1950 to an all-time peak of just under 500 million tons by the time the 1974 oil crisis impacted. Steel is also one of the most energy-intensive industries. For two to three years after the first oil crisis, world steel output reflected the economic shock and plummeted almost 15 per cent from its peak of 1974–75. But by 1976, steel output had again begun a steady upward climb.

A similar pattern occurred in world sea-borne trade, with a sharp decline in total ton-miles of ocean ships in response to the 1974 oil shock and the severe world economic downturn, followed by a similar slow but steady recovery up to 1977–78. The year 1975 witnessed the first major decline in world trade since the end of the war in 1945, a significant drop of 6 per cent, followed by a slow resumption.[1]

But one sector which had not recovered from the greatest financial and inflation shock of the postwar period was the fragile countries south of the equator, most especially those which had no significant indigenous oil supplies. For the vast majority of the developing sector, the oil crisis spelled an end to development, inability to finance industrial and agriculture improvement, and a reversal of the hopes for a better life which had emerged in many parts during the 1960s.

As though some perverse fate had struck, this oil crisis coincided during the years 1974–75 with the onset of the worst global drought in decades, leading to severe harvest shortfalls, especially in Africa, South America and parts of Asia, just as the economic impact of the oil shock was at its greatest. With the desperate need to import record volumes of grain and other food from the United States and western Europe, most underdeveloped countries found themselves faced with famine, unable to finance increased food imports, to say nothing of financing the oil shock.

The dynamic created by the Anglo-American decoupling of the dollar from gold in August 1971, followed by the 400 per cent forced inflation of the price of oil, had created a catastrophe for the majority of the world's population who lived in the developing sector.

Bank of Italy chairman Guido Carli noted at the time that the 'banking community has increasingly come to be regarded with hostility ... The feeling of mistrust derives from a conviction that the commercial banks have appropriated too large a share of monetary sovereignty.' Carli described the effects of the oil shock on world financial flows in an address to fellow bankers during early 1976. In the context of the 1971 dollar–gold decoupling and the floating of exchange rates, the new oil prices had created a worldwide shortage of liquidity. 'The shortage of international liquidity was made up by the banks,' Carli noted, 'and in large measure by American banks through their overseas branches.'

Carli remarked that some saw this process as 'corroboration of the evil intentions' of those who were behind the push for creation of the new gold-free dollar monetary order, 'maintaining that the eradication of gold from the system and the failure to replace it with official instruments confirm a malicious design to strengthen the dominant position of the American banks.'[2]

Indeed, some did see it as malicious. While industrial countries had experienced a certain slow recovery from the initial oil shock by 1975, the overall position of developing economies deteriorated as a result of the quadrupling of primary oil prices. The total current-account deficit of all developing countries rose from an average of some $6 billion per year during the early 1970s to more than $26 billion in 1974 (again a quadrupling, in parallel with the price of oil), and to $42 billion, an unbearable seven-fold increase, by 1976. The vast majority of this deficit was in countries of the developing sector, whose per capita income levels were the lowest in the world.

Under the threat of losing access to further borrowings from the World Bank and the private banks of the industrial nations, these less-developed countries were forced to divert precious funds from industrial and agricultural development into simply reducing this balance-of-payments deficit. Their oil imports had to be paid, and paid in dollars, while the cost of their raw materials exports had fallen sharply in the global recession of 1974–75.

Private U.S. and European banks stepped into the breach to lend to these countries, under the Bilderberg 'petrodollar recycling' strategy, but only to 'balance' accounts which had been left in shambles by the Anglo-American oil shock, not to finance the creation of necessary production infrastructure or technology development. These private petrodollar loans came from the London-based U.S. and British Eurodollar banks. OPEC oil revenues, paid to Saudi Arabia, Kuwait and other countries, were paid in dollars and those dollars were channeled and 'guided' into offshore London Eurodollar banks for relending to the victims of the oil crisis in the developing sector.

Dr. Kissinger and his friends left nothing to chance in the process. A senior partner of an American investment bank at the center of the Eurodollar markets, David Mulford, at the time the head of White Weld & Co.'s London Eurodollar operations, was appointed director and principal investment adviser of the Saudi Arabian Monetary Agency (SAMA), the central bank of Saudi Arabia, the largest OPEC oil producer and a country dominated by American Big Oil. Little publicity was given to this rather unusual appointment of a national of the country against which Saudi Arabia had only months earlier enjoined an oil embargo. Along with White Weld, SAMA enjoyed the confidential investment advice of the elite London merchant bank, Baring Brothers.

As director of the Saudi Arabian Monetary Agency, David Mulford was in a critical position to ensure that the Saudi authorities made 'wise' use of their new financial windfall. To make Mr. Mulford's task easier, Citibank, the New York bank closely tied to Exxon and the American oil companies involved in Saudi Arabia's Arab American Oil Company (ARAMCO), was curiously enough able to operate in this period as the only wholly owned foreign bank with operations in Saudi Arabia. Not surprisingly, in 1974 fully 70 per cent of OPEC oil surplus revenues were invested abroad in stocks, bonds, real estate and the like. Of this enormous sum of $57 billion, no less than 60 per cent went directly to financial institutions in the United States and Britain.[3]

As early as June 8, 1974, in his capacity as U.S. secretary of state, Henry Kissinger had signed an agreement establishing a little-noted U.S.–Saudi Arabian Joint Commission on Economic Cooperation, whose official mandate included, among other projects, 'cooperation in the field of finance.' (Kissinger retained the unprecedented dual posts of national security adviser to the president and secretary of state well into Gerald Ford's presidency.)

By December 1974, the nature of this cooperation had been defined more clearly, though strict secrecy was maintained by both Saudi and Washington governments. The U.S. Treasury had signed an agreement in Riyadh with the Saudi Arabian Monetary Agency, whose mission was 'to establish a new relationship through the Federal Reserve Bank of New York with the [U.S.] Treasury borrowing operation. Under this arrangement, SAMA will purchase new US Treasury securities with maturities of at least one year,' explained assistant secretary of the U.S. Treasury, Jack F. Bennett, later to become a director of Exxon. Bennett's memo explaining the arrangements agreed two months before was dated February 1975 and addressed to Secretary of State Kissinger.[4]

No less astonishing than these U.S.–Saudi 'arrangements' to one ignorant of the real history of Anglo-American interests in the Persian Gulf was the exclusive policy decision by the OPEC oil states to accept only U.S. dollars for their oil—not German marks, despite their clear value, not Japanese yen, French francs or even Swiss francs, but only American dollars.

Dollar oil pricing was initially a practice encouraged after the Second World War by the American oil majors and by their bankers in New York. But when, following the oil crisis of early 1974, leading European governments began to enter into serious negotiations with Arab oil suppliers to secure long-term oil purchase contracts to cover their import needs, to be paid in their own national currency—an eminently sensible move which would have enormously lessened the European impact of the oil shock—something extraordinary occurred within OPEC. Germany or France would have had far less difficulty in securing domestic funds for the payment of its oil imports in Deutschmarks or francs than in buying dollars for the same oil. This makes it all the more curious that OPEC ministers, meeting in 1975, agreed to accept no other currency than the U.S. dollar in payment for deliveries of its oil, not even the British pound.

This arrangement, needless to say, proved enormously valuable for the United States dollar and for the financial institutions of New York and the London Eurodollar markets. The world was forced to buy huge amounts of dollars more or less continuously, in order to purchase essential energy supplies. Even more extraordinary, this OPEC dollar-pricing agreement remained in force despite the subsequent enormous losses to OPEC as the dollar gyrated up and down through the next decade and more.

One consequence of the directed recycling of these petrodollars into London and New York was the emergence of American banks as the giants of world banking, paralleling the emergence of their clients, the Seven Sisters oil multinationals, as the giants of world industry. The Anglo-American oil and banking combination so overwhelmed the scale of ordinary enterprise that their power and influence seemed invincible.

In effect, through such secret arrangements as the U.S.–Saudi Joint Agreement with the Treasury and the activities of David Mulford, as well as OPEC's strange dollar-pricing mandate, Washington and the New York banks had exchanged their flawed postwar Bretton Woods gold exchange system for a new, highly unstable petroleum-based dollar exchange system, which, unlike the gold exchange system, they reckoned they could control. Kissinger and the financial establishment of London and New York had in effect replaced the old gold exchange standard of the postwar world with their own 'petrodollar standard.'

After all, who really controlled OPEC? Only the politically naive could believe that Arab countries would suddenly be allowed to exercise independence on issues of such importance to British and American interests. Had they really regarded the oil shock as a life-threatening matter, Washington could have found numerous ways in which to restore a reasonable OPEC oil price. They wanted the high oil price and they wanted OPEC to take the blame for it.

The two reserve currencies of Bretton Woods, the British pound sterling and the U.S. dollar, remained at center stage in the new petrodollar order of the 1970s. Sterling conveniently gained from the vast exploitation of North Sea oil, which came on line just in time to benefit from the 400 per cent oil price inflation, as noted earlier. The British pound became known as a 'petrocurrency.'

The dollar gained for the reasons just mentioned. Clearly, the May 1973 Bilderberg deliberations in Saltsjöbaden had calculated the winners and losers. No matter to them that their artificial oil price inflation was a manipulation of the world economy of such a hideous dimension that it created an unprecedented transfer of the wealth of the entire world into the hands of a tiny minority. Was this not, after all, what Adam Smith meant by the 'magic' of the market?

If the methods look more than a little like a perverse variation on the old mafia 'protection racket' game, this is understandable. The same Anglo-American interests which manipulated political events to create a 400 per cent increase in the oil price then turned to the countries which were the victims of assault and 'offered' to lend them petrodollars to finance the purchase of the costly oil and other vital imports—at a vastly inflated interest cost, of course.

Real industrial and agricultural development for a vast majority of the world, living in less-developed regions, suffered the consequences of the Anglo-American oil policy. The petrodollars went simply to refinance deficits, rather than to finance the creation of new infrastructure, to assist agriculture or to improve the living standards of the world's population.

During 1975, the policy organ of the Anglo-American liberal establishment, the New York Council on Foreign Relations, under the direction of New York attorney Cyrus Vance, drafted a series of policy blueprints for the 1980s, much as they had done at the critical turning point during the late 1950s recession. In their account of the future of the global monetary order, the council stated, 'A degree of "controlled dis-integration" in the world economy is a legitimate objective for the 1980's.' What was disintegrating, however, was the entire fabric of traditional industrial and agricultural development, most clearly in the developing sector.[5]

During the following August, in Colombo, Sri Lanka, heads of state and senior cabinet officials of 85 nations, members of the so-called Group of Non-Aligned Nations, met under the host government of Prime Minister Sirimavo Bandaranaike. Among the leaders present were India's Indira Gandhi and numerous heads of state or officials of African, Asian and Latin American governments, including Algeria and Iraq.

## FROM COLOMBO COMES A POLITICAL EARTHQUAKE

The Colombo gathering began with little fanfare. It hardly seemed any different from one of the endless rounds of bickering and rhetoric among the numerous former colonial states. But Prime Minister Bandaranaike, a veteran of earlier struggles against British and American interests, having expropriated British and U.S. oil companies in the early 1960s, had decided to make the August summit an intervention into the deteriorating economic state of the developing countries in the aftermath of Kissinger's oil crisis.[6]

The final declaration of the Colombo meeting, dated August 20, 1976, was a document unlike any produced by developing-country heads of state in the postwar period. The central theme of the 85 non-aligned states had been publicly announced as 'A fair and just economic development.' The resolution declared that 'economic problems have become the most difficult aspect of international relations ... The developing countries have become the victim of this worldwide crisis,' a crisis which was preventing the attempts of these countries to eliminate hunger, sickness and illiteracy.

In this context, noting the near doubling of the burden of foreign debt since the onset of the 1973 oil shock and the catastrophic worsening of terms of trade for raw materials export, the declaration proposed several concrete steps towards the creation of a new international economic order.

The existing order, it noted correctly, had collapsed, and this was leading to restrictive protectionist policies, recession, inflation and unemployment. Therefore the declaration called for a 'fundamental reorganization of the international trade system in order to improve terms of trade ... a worldwide reorganization of industrial production which would incorporate improved access by the developing nations to industrial products and technology transfer.' Addressing the chaos of the existing Bretton Woods system, with its 'anarchy of floating exchange rates,' the declaration called for a radical overhaul of the international monetary system in order, among other things, to guarantee an adequate transfer of investment capital to developing nations. But the most alarming aspect of the Colombo declaration, from the standpoint of the New York and London financial establishment, was a call for a 'satisfactory resolution of the problem of the public indebtedness, especially for the least developed and most severely affected countries.' The explosive issue of foreign debt had been placed on the negotiating table for the first time, not by a single government, but by 85 governments acting collectively.

Bandaranaike's Sri Lanka (a former British colony) and India under the leadership of Prime Minister Indira Gandhi, had carefully prepared the agenda for debate among the 85 heads of state, in concert with the government of another former British colony on the northeast coast of South America, Guyana. The crucial negotiator for Guyana in Colombo was its minister of foreign affairs, Frederick Wills. Significantly, the newly independent governments of three former British colonies led the Colombo initiative to create a powerful new alignment of forces, which would potentially redirect priorities towards industrialization and development.

The important next step for the non-aligned initiative was decided. The annual meeting of the United Nations General Assembly in New York the following month would be the forum at which to present their proposal to the world community of nations. At the end of September 1976, Wills was designated to present the position of the Colombo group. Carefully declaring their 'non-alignment' from either major superpower bloc of the postwar era, Wills then proceeded to present to the assembled delegates the results of the recently passed Colombo declaration.

Citing repeated attempts from developing countries over the past years to reach a satisfactory resolution of their economic future, which was also in the interests of the economic security of the industrial nations, Wills then dropped his political bombshell:

The International Monetary Fund and the monetary system of Bretton Woods must provide a place for alternative structures such as international development banks, which have as their goal, not the recovery and reconstruction of Europe or preferential agreements for development of a market economy, but rather, the just division of the gains from an unequal global economic system.

Wills concluded his remarks:

> The burning problem of the debt and debt service has taken on a special importance. Developing countries are not able to manage their basic requirements, as noted in Colombo, without resort to some form of debt restructuring or moratoria. We must make every effort to oppose attempts to divide us through 'case-by-case' techniques. We cannot allow ourselves to mortgage future unborn generations to the burdensome debt repayment and destructive debt service. The time for a debt moratium has arrived.

The impact of the combined Colombo and UN declarations was immediate. On Wall Street, traders spoke of a 'crisis of confidence.' Share prices for U.S. banks began to fall, especially those most involved in Eurodollar lending to the developing countries: Citicorp, Morgan Guaranty, Bankers Trust and Chase Manhattan. The Federal Reserve bank was forced to intervene to support the falling dollar. The implications of a concerted action by developing states on the dollar debt had sent shock waves through the financial system.

But the Colombo resolution of the 85 non-aligned states which Wills presented at the United Nations that autumn was only one part of what was rapidly becoming a potential alliance of the key oil-producing states with certain European industrial nations and possibly Japan—a combination which would have decisively challenged the Anglo-American Bretton Woods order as never before.

In reviewing what had taken place in 1976, Wills some years later told this author:

> In what became known as the Third World, approximately 80 per cent of mankind lived on the flanks of superpower rivalry, supplying raw materials for the processing economies of the First and Second Worlds, and striving to become market extensions of the market economies of the First World.
>
> Third world politicians at that time had a different view about their international role, however. They regarded political independence as merely one essential step in the path of growth and development. They sought generalized technological advance, which should be coterminous with diversification of agriculture and the insertion of such infrastructure as would lead to the industrialization, and thereby closing of the huge gaps that separated the different worlds.

Wills went on to explain how all this was to be paid for:

> Led by Britain and France, the economic theorists of the First
> World determined that the export receipts of the Third World
> should decide the pace and quality of development and, when
> these fell below expectations, resort should be had to the Bretton
> Woods system whose machinery had been set up in the late 1940s.
> Above all, this meant the requirement of the stamp-of-approval
> of the International Monetary Fund (IMF) and submission to the
> barbarous conditionalities which were the underpinning of IMF
> intervention.
>
> This was the context within which the Summit of the Non-
> Aligned Nations was held at Colombo in Sri Lanka in 1976. There
> was a call for a new funding institution—an international resources
> bank—to replace the iniquitous neocolonialism of the IMF. There
> was also a call for diminution of the vertical and structural economic
> dependence of the Third World on Britain, France and the USA, and
> an increase in horizontal linkages between Third World countries.
> There were calls for regional *Zollvereins* or customs unions to protect
> Third World industries, and for technology transfers in order to
> remove the harshness of underdevelopment.
>
> The United Nations was chosen as the arena where it was hoped
> that a new era of global cooperation would emerge. These hopes
> were never realized. One by one, the outstanding advocates of
> Third World development were removed from the seats of domestic
> power, and their solidarity was defeated in detail by the age-old
> principle of 'divide and conquer.' Export receipts and import prices
> were manipulated to create enormous gaps in balances of payments,
> and Third World countries were told that they must get the seal of
> approval of the IMF before any government or private institution
> would advance further loans. The IMF insisted on austere programs
> based on currency devaluations which increased misery in the
> Third World, was directly responsible for the spread of disease
> and was also successful in encouraging drug cultivation, as those
> unfortunate countries sought the chimera of a quick cash crop as
> a panacea for their fiscal difficulties.

On the role of the petroleum-exporting countries of the Third
World, Wills added:

The only Third World raw material that did well in the economic arena was oil, but the large oil reserves were centered in the Middle East, and manipulation of inter-Arab and Arab–Israeli conflicts, together with inculcation of a penchant for prestige projects, meant that Third World oil reserves could not be used as factors in Third World development. One by one Third World countries were gripped by inflation and starvation, by low life-expectancy and high infant mortality. The old order of Canning and Castlereagh, Pitt and Disraeli remains.

The reference to the methods of British nineteenth-century foreign minister, Castlereagh, the master artisan of British balance-of-power diplomacy at the 1815 Congress of Vienna, was appropriate. The principal active opponent who deployed the full power and force of the U.S. government, intelligence services and economic clout to destroy the dynamic set off at Colombo in 1976 was the secretary of state, Henry Kissinger, a devout student of Castlereagh.

When the foreign ministers of the European Community met in December 1976 to discuss, among other issues, a possible cooperation with the call of the non-aligned nations, Kissinger sent a telegram to the delegates, warning:

The United States believes it would be dangerous for the industrial countries to strengthen the ties between the CIEC [Conference for International Economic Cooperation—the North–South Conference] and OPEC. A number of OPEC spokesmen have publicly sought to make clear that the final decision about the oil price in a great degree will depend on concessions from the industrial nations toward the CIEC. This would create the opposite of our desired link [to OPEC countries] and strengthen instead the links between OPEC and other underdeveloped countries.

Kissinger's veiled threat succeeded in disrupting any active support from the nations of Europe for the potential alliance of OPEC and the non-aligned group. Diplomats personally involved in these talks at the time report that the two governments most open and responsive to such a call for cooperation with the non-aligned were Italy and West Germany. On December 12, Italian papers reported a meeting of leading representatives of government, industry and trade unions, convened by the German and Italian governments on the subject of the creation of a European defense against the damaging impact of the unstable oil-linked U.S. dollar. The government of Helmut Schmidt was reportedly told privately at this time by Washington, that Bonn risked a pull-out of U.S. troops if it dared to pursue the non-aligned offer in any serious way. Andreotti's Italy was isolated and unable to act alone. The Kissinger tactic of 'divide and conquer' had again prevailed, at least for the moment.

As for the key strategists of the bold Colombo non-aligned declaration, within months each had been forced out of office, 'case-by-case,' to use Kissinger's phrase. In India, Prime Minister Indira Gandhi was forced into elections in February 1977 and in the midst of this, several key members of her Congress Party led by Jagjivan Ram, staged a public party defection to form an opposition coalition with the radical Janata. The key issue was the imposition of IMF-dictated domestic austerity. Gandhi was out by that March, less than six months after the UN declaration of the non-aligned. In Sri Lanka, Mrs.Bandaranaike's ruling Freedom Party and the entire country were paralyzed by a wave of strikes in early January led by a 'Trotskyite' party linked to the trade unions, which reportedly enjoyed intimate ties with Anglo-American intelligence. Bandaranaike at the time, in a futile effort to restore order, charged 'foreign interference.' By May 1977 she was out. And in Guyana, on Valentine's Day, February 14, 1978, after repeated external pressures on the government of Prime Minister Forbes Burnham, Frederick Wills, the third key strategist of the non-aligned initiative on economic development, was forced to resign.

According to diplomatic sources familiar with the situation, the heavy hand of Henry Kissinger was present in each case. 'But this was done in close coordination with the British,' according to these observers. 'The British, you know, were very clever. They were willing to let the Americans do the public dirty work and take the blame, while they worked very effectively on a more discreet level. It wasn't people like Jim Callaghan [the British Labour prime minister] who did this. It was the people of [Royal Institute for International Affairs'] Chatham House, people such as Michael Howard, and families such as Lord Cecil's, and the MI5 intelligence circles, who went into action against the Colombo initiative.'[7]

The Third World threat to the Anglo-American order and their regime of global taxation through petrodollars had apparently been beaten back. The leading Eurodollar banks of London and New York opened the floodgates, lending ever greater sums to select states of the Third World who agreed to the draconian IMF terms, to refinance their oil-related deficits.

## ATOMS FOR PEACE BECOMES A *CASUS BELLI*

But there were growing signs in too many parts of the world that the potential still existed for stronger and potentially decisive initiatives in technology transfer from the key European industrial nations, as well as from Japan, to select developing countries. While the broad front presented at Colombo had been nominally defeated, the idea of specific North–South economic cooperation was taking hold in dramatic new ways.

During late 1975, the government of Brazil entered into a major agreement with the German government of Helmut Schmidt for construction of a complex of nuclear power stations, fuel enrichment plants and other related technologies. The German nuclear reactor manufacturer, KWU, signed what at the time was the largest single nuclear contract in the world. Germany was to provide 'turnkey' construction of eight nuclear power reactors and facilities for the entire nuclear fuel cycle, including enrichment. Valued at a total cost of $5 billion, the entire project was to be completed by 1990. The European uranium enrichment consortium, Urenco, was to supply the initial uranium fuel. Also in 1975, Brazil signed a $2.5 billion cooperation agreement with France for the construction of an experimental fast breeder reactor. Washington responded with unprecedented efforts to force Germany as well as Brazil to cancel the program. Brazil threatened to become an economic power independent of Anglo-American control and, significantly, independent of their oil blackmail.

Mexico, which during the early 1970s was not yet a significant exporter of oil, for sound economic reasons made the decision to develop nuclear power for electricity as part of its plan for rapid industrialization, while conserving its oil 'patrimony' for other uses, such as earning export dollars. As an initial part of its nuclear program, Mexico entered into contracts with Mitsubishi of Japan and Siemens of Germany. In 1975, in the wake of the first oil shock, Mexico's National Energy Commission decided that it was wasteful and inefficient to burn hydrocarbons to produce electricity. They announced plans to build 15 new nuclear power reactors over a 20-year period.

Pakistan, under the government of Prime Minister Zulfikar Ali Bhutto, responded to the 1974 oil shock by accelerating work on an earlier small-scale nuclear energy program. Bhutto had withdrawn Pakistan from the British Commonwealth of Nations, in order to pursue an independent national development policy.

The Bhutto government entered negotiations with France on construction of a nuclear fuel enrichment plant for Pakistan, which were finalized in March 1976. Pakistan was developing into an effective lobby throughout the Middle East on the importance of developing nuclear energy in addition to oil resources. By August 1976, the U.S. State Department, and Henry Kissinger in person, launched a major pressure campaign on both France and Pakistan to abort the nuclear deal, claiming it was related to nuclear weapons ambitions, despite Pakistan's approval from the International Atomic Energy Agency that there were sufficient safeguards to ensure that this would not be the case. According to Pakistani accounts, earlier that year in Lahore, Kissinger had delivered a direct threat 'that he would make a horrible example of Pakistan' if Bhutto did not abandon the nuclear reprocessing project negotiations with France.

In 1977, Bhutto was overthrown in a military coup led by General Zia ul-Haq. Before his death by hanging, Bhutto accused U.S. Secretary of State Henry Kissinger of being behind his overthrow because of Bhutto's insistence on developing Pakistan's independent nuclear program. Writing his defense from his prison cell before his execution, Bhutto declared:

> Dr. Henry Kissinger, the Secretary of State for the United States, has a brilliant mind. He told me that I should not insult the intelligence of the United States by saying that Pakistan needed the Reprocessing Plant for her energy needs. In reply, I told him that I will not insult the intelligence of the United States by discussing the energy needs of Pakistan, but in the same token, he should not insult the sovereignty and self-respect of Pakistan by discussing the plant at all ... I got the death sentence.[8]

General Zia reversed Bhutto's independent foreign policy and quickly embraced Washington. Abundant U.S. military assistance followed.

But by all measures, the most impressive commitment to nuclear energy by a developing sector country in the wake of the 1974 oil shock came from the Shah of Iran. The Shah, who owed his position to the coup staged by British and American intelligence in 1953 to overthrow the nationalist Mossadegh regime and reinstate a 'pro-American' monarchy, had appeared to be a grateful recipient of American military supplies and other support over more than 20 years. He had even agreed to initiate Henry Kissinger's call for an increase in the OPEC benchmark oil price to $11.65 per barrel at the January 1974 OPEC meeting.

But with the new oil revenues flowing in to the state treasury, the Shah saw the opportunity to realize an old dream. Iran would use its oil wealth to create one of the world's most modern energy infrastructures, built upon nuclear power generation, which would transform the electricity and other power needs of the entire Near East.

By 1978, Iran had the fourth largest nuclear power program in the world and the largest by far among Third World nations. The Shah's plan called for the installation of 20 nuclear power reactors by 1995, to provide some 23,000 megawatts of electricity. The Shah saw nuclear electricity as the rational means to diversify Iran's dependence on petroleum, and as a means to counter the enormous pressure from Washington and London to recycle his petrodollars to New York and London banks.

The major negotiating partners with whom the Shah negotiated his nuclear program were France and Germany. As early as 1974, Iran had signed a provisional agreement with France to construct five nuclear power reactors and a nuclear research center. This was expanded in 1975 to eight reactors, for a total cost of $8.6 billion. In addition, Iran purchased a 10 per cent share in the French uranium enrichment facility being constructed at Tricastin, and lent $1 billion for its construction.

In 1976, Iran signed a contract with the German nuclear firm, KWU, for 7.8 billion Deutschmarks, for two reactors and infrastructure; this was followed in 1977 by a contract to supply four more reactors for an added 19 billion Deutschmarks. In addition, Iran under the Shah invested in key European industrial companies, including a 25 per cent stake in the German Krupp, and in French nuclear enrichment facilities. The economic bonds between Iran and Continental Europe were growing in importance. During this time, under the strict antinuclear regime of U.S. President Carter, the United States did not participate in backing the export of U.S. nuclear reactor technology, and Washington tried strenuously to block the German and French deals, to no avail.

In the wake of the 1973 oil crisis, nuclear technology was threatening to become the most rapidly growing source for non-oil energy infrastructure in country after country, both in western Europe and in the developing sector.

## GOLD, DOLLAR CRISIS AND DANGEROUS
## NEW POTENTIALS FROM EUROPE

At a private closed-door gathering convened in Tokyo in April 1975 and organized by Chase Manhattan Bank chairman David Rockefeller and Bilderberg founder George W. Ball, a handpicked group of policy spokesmen met to discuss a special project. Lord Roll of Ipsden, chairman of the S.G. Warburg bank and a director of the Bank of England, was present; David Ormsby Gore, Lord Harlech, who was London's ambassador to Washington during the fateful Kennedy years of the early 1960s, was also present. Barclays Bank chairman Sir Anthony Tuke also attended the secretive Tokyo discussions that April, as did the Earl of Cromer, George Baring, a man closely tied to Morgan Guaranty Trust in New York and to Royal Dutch Shell. (Baring had been ambassador to Washington during the time of Kissinger's oil shock, when the U.S. secretary of state acknowledged his unusually close policy coordination with the British Foreign Ministry.) Present too at the fateful Tokyo talks was John Loudon, chairman of Royal Dutch Shell, who also sat on the Advisory Committee of David Rockefeller's Chase Manhattan Bank.

What concerned the hundred or so influential policy makers at the April meeting of Rockefeller's newly formed Trilateral Commission was the dangerous risk to the Anglo-American establishment of continuing the offensive U.S. foreign policy stance against the rest of the world associated with Secretary of State Henry Kissinger and the Republican administration. Kissinger's hard-line 'divide and rule' tactics had been to isolate one country after another, whether European, developing sector or OPEC, and to portray OPEC as the villain to developing countries whose economic growth had been destroyed by the Bilderberg group's 1973 oil policy.

By 1975, Kissinger's thinly-veiled 'thug' approach to international diplomacy was risking creating an enormous international backlash. A new 'image' was needed to persuade the world of the need for continued American hegemony. Therefore, at the Tokyo gathering of the Trilateral Commission that April, little more than a year and a half from the 1976 American presidential elections, David Rockefeller introduced a man to his influential international friends as the next president of the United States. Few Americans, not to mention foreigners, had ever heard of the small-town Georgia peanut farmer who preferred to be called 'Jimmy' Carter.[9]

Following his initiation at the 1975 Tokyo meeting, Carter received an extraordinary public relations buildup from establishment media such as the liberal *New York Times*, which hailed him as a dynamic exponent of America's 'New South.' In November 1976, despite allegations of voting irregularities, Carter became president.

Carter brought with him such a large number of advisers who were members of the Trilateral Commission that his presidency was dubbed the 'Trilateral Presidency.' Not only was Carter's vice president, Walter Mondale, like himself, a member of the elite secretive Trilateral organization, but his national security adviser, Zbigniew Brzezinski, his secretary of state, Cyrus Vance, his treasury secretary, Michael Blumenthal, his defense secretary, Harold Brown, his United Nations' ambassador, Andrew Young and State Department senior officials Richard Cooper and Warren Christopher were all part of the exclusive Trilateral club.

The public profile of Carter's presidency was 'human rights' for the Third World, 'negotiation, not confrontation.' He portrayed himself as an 'outsider' to the Washington power establishment, but the content of U.S. policy under Carter, with his preselected crew of establishment advisers, was to maintain the American century at all costs. Under a rhetorical facade of 'reforming the old order' of U.S. foreign policy, the Carter administration continued the basic Anglo-American neo-Malthusian strategy initiated by Kissinger at the National Security Council under National Security Study Memorandum 200. Third World development was to be blocked, and a 'limits to growth' postindustrial policy was to be imposed, to maintain the hegemony of the dollar imperium. Carter's 'human rights' was to become a bludgeon to justify unprecedented U.S. intervention into the internal affairs of targeted Third World nations. The strategy was to fail miserably.

A significant problem arose in the immediate wake of the oil shock, which threatened to undo the edifice of the new Anglo-American 'petrodollar monetary system.' Already in 1974, the Commission of the European Community proposed to the member country central banks a system for settling intra-EEC trade balances with gold, at a market price that was then around $150 per fine ounce. The European proposal would have greatly eased the oil payment burden for a number of European countries, and reduced the influence of the dollar. The U.S. Treasury, for the political reason of dollar hegemony, adamantly insisted that the central banks value gold at the artificially low price of $42.22 per fine ounce. A valuation of gold at the higher price might have opened the door for the EEC to significant trade possibilities with two leading gold-producing countries, South Africa and the Soviet Union. The U.S. Treasury under-secretary, Paul Volcker, went to London in the autumn of 1974 to deliver a blunt warning against any such European moves to bring gold back into the monetary system in the wake of the oil crisis.

But the idea, naturally, did not die. Rather the opposite. The South African government of John Vorster, dependent on imported oil, was at the time struggling to maintain economic stability in the wake of the severe oil price increase. At the same time, it was extending tentative feelers to neighboring black African states for some form of economic development cooperation, despite the rigid regime of apartheid at home.

Angola was rich in oil; South Africa had industrial technology and infrastructure needed by Angola and other African states. The region required financial investment and secure foreign trade outlets for it to work. In late 1974, South African Finance Minister Nicolaas Diederichs publicly called for a revaluation of the international central bank gold price to a market level, echoing the debate in Europe:

I have consistently pressed for monetary authorities to be allowed to sell gold among themselves at a market-related price ... gold in official vaults of central banks would be revalued; and there would be much more money to pay the Arabs; secondly, the dollar would lose value.

At the same time, Germany and Italy initiated a bilateral agreement under which gold was used as collateral for a German loan, valued at 80 per cent of the current market price of $150 per ounce. European discussion about the effective use of gold as an alternative to the tyranny of the dollar standard were clearly gaining momentum.

But these possibilities of closer trade and economic linkage between Continental Europe and South Africa received a devastating blow. Soviet and Cuban support for Angola's Marxist Movement for the Popular Liberation of Angola (MPLA) brought that country under the control of a regime hostile to Pretoria. In addition, repeated unannounced sales of official U.S. gold reserves, which dumped large quantities onto the market, severely depressed the world gold price and brought growing economic difficulties for the vital South African mining industry. Then, in May 1976, riots erupted in the South African township of Soweto. The riots, curiously enough, coincided with a visit of U.S. Secretary of State Kissinger to South Africa. The international political backlash of a brutal South African police repression of the rioters at Soweto made effective economic linkage between South Africa and European governments more difficult. But the talks continued as the situation stabilized to some extent over the following months; the involvement of the world's largest gold-producing country in any attempt to stabilize world monetary relations was absolutely crucial.

In July 1977, a South African business monthly, *To the Point International*, published an interview with a leading West German banker, Dresdner bank chairman Jürgen Ponto. In the interview, Ponto outlined his vision of a development solution to the economic and racial crises then enveloping all of southern Africa. Speaking of the vital role which Europe must play in resolving the crisis of Africa, Ponto stressed that first Europe must restore order in its economies following the oil and related economic crises. In order to do this, Ponto stated,

> priority must be given to the creation of a stable monetary system; when a smaller but economically important region of the world such as the European Community starts the stone rolling, by eliminating its own monetary chaos, then we will be on the way to realize this.

Ponto further elaborated the concept of European economic development initiatives for the entire southern African region, including the wealthy African states such as South Africa, Ivory Coast and Algeria, which would enable those countries to develop the poorest states: 'They can produce sufficient food, employment and education possibilities for the entire Continent, provided that the restrictions can be removed in the course of developments.' Ponto was a close personal friend of the South African finance minister, Nicolaas Diederichs, and Diederichs' designated successor, Robert Smit. Advanced discussion was clearly taking place between influential European banking and industry and the resource-rich governments of Southern Africa. A potential combination was emerging which could have changed the geopolitical map of the entire Anglo-American world, to the clear disadvantage of London and New York.

But on July 31, in Frankfurt, Jürgen Ponto was assassinated by terrorists claiming to belong to the Baader-Meinhof gang. Some weeks later, in Cologne, the chairman of the German employers' federation, Hanns-Martin Schleyer, was kidnapped and later murdered by the same organization. While the assassins' trail led back to the East, there was significant reason to believe that certain powerful Western intelligence services had a role in both assassinations. In the event, West Germany was plunged into political chaos and gripped by fear as never before in the postwar period. The possibility of any significant development initiative towards South Africa had been killed along with Ponto and Schleyer. The initiative to break with the dollar imperium had been stalled for the moment.

## THE CRASH OF 1979: IRAN AND VOLCKER

One major aspect of what Ponto alluded to in his last interview did come to pass. In June 1978, in response to growing frictions and outright policy clashes with the Carter administration on nuclear energy policy, international monetary policy, the free fall of the dollar, and just about every foreign policy issue of importance to Continental Europe, the member governments of the European Community, on the initiative of France and Germany, took steps to create the first phase of what was seen as a European currency zone, a first attempt to insulate Continental Europe from the shocks of the dollar regime.

German Chancellor Helmut Schmidt and France's President Giscard d'Estaing proposed the establishment what became Phase I of the European Monetary System (EMS), in which the central banks of nine European Community member countries agreed to stabilize their currencies in relation to one another. With growing trade flows concentrated inside the community, the EMS provided a minimal basis for defending intra-European trade and monetary relations.

In early 1979 the EMS became operational and its effect in stabilizing European currencies was notable. But the future possibilities of the EMS were what worried certain circles in London and Washington. It had ominous overtones of becoming a seed crystal for an alternative world monetary order which could threaten the existing hegemony of the 'petrodollar monetary system.' Indeed, one German official at the time privately referred to the new EMS as the 'seed crystal for the replacement of the International Monetary Fund.' And the French government openly said as much at the time. The EMS established a European Monetary Fund with initial capitalization consisting of 20 per cent of each member country's gold and dollar reserves, valued at some $35 billion. Further, Switzerland too linked its currency de facto to the new EMS parities.

As early as 1977, the governments of France and Germany had begun to explore the possibility of an agreement with select oil-producing OPEC states under which western Europe would supply high-technology exports to OPEC, in return for long-term oil supply agreements at a stable price. In turn, under this arrangement, OPEC would deposit their financial surpluses into Continental European banks and, ultimately, into the new EMS, to build a fund which could be used for long-term industrial credits to other developing countries.

London opposed the new EMS concept of France and Germany at every step. Unable to stop its implementation, London refused to join the new stabilization arrangement. The City of London establishment had other ideas.

At a September 1978 Aachen Summit between Giscard d'Estaing and Schmidt, the two countries agreed on plans for joint scientific and technical education, as well as joint nuclear energy cooperation. Furthermore, the UDF party of Giscard in France had proposed a $100 billion five-year development program for Continental Europe and the developing sector. A state visit by President Carter to Bonn and West Berlin in July 1978 only reinforced French and German resolve to pursue an independent policy.

Carter had unsuccessfully sought to persuade the Schmidt government, under the Carter administration's new Nuclear Non-Proliferation Act, to abandon export of virtually all nuclear technology to the developing sector, on the false argument that peaceful nuclear plant technology threatened to proliferate nuclear weapons, an argument which uniquely stood to enhance the strategic position of the Anglo-American petroleum-based financial establishment.

Thus, despite all efforts since the early 1970s, the 'danger' of independent industrial and trade growth which undercut the prized domination of the dollar imperium was clearly becoming real in the minds of policy shapers in Washington and London. Even more drastic shocks were required to stop the determination of nations to pursue scientific and industrial development.

Drastic shocks they were.

In November 1978, President Carter named the Bilderberg group's George Ball, another member of the Trilateral Commission, to head a special White House Iran task force under the National Security Council's Brzezinski. Ball recommended that Washington drop support for the Shah of Iran and support the fundamentalist Islamic opposition of Ayatollah Khomeini. Robert Bowie from the CIA was one of the lead 'case officers' in the new CIA-led coup against the man their covert actions had placed into power 25 years earlier.

Their scheme was based on a detailed study of the phenomenon of Islamic fundamentalism, as presented by British Islamic expert, Dr. Bernard Lewis, then on assignment at Princeton University in the United States. Lewis's scheme, which was unveiled at the May 1979 Bilderberg meeting in Austria, endorsed the radical Muslim Brotherhood movement behind Khomeini, in order to promote balkanization of the entire Muslim Near East along tribal and religious lines. Lewis argued that the West should encourage autonomous groups such as the Kurds, Armenians, Lebanese Maronites, Ethiopian Copts, Azerbaijani Turks, and so forth. The chaos would spread in what he termed an 'Arc of Crisis,' which would spill over into the Muslim regions of the Soviet Union.

The coup against the Shah, like that against Mossadegh in 1953, was run by British and American intelligence, with the bombastic American, Brzezinski, taking public 'credit' for getting rid of the 'corrupt' Shah, while the British characteristically remained safely in the background.

During 1978, negotiations were under way between the Shah's government and British Petroleum for renewal of the 25-year oil extraction agreement. By October 1978, the talks had collapsed over a British 'offer' which demanded exclusive rights to Iran's future oil output, while refusing to guarantee purchase of the oil. With their dependence on British-controlled export apparently at an end, Iran appeared on the verge of independence in its oil sales policy for the first time since 1953, with eager prospective buyers in Germany, France, Japan and elsewhere. In its lead editorial that September, Iran's *Kayhan International* stated:

In retrospect, the 25-year partnership with the [British Petroleum] consortium and the 50-year relationship with British Petroleum which preceded it, have not been satisfactory ones for Iran ... Looking to the future, NIOC [National Iranian Oil Company] should plan to handle all operations by itself.

London was blackmailing and putting enormous economic pressure on the Shah's regime by refusing to buy Iranian oil production, taking only 3 million or so barrels daily of an agreed minimum of 5 million barrels per day. This imposed dramatic revenue pressures on Iran, which provided the context in which religious discontent against the Shah could be fanned by trained agitators deployed by British and U.S. intelligence. In addition, strikes among oil workers at this critical juncture crippled Iranian oil production.

As Iran's domestic economic troubles grew, American 'security' advisers to the Shah's Savak secret police implemented a policy of ever more brutal repression, in a manner calculated to maximize popular antipathy to the Shah. At the same time, the Carter administration cynically began protesting abuses of 'human rights' under the Shah.

British Petroleum reportedly began to organize capital flight out of Iran, through its strong influence in Iran's financial and banking community. The British Broadcasting Corporation's Persian-language broadcasts, with dozens of Persian-speaking BBC 'correspondents' sent into even the smallest village, drummed up hysteria against the regime in exaggerated reporting of incidents of protest against the Shah. The BBC gave the Ayatollah Khomeini a full propaganda platform inside Iran during this time. The British government-owned broadcasting organization refused to give the Shah's government an equal chance to reply. Repeated personal appeals from the Shah to the BBC yielded no result. Anglo-American intelligence was committed to toppling the Shah. The Shah fled in January, and by February 1979, Khomeini had been flown into Tehran to proclaim the establishment of his repressive theocratic state to replace the Shah's government.

Reflecting on his downfall months later, shortly before his death, the Shah noted from exile,

> I did not know it then—perhaps I did not want to know—but it is clear to me now that the Americans wanted me out. Clearly this is what the human rights advocates in the State Department wanted … What was I to make of the Administration's sudden decision to call former Under Secretary of State George Ball to the White House as an adviser on Iran? … Ball was among those Americans who wanted to abandon me and ultimately my country.[10]

With the fall of the Shah and the coming to power of the fanatical Khomeini adherents in Iran, chaos was unleashed. By May 1979, the new Khomeini regime had singled out the country's nuclear power development plans and announced cancellation of the entire program for French and German nuclear reactor construction.

Iran's oil exports to the world were suddenly cut off, some 3 million barrels per day. Curiously, Saudi Arabian production in the critical days of January 1979 was also cut by some 2 million barrels per day. To add to the pressures on world oil supply, British Petroleum declared force majeure and cancelled major contracts for oil supply. Prices on the Rotterdam spot market, heavily influenced by BP and Royal Dutch Shell as the largest oil traders, soared in early 1979 as a result. The second oil shock of the 1970s was fully under way.

Indications are that the actual planners of the Iranian Khomeini coup in London and within the senior ranks of the U.S. liberal establishment decided to keep President Carter largely ignorant of the policy and its ultimate objectives. The ensuing energy crisis in the United States was a major factor in bringing about Carter's defeat a year later.

There was never a real shortage in the world supply of petroleum. Existing Saudi and Kuwaiti production capacities could at any time have met the 5–6 million barrels per day temporary shortfall, as a U.S. congressional investigation by the General Accounting Office months later confirmed.

Unusually low reserve stocks of oil held by the Seven Sisters oil multinationals contributed to creating a devastating world oil price shock, with prices for crude oil soaring from a level of some $14 per barrel in 1978 towards the astronomical heights of $40 per barrel for some grades of crude on the spot market. Long gasoline lines across America contributed to a general sense of panic, and Carter energy secretary and former CIA director, James R. Schlesinger, did not help calm matters when he told Congress and the media in February 1979 that the Iranian oil shortfall was 'prospectively more serious' than the 1973 Arab oil embargo.[11]

The Carter administration's Trilateral Commission foreign policy further ensured that any European effort from Germany and France to develop more cooperative trade, economic and diplomatic relations with their Soviet neighbor, under the umbrella of détente and various Soviet–west European energy agreements, was also thrown into disarray.

Carter's security adviser, Zbigniew Brzezinski, and secretary of state, Cyrus Vance, implemented their 'Arc of Crisis' policy, spreading the instability of the Iranian revolution throughout the perimeter around the Soviet Union. Throughout the Islamic perimeter from Pakistan to Iran, U.S. initiatives created instability or worse.

Then came Brzezinski's 'China card' policy tilt, with U.S. diplomatic recognition of communist China in December 1978, together with U.S. withdrawal of recognition of the nationalist Chinese regime on Taiwan, thereby giving communist China the UN Security Council veto and access to U.S. technology and military aid. At a summit meeting in January 1979, German Chancellor Schmidt delivered a strong protest to President Carter that his new 'China card' policy was proving extremely destabilizing for fragile German–Soviet relations, by creating the impression in Moscow that NATO was aggressively encircling the USSR in an arc of chaos and military hostility.

In October 1979, a devastating new Anglo-American financial shock was unleashed on top of the second oil crisis of that year. That August, on the advice of David Rockefeller and other influential voices of the Wall Street banking establishment, President Carter appointed Paul A. Volcker, the man who, back in August 1971, had been a key architect of the policy of taking the dollar off the gold standard, to head the Federal Reserve. Volcker, a former official at Rockefeller's Chase Manhattan Bank, and, of course, a member of David Rockefeller's Trilateral Commission, was president of the New York Federal Reserve at the time of his appointment as head of the world's most powerful central bank.

Despite the fact that an oil price of $40 per barrel represented a dramatic increase in dollar terms, the size of the oil crisis, combined with the growing international alarm over the incompetent Carter administration, led to a further weakening of the dollar. Since early 1978, the dollar had already dropped more than 15 per cent against the German mark and other major currencies. The price of gold was rising rapidly and in September 1979 was at the record high of almost $400 per ounce. Arab and other investors were preferring to invest in gold rather than dollars. In September 1978 the dollar fell in a near panic collapse, when it became known that Saudi Arabia's Monetary Agency had begun liquidating billions of dollars of U.S. treasury bonds. It appeared that Mr. Carter's presidency was proving too much even for these staunch U.S. allies.

The policy strategists based in the City of London and New York then resolved to impose a Malthusian monetary shock on top of the oil crisis, to tilt the balance of world development decisively to their relative advantage.

In October 1979, Volcker unveiled a radical new Federal Reserve monetary policy. He deceived a shocked Congress and a desperate White House by insisting that his radical monetarist cure was aimed at 'squeezing inflation out of the system.' It was aimed at making the U.S. dollar the most eagerly sought currency in the world and to stop industrial growth dead in its tracks, in order that political and financial power flow back to the dollar imperium. Volcker's cold rationalization to Congress was that 'restraint on growth in money and credit, maintained over a considerable period of time, must be an essential part of any program to deal with entrenched inflation and inflationary expectations.'

The defect in Volcker's monetary shock therapy was that he never addressed the fundamental origins of the soaring inflation—two oil price shocks since 1973, which had raised the price of the world's basic energy and transportation by 1,300 per cent in six years. And Volcker's insistence on restricting the U.S. money supply by cutting credit to banks, consumers and the economy, was also a calculated fraud. Volcker knew full well, as did every major banker in New York and London, that control of America's domestic dollar supply was a minor part of a far larger problem. Volcker knew that his actions had little control on the estimated $500 billion outside the United States, circulating in the so-called Eurodollar markets of London and the Cayman Islands and other offshore hot-money havens. At the time of the October 1979 Volcker monetary shock therapy, Morgan Guaranty Trust calculated the gross size of the Eurodollar offshore markets at fully 57 per cent of the entire domestic U.S. money supply. The American citizen was to pay the cost of this rampant offshore money pool, as though it never existed.

In both his objectives, Volcker succeeded. U.S. interest rates on the Eurodollar market soared from 10 per cent to 16 per cent, on their way up to levels of 20 per cent in a matter of weeks, as the world looked on in stunned disbelief. Inflation was indeed being 'squeezed' as the world economy was plunged into the deepest depression since the 1930s. And the dollar began what was to be an extraordinary five-year-long ascent.

The oil crisis and the Volcker shock were further strengthened by a decision of the leading circles of the establishment to 'take the bloom off the nuclear rose' once and for all, in order to ensure that the alarming trend of developing worldwide nuclear energy resources to replace reliance on Anglo-American oil was decisively ended.

Unprecedented diplomatic and legal pressures from the White House since 1977 had not succeeded in significantly blunting the attraction of nuclear power. But on March 28, 1979, in a town in the center of Pennsylvania, a bizarre event occurred, which was then portrayed to the world press in fictitious terms, as though it were a Hollywood movie script or a remake of Orson Welles' 1938 *War of the Worlds* radio broadcast.

Unit 2 of the Three Mile Island nuclear power reactor complex in Harrisburg underwent an improbable sequence of 'accidents.' Later investigation revealed that critical valves had been illegally and manually closed before the event, preventing emergency cooling water from entering the reactor's steam generator system. Within 15 seconds, emergency back-up systems had brought the nuclear fission process to a stop. But a plant operator then violated all procedure and intervened to shut off cooling water into the reactor core. The details of what happened next have been extensively documented elsewhere.

On August 3, 1979, in its official report on the event, the U.S. Nuclear Regulatory Commission posed sabotage or criminal negligence as one of six possible causes for the Three Mile Island event. But even after eliminating the other five possible causes, the government refused to consider the possibility of sabotage seriously.

News to the world's media during the entire Harrisburg drama was strictly controlled by the newly established White House Federal Emergency Management Agency (FEMA). No government or nuclear plant official was allowed to speak to the press, except when screened by FEMA censors. FEMA had been created by Presidential executive order, based on the blueprint of Trilateral Commission White House adviser Samuel Huntington. Curiously, the agency went into operation on March 27, five days before its stated date of operation, and the day before the Three Mile Island incident. Under the direction of National Security Adviser Brzezinski, FEMA controlled all news at Harrisburg. The agency ordered the evacuation of the surrounding population, although there was no indication of radiation danger, and refused to brief the media for days, permitting panic stories of fictitious items such as 'Gigantic Radioactive Hydrogen Bubble into Atmosphere,' and worse, to fill the headlines. Curiously too, that same month a spectacular Hollywood movie, *The China Syndrome*, starring Jane Fonda, portrayed a fictional account almost exactly parallel with the Harrisburg events, further fueling public hysteria over the dangers of nuclear energy.

By the end of 1979, the hegemony of the Anglo-American financial establishment over the world's economic and industrial potentials had been reasserted in a manner never before imagined. Control of world oil flows had again been a central weapon of their peculiar brand of Malthusian policy. Out of the chaos of Khomeini's Iran and Volcker's dollar shocks, these influential policy arbiters virtually saw themselves as gods on Mount Olympus. Within a short decade, however, their lofty mountain was to feel the rumblings of an underlying volcano.

# 11
# Imposing the New World Order

## VOLCKER BORROWS A BRITISH MODEL

Well before Karl Marx ever conceived of his notion of class warfare, British liberalism had evolved a concept of a society polarized into what they termed the 'upper classes' and the 'lower classes.' The essence of the nineteenth-century liberal free trade policies of Adam Smith and David Ricardo, which led to the abolition of the protective Corn Laws in Britain after 1846, and which opened the flood gates to ruinous cheap grain imports, led, as noted earlier, to the predictable impoverishment of the greater majority of British citizens, and to the concentration of the wealth of the society into the hands of a small minority, the so-called 'upper classes.' The political philosophy of what was called British liberalism was the justification for this economically inequitable process.

As the most influential American publicist of nineteenth-century British liberalism, the aristocratic Walter Lippmann defined this class society in a modern framework for an American audience. Society, Lippmann argued, should be divided into the great vulgar masses of a largely ignorant 'public,' which is then steered by an elite or a 'special class,' which Lippmann termed the 'responsible men,' who would decide the terms of what would be called 'the national interest.' This elite would become the dedicated bureaucracy, to serve the interests of private power and private wealth, but the truth of their relationship to the power of private wealth should never be revealed to the broader ignorant public. 'They wouldn't understand.'

The general population must have the illusion, Lippmann argued, that it is actually exerting 'democratic' power. This illusion must be shaped by the elite body of 'responsible men' in what was termed the 'manufacture of consent.' This was described by Lippmann, several decades before Paul Volcker ever set foot in Washington, as the 'political philosophy for liberal democracy.' In its concept of an elite specialized few, ruling on behalf of the greater masses, modern Anglo-American liberalism bore a curious similarity to the Leninist concept of a 'vanguard party,' which imposed a 'dictatorship of the proletariat' in the name of some future ideal of society. Both models were based on deception of the broader populace.[1]

More and more, following the turning point of the 1957 U.S. economic recession, the enormous power of a small number of international banks and related petroleum multinationals, concentrated in New York, defined the contents of an American 'liberalism,' based on adaptation of the nineteenth-century British imperial model. The American version of this enlightened liberal model would be shaped from an aristocracy of money, rather than the blue-blood aristocracy of birth. But increasingly, as a consequence of the economic policy decisions of the American East Coast liberal establishment—so-called because its center of power was built around the New York finance and oil conglomerates—the United States became transformed. America, once the ideal of freedom for much of the world, became, step-by-step, transformed into the opposite, and at a quickening pace during the 1970s and 1980s, while she retained a rhetorical facade of 'freedom and liberty.'

The combined impact of the two staggering oil shocks of the 1970s, and the resulting hyperinflation this set into motion, created, in effect, a new American 'landed aristocracy,' in which those who owned property suddenly saw themselves become millionaires overnight, not as a consequence of enterprise or successful manufacturing or scientific invention, but merely as the consequence of possession of land—real estate, dead dirt.

But if the oil shocks set off this polarization of society into a minority of the increasingly wealthy and a vast majority whose living standards were slowly sinking, the monetary shock therapy imposed on the United States by Paul Volcker after October 6, 1979 helped the task to its ultimate conclusion.

It would be a mistake to think that this policy was Volcker's own invention. It had been developed, and already implemented months before, in Britain. Volcker and his close circle of New York banking friends, including Lewis Preston of the Anglophile Wall Street firm, Morgan Guaranty Trust Company, merely imposed the Thatcher government's monetary shock model under U.S. conditions.

In early May 1979, Margaret Thatcher won the British general election against her Labour Party opponent, James Callaghan. She had campaigned on a platform of 'squeezing inflation out of the economy.' But Thatcher, and the inner circle of modern-day Adam Smith 'free market' ideologues which surrounded her, promoted a consumer fraud, insisting that government deficit spending, and not the 140 per cent increase in the price of oil since the fall of Iran's Shah, was the chief 'cause' of Britain's 18 per cent rate of price inflation.

According to the Thatcher government claim, inflated prices could again be lowered simply by cutting the supply of money to the economy, and since the major source of 'surplus money,' she argued, was from chronic government budget deficits, government expenditure must be savagely cut in order to reduce 'monetary inflation.' The Bank of England, as their contribution to the remedy, simultaneously restricted credit to the economy by a policy of high interest rates. Predictably, the effect was depression; but it was called instead the 'Thatcher revolution.'

Cut and squeeze. Thatcher did just that. In June 1979, only one month after taking office, Thatcher's chancellor of the exchequer, Sir Geoffrey Howe, began a process of raising base rates for the banking system a staggering five percentage points, from 12 per cent up to 17 per cent, over a matter of twelve weeks. This amounted to an unprecedented 42 per cent increase in the cost of borrowing for industry and homeowners. Never in modern history had an industrialized nation undergone such a shock in such a brief period, outside the context of a wartime economic emergency.

The Bank of England simultaneously began to cut the money supply, to ensure that interest rates remained high. Businesses went bankrupt, unable to pay borrowing costs; families were unable to buy new homes; long-term investment in power plants, subways, railroads and other infrastructure ground virtually to a halt as a consequence of Thatcher's monetarist revolution.

But the principal problem with the British economy at the end of the 1970s was not government ownership of companies such as the British Leyland car group, Rolls-Royce or the many other enterprises which have since been auctioned off to private investors. The main problem was lack of investment by the government in upgrading public infrastructure, in the education of its skilled labor force, and in scientific research and development. It was not 'government,' but rather wrong government policy, in response to the economic shocks of the previous ten or more years, which was at fault.

Thatcher's 'economic revolution' applied the wrong medicine to 'cure' the wrong disease. But the international financial interests of the City of London and the powerful petroleum companies grouped around Shell, British Petroleum and their allies were the intended real beneficiaries, as was the perceived strategic British 'balance-of-power' calculus. Thatcher was a simple grocer's daughter, groomed by her cynical patrons to act out a role for their greater geopolitical designs.

As Thatcher imposed the policies which earned her the name 'Iron Lady,' unemployment in Britain doubled, rising from 1.5 million when she came into office to a level of 3 million by the end of her first 18 months. Labor unions were targeted under Thatcher as obstacles to the success of the monetarist 'revolution,' a prime cause of the 'enemy,' inflation. All this time, with British Petroleum and Royal Dutch Shell exploiting the astronomical price of $36 or more per barrel for their North Sea oil, never a word was uttered against Big Oil or the City of London banks, which were amassing huge sums of capital as a result of the situation. Thatcher also moved to accommodate the big City banks by removing exchange controls, so that instead of capital being invested in rebuilding Britain's rotten industrial base, funds flowed out in speculation on real estate in Hong Kong or lucrative loans to Latin America.[2]

Beginning in Britain, then moving to the United States, and from there radiating outward from the Anglo-American world, the radical monetarism of Thatcher and Volcker spread like a cancer, with its insistent demands to cut government spending, lower taxes, deregulate industry and break the power of organized labor. Interest rates rose around the world to levels never before considered possible.

In the United States, Volcker's monetary shock policy had driven U.S. interest rates up to British levels by early 1980, and some months later even higher, to an astonishing 20 per cent level for select interest rates. The economics of this interest rate austerity were soon obvious to all. Interest rates of 20 per cent, or even 17 per cent, meant that any normal investment requiring more than four or five years to complete was simply not profitable. Interest charges on the construction alone prohibited this.

With regulatory changes in nuclear power plant construction in the United States after the Three Mile Island antinuclear hysteria adding years of delay in the completion of existing power plants, nuclear energy as an investment for America's electric utility companies became prohibitive under the Volcker interest rate regime. After 1979, not one new nuclear reactor was ordered in the United States, and scores of half-built or planned nuclear projects were cancelled midstream because of prohibitive financing costs. One of the most advanced sectors of the productive economy was allowed to die.

Volcker's shock medicine was imposed on a desperate and ignorant President Carter, who in March 1980 willingly signed an extraordinary piece of legislation, the Depository Institutions Deregulation and Monetary Control Act of 1980. This law empowered Volcker's Federal Reserve to impose reserve requirements on banks, even if not in the Federal Reserve system, including savings and loan banks, ensuring that Volcker's credit choke succeeded. In addition, the new law phased out all legal ceilings on interest rates which the banks could charge customers under what the Federal Reserve called 'Regulation Q,' as well as repealing all state laws which had set interest rate limits, the so-called anti-usury laws.

The sky was the interest rate limit under the religious dogma of the new Anglo-American monetarism; money was to king, and the world, or at least, the payer of usurious interest rates to the banks of London and New York, its dutiful servant.

Long-term government-funded infrastructure and capital investment, such as railroad, highway, bridge, sewer and electricity plant construction, was devastated by this Thatcher–Volcker policy offensive in the early 1980s. From the time of the first oil shock in 1975 until 1985, the International Iron and Steel Institute calculated that the total share of all government expenditure in major industrial nations devoted to the construction of public infrastructure had fallen to one half of its level in the mid 1970s. The world production of steel, shipping ton miles and other indicators of real physical economic flows reflected the catastrophic Anglo-American monetary shock policy. The world steel industry was forced deeper into its worst depression since the 1930s.[3]

Paul Volcker's monetary shock and the ensuing U.S. economic downturn were major factors in the November 1980 election defeat of Jimmy Carter. The new 'conservative' Republican president, a former Hollywood movie actor named Ronald Reagan, had little difficulty backing the Volcker shock treatment. Reagan had been tutored while governor of California by the guru of monetarism, Mont Pelerin economist Milton Friedman. Britain's Margaret Thatcher deliberately cultivated what she called a 'special relationship' with Reagan. She 'encouraged' his support of the shock therapy of Volcker and government austerity, as well as his propensity for antiunion policies. To ensure a unified Anglo-American offensive on policy during this period, Reagan and Thatcher also shared some of the same economic advisers, from a circle of dogmatic Mont Pelerin economists which included Karl Brunner, Milton Friedman, Sir Alan Walters and others.

One of Reagan's first acts as president in early 1981 was to use his powers of office to dissolve the trade union of the airline traffic controllers, PATCO. This served to signal other unions not to attempt to seek relief from the soaring interest rates. Reagan was mesmerized by the same ideological zeal to 'squeeze' out inflation as was his British counterpart, Thatcher. Some informed people in the City of London even suggested that a major reason for the Thatcher government's existence in the first place was to influence the monetary policy of the world's largest industrial nation, the United States, and to shift economic policy throughout most of the industrial world away from the direction of long-term nuclear and other industrial development.

If that was in fact the plan, it succeeded. Six months after Thatcher took office, Ronald Reagan was elected. Reagan as president reportedly enjoyed repeating at every opportunity to his cabinet the refrain, 'Inflation is like radioactivity. Once it starts, it spreads and grows.' Reagan kept Milton Friedman as an unofficial adviser on economic policy. His administration was filled with disciples of Friedman's radical monetarism, much as Carter's had been with exponents of David Rockefeller's Trilateral Commission.[4]

This entire radical monetarist construct, first advanced in the early 1980s by the British regime of Thatcher and soon afterwards by the U.S. Federal Reserve and the Reagan administration, was one of the most cruel economic frauds ever perpetrated. But its aim was other than what its ideological 'supply-side' economics advocates claimed.

The powerful liberal establishment circles of the City of London and New York were determined to use the same radical measures earlier imposed by Friedman to break the economy of Chile under Pinochet's military dictatorship, this time in order to inflict a devastating second blow against long-term industrial and infrastructure investment in the entire world economy. The relative power of Anglo-American finance was thus to become again hegemonic, they reasoned. What was to follow in the 1980s would have appeared inconceivable to a world which had not already been stunned and disoriented by the shocks of the 1970s.

## GUNBOAT DIPLOMACY AND A MEXICAN INITIATIVE

It would be no exaggeration to say that there would not have been a Third World debt crisis during the 1980s had it not been for Margaret Thatcher's and Paul Volcker's radical monetary shock policies.

As the average cost of their petroleum imports, denominated in US dollars, rose some 140 per cent following the Iran oil shock in early 1979, developing countries this time around found that the dollar itself, in terms of their local currencies, was also rising like an Apollo rocket because of the high U.S. interest rates caused by Volcker's policy. Not only could most struggling developing countries barely manage the borrowings to finance the oil deficits built up from the 1974 oil crisis; by 1980, an entirely new element faced them—floating interest rates on their Eurodollar borrowings.

As noted earlier, as early as 1973 the Anglo-American financial insiders of the Bilderberg group had discussed using the major private commercial banks of New York and London, in the London-centered Eurodollar market, to recycle what Henry Kissinger and others referred to as the new OPEC petrodollar surpluses. The sudden glut of new OPEC oil funds, which was steered into the London Eurodollar banks during the oil crises of the 1970s, was to be the source of the greatest unregulated lending spree since the 1920s.

London had evolved as the geographical center for this Eurodollar 'offshore' market because the Bank of England, over a period since the 1960s, had made it clear that it would not attempt to regulate or control the flows of foreign currencies in the London Eurodollar banking market. It was part of their strategy of reconstructing the City of London as the center of world finance. This meant, despite vague public utterances of various bankers about the safeness of Eurodollar loans, that the billions of dollars flowing out of the London-based Eurodollar banks to the accounts of developing country borrowers during the 1970s, had no 'lender of last resort'—no single sovereign government was legally bound to make good the losses in the event of a major default on the bank loans.

Nobody seemed concerned, as long as this Eurodollar roulette wheel kept turning. Foreign debts incurred by developing countries expanded some five-fold, rising from $130 billion in the 'halcyon' days of 1973, before the first oil shock, to some $550 billion by 1981, and to over $612 billion by the decisive year 1982, according to International Monetary Fund calculations. Even this omitted significant short-term lending of less than one year. The leading banker of New York at the time, Citicorp's Walter Wriston, justified the private bank lending to countries such as Mexico and Brazil by arguing that 'governments have assets that are in excess of their liabilities, and this is, shorthand, governments don't go bankrupt ...'

A crucial feature of these private Eurodollar loans to developing countries was ignored in the aftermath of the first oil shock. Manufacturers Hanover Trust of New York, a major Eurodollar bank, had pioneered the petrodollar recycling of huge sums to developing countries such as Mexico, Brazil, Argentina, even Poland and Yugoslavia. While developing countries were able to borrow on far more favorable terms than if they had submitted their economies to the conditionalities of the International Monetary Fund, the Anglo-American bank syndicates extracted a little-noticed concession, pioneered by Manufacturers Hanover. All Eurodollar loans to these countries were fixed at a specified premium over and above the given London Inter-Bank Offered Rate (LIBOR). This LIBOR rate was a 'floating' rate, which would fall or rise, as determined by short-term interest-rate levels in New York and London. Before the summer of 1979, this seemed an innocuous precondition to borrowing needed funds to finance oil deficits.

But with the application of the Thatcher government's interest-rate monetary shock beginning June 1979, followed that October by the same policy from Paul Volcker's Federal Reserve, the interest rate burdens of Third World debt compounded overnight, as interest rates on the London Eurodollar market climbed from an average of 7 per cent in early 1978 to almost 20 per cent by early 1980.

Due to this one factor alone, Third World debtor countries would have collapsed into default as the altered debt service conditions imposed on them by the creditor banks added an unpayable new amount to their previous onerous debt burden. But even more unsettling were the uncanny parallels of policy then imposed by the leading London and New York bankers, virtually a letter-by-letter rerun of the same banks' Versailles war reparations debt-recycling folly of the 1920s, which had collapsed into chaos in October 1929 with the crash of the New York stock market.

As interest rate burdens on their foreign debt obligations soared to the stratosphere after 1980, the market for Third World debtor country commodity exports to the industrial countries, which were critical to repaying those debt burdens, collapsed, as the industrial economies were plunged into the deepest economic downturn since the world depression of the 1930s—a result of the impact of the Thatcher–Volcker monetary shock 'cure.'

Third World debtor countries began to get squeezed in the blades of a vicious scissors of deteriorating terms of trade for their commodity exports, falling export earnings, and a soaring debt service ratio. This, in short, was what Washington and London preferred to call the 'Third World debt crisis.' But the crisis had been made in London, New York and Washington, not in Mexico City, Brasilia, Buenos Aires, Lagos or Warsaw.

Events came to a predictable head during the summer of 1982. As it became obvious that the Latin American debtor countries would soon explode under the onerous new debt repayment burdens, influential circles around Margaret Thatcher and the Reagan Administration, notably Secretary of State Alexander Haig, Vice President George Bush and CIA Director William Casey, began to prepare an 'example,' to deter debtor countries from considering nonpayment of their debts to the major U.S. and UK banks.

In April of 1982, Prime Minister Thatcher told the British House of Commons, 'Britain won't flinch from using force' to retake the disputed Malvinas Islands in the desolate waters of the south Atlantic off Argentina's coast, known as the Falklands in Britain. The issue was not that Argentina's Galtieri government had, with justification, claimed sovereignty over the islands, and retaken them on April 1, after years of unsuccessful attempts at negotiation of the issue. Nor was the issue that the surrounding area was believed by some to contain rich untapped petroleum reserves. The real issue of Thatcher's military confrontation with Argentina was to enforce the principle of the collection of Third World debts by a new form of nineteenth-century 'gunboat diplomacy.' Two-thirds of Britain's Naval fleet was dispatched to the south Atlantic during April 1982, for a shooting war with Argentina which Britain nearly lost due to Argentine deployment of French Exocet missiles.

The British intent was to trigger a crisis in order to attempt to place the military might of all NATO behind the policing of Third World debt repayment, under the changed terms of sky-high floating interest rates. Argentina was the third largest debtor nation at the time, with $38 billion in foreign debts, and the country which appeared closest to default. Thatcher had been advised to make a test case of Argentina. The staged Malvinas conflict, details of which were to emerge almost ten years later, was merely the pretext to persuade other NATO members to back what was termed 'out of area' NATO military response. A tentative step in that direction came at a May 7 NATO Nuclear Planning Group meeting that spring in Brussels, but aside from American backing, Britain largely stood alone in its demand to expand the purview of NATO beyond the defense of western Europe.

What did result from the British military action against Argentina in the spring of 1982 was the severe worsening of Washington's relations with its Latin American neighbors. The Reagan administration had been persuaded, after much internal wrangling, to come out on the side of British gunboat diplomacy against Argentina, in de facto violation of the United States' own Monroe Doctrine.

Perhaps unknown to President Reagan, Assistant Secretary of State Thomas Enders had traveled to Buenos Aires in March that year to privately assure the Galtieri government that the dispute between Argentina and Britain over the Malvinas would not draw U.S. participation. This assurance was considered in Buenos Aires as the 'green light' from Washington to proceed. It bore remarkable parallels to similar 'assurances' which a U.S. ambassador was to give to Iraq's Saddam Hussein in July 1990, some days before the Iraqi invasion of Kuwait. Certain circles in the Washington establishment were in full accord with the London Foreign Office policy. Argentina had to be maneuvered into giving the pretext for military action by Britain.

One country which did not appreciate Washington's support for Thatcher's replay of nineteenth-century British colonialism was Mexico, which shared a border with the United States. Under the presidency of José López Portillo, beginning late 1976, Mexico had undertaken an impressive modernization and industrialization program. López Portillo's government had determined to use its 'oil patrimony' to industrialize the country into a modern nation. Ports, roads, petrochemical plants, modern irrigated agriculture complexes, and even a nuclear power program were undertaken. Significant and nationally controlled oil resources were to be the means for modernizing Mexico.

By 1981, after the Volcker interest rate shock, certain Washington and New York policy circles determined that the prospect of a strong industrial Mexico, a 'Japan on our southern border,' as one American establishment person derisively called it, would 'not be tolerated.' As with Iran earlier, a modern independent Mexico was considered by certain powerful Anglo-American interests to be intolerable. The decision was made to intervene to sabotage Mexico's industrialization ambitions by securing rigid repayment, at exorbitant rates, of her foreign debt.

A well-prepared run on the Mexican peso was orchestrated beginning the fall of 1981, signaled by a *New York Times* interview with former CIA chief William Colby, then a consultant on 'political risk' to multinational corporations. Colby stated that he was advising his clients regarding investment in Mexico to 'expect a devaluation of Mexico's currency before next year's general election.' Colby's theme was echoed by articles throughout the U.S. media, including the *Wall Street Journal*.

Colby had been connected with a 'private' international consultancy, known as Probe International, on whose board sat Lord Caradon (Hugh Foot), a British Foreign Office intelligence specialist in Middle East and American affairs, and a leading advocate of Malthusian population reduction policies in the developing sector, as opposed to increasing industrial and agricultural productivity.

Probe's president, a former U.S. State Department senior official named Benjamin Weiner, planted a series of articles in U.S. papers during the early weeks of 1982, fostering the idea that knowledgeable Mexican businessmen were rushing to smuggle their funds, converted into dollars, out of Mexico into Texas and California real estate, before the country exploded. The articles were dutifully reported in major Mexican dailies, further fueling capital flight. President López Portillo, in a speech broadcast nationally on February 5 that year, attacked what he termed 'hidden foreign interests' who were trying to destabilize the country through panic rumors and flight of capital out of the country and to force a devaluation of the peso against the U.S. dollar. Three years earlier, the same Probe International had played a critical role in fueling the capital flight which helped to weaken the Shah of Iran, preparing the way for the Khomeini revolution.

By February 19, 1982, the Mexican government was forced to impose a draconian austerity program, in the desperate hope of stabilizing the flood of flight capital out of Mexico into the United States. Powerful vested financial interests exerted strong pressure on López Portillo to prevent his taking what would have been the necessary defense of reimposing Mexican foreign exchange controls. The capital flight accelerated.

That February 19, the López Portillo government cracked under the pressure. The Mexican peso was devalued by an immediate 30 per cent to try to stem the capital outflow and stabilize the situation. The domestic consequence was that private Mexican industry, which had borrowed dollars to finance investment in the previous years, led by the once-powerful Alfa Group of Monterrey, was made bankrupt overnight. Its earnings were in pesos, and its debt service in the vastly more costly dollars. Simply to maintain its previous debt-service position, a company would have had to increase peso prices by 30 per cent, or cut costs by reducing its workforce. The devaluation also forced reduction in Mexico's industrial program, cuts in living standards, and increased domestic inflation. Mexico, only months earlier the most rapidly growing economy in the developing world, had been plunged into chaos by the spring of 1982. A Mexican case officer with the International Monetary Fund declared after the severe measures, 'This was just the right thing to do.'[5]

Mexico was now put firmly under the international spotlight as a 'problem borrower' and a 'high-risk country.' Leading Eurodollar banks in London, New York, Zurich and Frankfurt, as well as in Tokyo, quickly cut back their lending plans. Mexico, under the double pressures of peso devaluation, loss of billions of dollars in needed capital through capital flight, and the decision by the major international banks not to roll over the old debt, by August faced a debt payments crisis of titanic dimension.

On August 20 that summer, at the headquarters of the New York Federal Reserve, more than 100 of the United States' leading bankers had been summoned to a closed-door meeting to hear a report from Jesús Silva Herzog, the Mexican finance minister, on Mexico's prospects for repaying its $82 billion foreign debt. Silva Herzog told the assembled gentlemen of international finance that his country could not even meet the next installment due on its foreign debt. Its foreign exchange reserves were gone.

In Mexico, President López Portillo, facing growing economic chaos, decided to act to stem the capital flight, then at crisis proportions. The president announced to the Mexican nation on September 1 that the country's private banks were being nationalized, with compensation, along with the then private central bank, the Bank of Mexico, as part of a series of emergency measures to restore financial order and stop the outflow of flight capital from collapsing the nation's entire economy.

In his nationally televised three-hour speech that day, he attacked the private banks as being 'speculative and parasitical' and detailed the capital flight which they had funneled out of Mexico's industrialization effort into dollars and U.S. real-estate speculation. The total was $76 billion, which compared with the entire total of foreign debt contracted in the previous ten years for the country's industrialization.

López Portillo had established a friendly rapport of sorts with Ronald Reagan, and had informed Reagan personally of his dramatic action to make clear that this was an issue of national emergency, not of irresponsible radicalism against the United States.

Then, appearing before the New York annual General Assembly of the United Nations on October 1, President López Portillo called on the nations of the world to act in concert to prevent a 'regression into the Dark Ages.' He effectively blamed the crisis of the financial system on the policy of unbearably high interest rates and the collapsing prices of raw materials.

These were 'two blades of a pair of scissors that threatens to slash the momentum achieved in some countries, and to cut off the possibilities for progress in the rest,' the Mexican president stated. Then he bluntly warned of the possibility of unilateral suspension of Third World debt payments, if a commonly beneficial solution were blocked. 'Payment suspension is to no one's advantage and no one wants it. But whether or not this will happen is beyond the responsibility of the debtors. Common situations produce common positions, with no need for conspiracies or intrigue.'

López Portillo attacked the arbitrary imposition of the new debt terms under Thatcher and Volcker.

Mexico and many other countries of the Third World are unable to comply with the period of payment agreed upon under conditions quite different from those that now prevail ... We developing countries do not want to become vassals. We cannot paralyze our economies or plunge our peoples into greater misery in order to pay a debt on which servicing has tripled without our participation or responsibility, and on terms that are imposed on us ... Our efforts to grow in order to conquer hunger, disease, ignorance and dependency have not caused the international crisis.

López Portillo then addressed the self-interest of the United States and other industrial creditor nations in working together for solutions which allowed countries such as Mexico to grow their way out of the crisis. His comments were echoed by the head of state of the largest debtor nation, Brazil's João Baptista Figueiredo, who then spoke of 'symptoms dramatically reminiscent of the 1930s', in which 'production investment is being asphyxiated on a global scale under the impact of high interest rates.'

Throughout the summer months of 1982, a behind-the-scenes White House policy debate continued over what to do about the explosive debt crisis. With the U.S. economy falling deeper into decline under the weight of the severe Federal Reserve interest rate levels, a group around President Reagan lobbied for a resolution of the impending Mexican and Latin American debt crisis, which would simultaneously spark increased U.S. industrial investment and export flows.

The voices of Wall Street and of Henry Kissinger's friends in the British Foreign Office and the City of London had more influence over the vacillating Reagan. As part of his preelection 'deal' to win backing of the powerful Wall Street establishment, Reagan had agreed to name former Merrill Lynch Wall Street chairman, Don Regan, as his Treasury secretary, along with a number of other key appointments, not least, those of former Trilateral Commission member George Bush as vice president, and Bush's close friend James Baker as White House chief of staff. They argued, 'We must save the New York banks at all costs.' By October 1982, their approach to the exploding Mexico and other debt crises had become Reagan administration policy.[6]

The day before López Portillo addressed the UN General Assembly, the newly named U.S. secretary of state delivered the American response. George Shultz, a former University of Chicago economist and friend of Milton Friedman, and one of the figures behind the fateful August 15, 1971, Nixon decoupling of the dollar from gold, announced the final Reagan administration response to the assembled United Nations delegates. Shultz unveiled Wall Street's simple 'solution' to the debt crisis.

After the Mexican declaration of insolvency in early August, Paul Volcker had met with senior Reagan administration officials and worked out a plan to gradually ease the strains on the major New York banks. This was announced by Shultz as the 'Reagan economic recovery.' Rather than addressing the root causes of the crisis in either the United States or the nations of the South, Shultz offered International Monetary Fund policing of debtor country debt repayment combined with a stimulation of U.S. consumer purchases. This, it was argued, would then draw in increased Third World commodity exports as part of the planned 'recovery.'

It was to be the most costly 'recovery' in world history.

### WALL STREET REPLAYS THE 1920s, IMF-STYLE

Shultz's fateful UN announcement was a carefully staged counter to the anticipated UN address of López Portillo and other Latin American heads of state. What then followed was almost beyond belief to anyone not directly familiar with negotiations between creditor bankers and debtor countries at that time.

José López Portillo failed in his call for Latin American unity following his UN speech. He was in any case a lame-duck president, who left office two months later. In the meantime, Brazil and Argentina were visited by a virtual army of U.S. officials and others, who exerted extraordinary blackmail and other pressure to dissuade them from joining Mexico in demanding a common solution to the debt crisis.

Henry Kissinger had formed a high-powered new consultancy firm, Kissinger Associates Inc., which numbered on its select board Aspen Institute chairman and oil magnate Robert O. Anderson, Thatcher's former foreign secretary, Lord Carrington, together with Bank of England and S.G. Warburg director, Lord Roll of Ipsden. Kissinger Associates worked together with the New York banks and circles of the Washington administration to impose, 'case-by-case,' the most onerous debt collection terms since the Versailles reparations process of the early 1920s.

Following the September 30 UN speech of Secretary of State Shultz, the powerful private banking interests of New York and London overruled any voices of reason. They managed to bring in the Federal Reserve, the Bank of England and, most importantly, the powers of the International Monetary Fund, to act as the international 'policemen,' in what was to become the most concerted organized looting operation in modern history, far exceeding anything achieved during the 1920s.

Contrary to the carefully cultivated impression in the media of western Europe and the United States, the debtor countries paid the modern-day Shylocks of New York and London many times over, with blood and the proverbial 'pound of flesh.' It was not the case that after August 1982, large Third World debtor nations refused to pay. They had a 'pistol to the head,' under IMF pressure, to sign what the banks euphemistically termed 'debt work-outs' with the leading private banks, most often led by Citicorp or Chase Manhattan of New York.

After October 1982, the onslaught against debtor nations of the developing sector involved several identifiable stages. The first crucial step was the move by the private banks of New York and London to 'socialize' their debt crisis. By publishing numerous interviews in the world media warning of the dire consequences to the international banking system of a widespread debt moratorium, the banks secured unprecedented international support for the debt collection strategy elaborated by Citicorp, Chase Manhattan, Manufacturers' Hanover, Lloyds Bank and others.

These powerful private interests used the crisis to turn the power of major public institutions to enforce the minority interests of that private elite, the creditor banks. These banks banded together, following a closed-door meeting in England's Ditchley Park that fall, to create a de facto creditors' cartel of leading banks, headed by the New York and London banks, later called the Institute for International Finance or informally, the Ditchley Group. They proceeded to impose what one observer characterized as a peculiar form of 'bankers' socialism,' in which the private banks socialized their lending risks to the majority of the taxpaying public, while privatizing all the gains for themselves. And the gains were considerable, despite the appearance of crisis.

Once the bankers and their allies inside the Reagan administration, such as Treasury Secretary Donald Regan, had sufficiently terrorized President Reagan about the situation, the White House called on Paul Volcker, the banks and the IMF to impose a program of strict 'conditionalities' on each debtor country. The idea of placing the IMF and its strict conditionalities in the middle of the debt-negotiating process, was an American idea. In substance, it was an almost exact copy of what the New York bankers did after 1919 against Germany and the rest of Europe under the ill-fated Dawes Plan, and later attempted under the Young Plan.

The IMF conditionalities, and a country's agreement to sign with the IMF, were part of a program developed by an American official then at the IMF, Irving Friedman, who was later to be rewarded for his work with a senior post at Citicorp. In late 1988, Friedman told an interviewer about his thinking at the onset of the debt crisis:

> My thought was that we would sort of hold out the use of the Fund resources as a kind of carrot to countries. You first have a very serious review of the country's economic situation. You identify the source of the difficulties, you point out what things have to be changed.

The IMF prescription, the 'conditionalities' medicine, was invariably the same. The victim debtor country was told that if it ever wanted to see a penny of foreign bank lending again, it must slash domestic imports to the bone, cut the national budget savagely, in most cases state subsidies for food and other necessities, and devalue the national currency in order to make its exports 'attractive' to industrial countries, while simultaneously making the cost of importing advanced industrial goods prohibitive. All of this, it was argued, would earn hard currency to service the debt. Parson Malthus no doubt smiled from his grave at the process.

This IMF Structural Adjustment Program was only Step One; it made the 'candidate' eligible for Step Two—an agreement with its creditor banks for 'restructuring' of the repayment schedule of their foreign debt, or a major portion of it. In this second stage, the banks contracted for huge future rights over debtor countries, as they added defaulted interest arrears onto the face amount of total debt owed.

The end result of the countless debtor restructurings since 1982 has been an enormous increase in the amount of debt owed to creditor banks, despite the fact that not one new penny of money had come into Latin America from those banks. According to data from a leading Swiss insurance firm, Swiss Re, total foreign debt of all developing countries, long term and short, rose steadily after 1982 from just over $839 billion to almost $1,300 billion by 1987. Virtually all this increase was due to the added burden of 'refinancing' the unpayable old debt.

Mexico, under this IMF regimen, was forced to slash subsidies on vital medicines, foodstuffs, fuels, and other necessities for its population. People, often infants, died needlessly for lack of the most basic medicine imports.

The IMF then dictated a series of Mexican peso devaluations to 'spur exports.' In early 1982, before the first 30 per cent devaluation, the peso stood at 12 pesos to one U.S. dollar. By 1986, an incredible 862 Mexican pesos were needed to buy one dollar, and by 1989 the sum had climbed to 2,300 pesos. But Mexico's total foreign debt, almost all of it 'taken over' by the national government from the Mexican private sector under demands from the New York banks and their Washington allies, grew from some $82 billion to just under $100 billion by the end of 1985. Mexico was rapidly going in the direction of Germany in the early 1920s.

The same process was repeated in Argentina, Brazil, Peru, Venezuela, most of black Africa, including Zambia, Zaire and Egypt, and large parts of Asia. The IMF had become the global 'policeman' to enforce payment of usurious debts through imposition of the most draconian austerity in history. With the crucial voting bloc of the IMF firmly controlled by an American–British axis, the institution became the global enforcer of Anglo-American monetary and economic interests in a manner never before seen. It was hardly surprising that victim countries shuddered when told that they were to receive an IMF inspection visit. In effect, the Anglo-American banks, far the largest group involved in lending to Latin America, blackmailed their bank counterparts in western Europe and Japan that they must 'solidarize' or face the prospect of the collapse of the international banking system.

In 1982 and the following years, the threat was indeed credible. No one dared challenge it; the countries of the creditor banks all closed ranks behind the New York banks and backed the Kissinger 'hard-line' approach to the debt. This allowed the Washington and New York banks and their friends in London to promote the useful rhetoric that the debt was solely the 'fault' of corrupt, irresponsible Third World governments.

So confident were the powerful banking interests of New York and London that they even refused at this time to increase their emergency loan–loss reserves against default on Third World debts. Citicorp and Chase Manhattan paid impressive dividends to their shareholders during the early 1980s, publicly declaring 'record profits,' as though nothing extraordinary were occurring. They had the full weight of the United States government and the IMF to police their debt collection. What could be more secure?

As debtor after debtor was coerced to come to terms with the IMF and the creditor banks of the Ditchley Group, a reversal in capital flows of titanic dimension took place. According to the World Bank, between 1980 and 1986, for a group of 109 debtor countries, payment to creditors of interest alone on foreign debts totaled $326 billion; repayment of principal on the same debts totaled another $332 billion—a combined debt service total payment of $658 billion on what originally was a debt of $430 billions. But despite this effort, these 109 countries still owed the creditors a sum of $882 billion in 1986. It was an impossible debt vortex. Thus worked the wonders of compound interest and floating rates.

An even more astonishing aspect of the 'debt crisis' of the 1980s, was the fact that much of the money never even left the New York or London banks. According to a direct participant in the procedures, the former Peruvian energy minister, Pedro Pablo Kuczinski, who took a lucrative post with the New York–Swiss bank, Credit Suisse First Boston:

Most of the money never came into Latin America. Out of $270 billion taken by Latin America between 1976 and 1981, we found only 8.4 per cent actually were cashed by Latin America—money which could have been used for productive investment. All the rest remained in the banks, never came to Latin America, only changed books.

The debtor countries had been caught in a debt trap, from which the only way out offered by the creditor banks of New York and London was to surrender national sovereign control over their economy, especially valuable resources such as the Mexican state oil monopoly. This the bankers called swapping the old 'debt for equity,' which was aimed at securing control of attractive resources of the debtor country.

A study by a Danish economist, commissioned by the Danish UNICEF Committee, illustrates the process.

In 1979 a net sum of $40 billion flowed from the rich North to the poorer South. That flow was reversed in 1983, when the under-developed countries sent $6 billion to the industrialized countries. Since then the amount has risen dramatically, according to UN estimates, approximately $30 billion a year. But if the transfer of resources due to falling raw material prices throughout the 1980's is taken into account, we are talking about a transfer of capital from the under-developed countries to the industrial countries of at least $60 billion a year. To this sum one should then add the capital flight of black money ...

This study, by Hans K. Rasmussen, pointed out that what has taken place since the early 1980s has been a wealth transfer from the capital-starved Third World, primarily into the financing of deficits in the United States, and to a lesser degree Britain. Rasmussen estimated that during the 1980s, the combined nations of the developing sector transferred a total of $400 billion into the United States alone. This allowed the Reagan administration to finance the largest peacetime deficits in world history, while falsely claiming credit for 'the world's longest peacetime recovery.'

With high U.S. interest rates, a rising dollar, and the security of American government backing, fully 43 per cent of the record high U.S. budget deficits during the 1980s were 'financed' by this de facto looting of capital from the debtor countries of the once-developing sector. As with the Anglo-American bankers in the post-First World War Versailles reparations debt process, the debt was merely a vehicle to establish de facto economic control over entire sovereign countries. The jaded New York bankers reasoned that they had little to fear from powerless Latin American or African countries. After all, business is business.[7]

In May 1986, a staff study prepared for the Joint Economic Committee of the U.S. Congress on the 'Impact of the Latin American Debt Crisis on the U.S. Economy' took note of some of these alarming aspects of how the problem was being handled by the Reagan administration. The report documented the devastating losses of U.S. jobs and exports as the IMF austerity measures forced Latin America to virtually halt industrial and other imports in order to service the debt. The authors noted:

> it is now becoming clear that Administration policies have gone above and beyond what was needed for protecting the money center banks from insolvency ... the Reagan Administration's management of the debt crisis has in effect, rewarded the institutions that played a major role in precipitating the crisis and penalized those sectors of the U.S. economy that had played no role in causing the debt crisis.

The study was promptly buried.

According to calculations by New York's Morgan Guaranty Trust Company, capital flight from Third World countries into the 'safe haven' of U.S. and other creditor countries amounted to at least another $123 billion in the decade up to 1985. More than one major New York bank and investment firm set up offices in cities such as Bogota, Medellin and other places in Latin America to profit from assisting black dollars to leave these countries. The rise of cocaine addiction in the industrial cities of the United States and western Europe (which, curiously enough, grew in parallel with the explosion of the Third World debt crisis beginning the early 1980s) bore a striking congruence to the rise in illegal dollars being 'laundered' out of South America through discreet transfers by the likes of Donald Regan's old firm, Merrill Lynch. The clients were given the more tasteful name of 'high net worth individuals.'

In a study of the capital flight out of Latin America, Professor Joe Foweraker at the University of California at San Diego, noted that facilitating capital flight flows for such clients had become one of the most profitable parts of the debt crisis for the large U.S. banks during the 1980s. He noted that in addition to some $50 billion annual interest payments from the hard-pressed debtor governments, these large banks, such as Citicorp, Chase Manhattan, Morgan Guaranty and Bank of America, were bringing in flight capital assets of some $100–120 billion from the very countries against whom they demanded brutal domestic austerity to 'stabilize' the currency. It was more than a little hypocritical, and more than a little lucrative for the banks.

The annual return for the New York and London banks on their Latin American flight capital business, kept in strictest secrecy, was reliably reported to average 70 per cent. As one such private banker said, 'Some banks would kill to get a piece of this business.' That was putting it mildly. In 1983 the London *Financial Times* reported that Brazil was far and away the most profitable banking part of Citicorp's worldwide operations.

If anything, Africa fared even worse than Latin America as a result of the Anglo-American debt strategy. Since nineteenth-century colonial times, when Britain and France, along with Portugal, dominated the continent, Africa, with the stubborn exception of South Africa, had been seen primarily as a primitive undeveloped source of cheap raw materials. The wave of independence during the 'decolonialization' of the 1960s and 1970s produced little substantial improvement in the economic prospects of black Africa.

But the oil shocks, and the ensuing shocks of 20 per cent interest rates and collapsing world industrial growth in the 1980s, dealt the literal death blow to almost the entire continent. Until the 1980s, black Africa remained 90 per cent dependent on raw materials export for financing its development. Beginning the early 1980s, the world dollar price of such raw materials—everything from cotton to coffee, copper, iron ore and sugar—began an almost uninterrupted fall. By 1987, raw materials prices had fallen to the lowest levels since the Second World War, as low as their level of 1932—a year of deep world economic depression.[8]

If the prices for such raw material exports had been stable, at merely the price levels of the 1980 period, black Africa would have earned an additional $150 billion during the decade of the 1980s. In 1982, at the beginning of the 'debt crisis,' these countries of Africa owed creditor banks in the United States, Europe and Japan some $73 billion. By the end of the decade, this sum, through debt 'rescheduling' and various IMF interventions into their economies, had more than doubled, to $160 billions—in short, almost exactly the sum which these countries would have earned at a stable export price level.

It begins to appear that a very different process was occurring than what the average citizen in a west European or American city was reading daily in the newspapers regarding the reality of this debt. Powerful British and U.S. multinationals followed the banks during the 1980s to set up child-labor sweatshops in places such as along the Mexican border with the United States. These *maquiladores*, as the low-skill assembly plants were named, employed desperate Mexican children aged 14 or 15 for wages of 50 cents an hour, to produce goods for General Motors or Ford Motor Company or various U.S. electrical companies. They were allowed by the Mexican government, because they 'earned' dollars needed to service the debt.

## REAGAN'S CHICKENS COME HOME TO ROOST

One of the most destructive consequences of the First World War and the Versailles war reparations aftermath, with the 1920s Dawes Plan of the London and New York banks, was the relative collapse of global long-term investment. More and more, owing to the absolute decline of world trade in the 1920s compared with prewar levels and the general economic and political instability which prevailed in Europe, money could be borrowed generally for only a short term, typically less than one year.

This produced a situation in which shortest-term speculative gains became the central criterion of all investment. This in turn fueled the great frenzy of the 1920s stock market boom in New York, a boom fueled by inflows of foreign funds from London and the Continent, seeking to make unheard-of gains on the ever rising New York bourse. All this came crashing down in October of 1929.

The aftermath of the oil shocks and the high interest rate monetary shocks of the 1970s, sometimes referred to as the 'great inflation,' was all too similar to the 1920s. In place of the Versailles reparations burden on world productive investment, the world had the onerous burden of the IMF Third World debt 'restructuring' process. The incredible rates of inflation during the early part of the 1980s, typically 12–17 per cent, dictated the conditions of investment returns. A fast and huge gain was needed.

Into this situation came the Reagan administration's bizarre collection of 'free market' economic conundrums, called by their advocates 'supply-side' economics. The idea was a thin veil behind which were unleashed some of the highest rates of short-term personal profiteering in history, at the expense of the greater good of the country's long-term economic health.

While the policies imposed after October 1982 to collect billions from Third World countries brought a huge windfall of financial liquidity to the American banking system, the ideology of Wall Street, and Treasury Secretary Donald Regan's zeal for lifting the government 'shackles' off the financial markets, resulted in the greatest extravaganza in world financial history. When the dust settled by the end of that decade, some began to realize that Reagan's 'free market' had destroyed an entire national economy. It happened to be the world's largest economy, and the base of world monetary stability as well.

On the simple-minded and quite mistaken argument that a mere removing of the tax burden on the individual or company would allow them to release 'stifled creative energies' and other entrepreneurial talents, President Ronald Reagan in August 1981 signed the largest tax reduction bill in postwar history. The bill contained provisions which also gave generous tax relief for certain speculative forms of real estate investment, especially commercial real estate. Government restrictions on corporate takeovers were also removed, and Washington gave the clear signal that 'anything goes,' so long as it stimulated the Dow Jones Industrials stock index.

By summer 1982, as the White House secured consent from Paul Volcker and the Federal Reserve for interest rate levels to begin a steady downward turn, the speculative bonanza was ready to go. The bankruptcy that spring of a small oil and real estate bank, Penn Square Bank in Oklahoma, had combined with the Mexico crisis to convince Volcker that it was time to ease up on his strangulation of the money supply. Between summer and December, the U.S. Federal Reserve discount rate was lowered an extraordinary seven times, to a level that was 40 per cent lower. The financial markets began to go wild with the low rates.

The reality of Reagan's 'economic recovery' was that it did nothing to encourage investment in improving the technology and productivity of industry, with the small exception of a handful of military aerospace firms which got record government defense contracts. Money went instead into speculation in real estate, into speculation in stocks, into oil wells in Texas or Colorado—all so-called 'tax shelters.'

As Volcker's interest rates went lower, the fever grew hotter. Debt was the new fashion. People reasoned it was 'cheaper' to borrow today and repay tomorrow at lower interest levels. It didn't quite work. American cities continued their 20-year-long decline, bridges fell in, roads cracked for lack of maintenance, new glass-enclosed shopping centers grew up, often sitting empty because some real estate developer could earn enough through generous tax write-offs.

A central feature of the Reagan supply-side credo, again echoing Margaret Thatcher in Britain, was to identify trade unions as 'part of the problem.' A British-style class confrontation was set up, and the result was the cracking of the organized labor movement.

Deregulation of government control over transportation was a central weapon of the policy. Trucking and airline transportation were 'set free.' Nonunion 'cut-rate' airlines and trucking companies proliferated, often with low or no safety standards. Accident rates climbed, wage levels of union workers plunged. While the Reagan 'recovery' was turning young stock traders into multimillionaires, seemingingly at the push of a computer key, it was reducing the standard of living of the skilled blue-collar workforce. No one in Washington paid much attention. After all, the conservative Reagan Republicans argued, trade unions were 'almost like communists.' A nineteenth-century British-style 'cheap labor' policy dominated official Washington as never before.

By 1982, the once-powerful International Brotherhood of Teamsters was humbled into accepting a three-year contract which virtually amounted to a wage freeze, in a climate of economic gloom and trucking deregulation which encouraged nonunion trucking. The United Auto Workers union, once one of the most advanced concentrations of skilled American labor, accepted wage cuts in their negotiations with Chrysler, Ford and General Motors in 1982. Steel unions and others followed with concessions, in a desperate attempt to secure benefits for older workers about to be pensioned off, or to avoid job cuts. The real living standard for the majority of Americans steadily decreased, while that of a minority rose as never before. Society was becoming polarized around income differentials.

The new dogma of a 'postindustrial society' was being preached from Washington to New York to California. No longer was America's economic prosperity linked to investment in the most modern industrial capacities. Steel had been declared a 'rust-belt' industry, as steel plants were allowed to rust or blast furnaces were actually dynamited. Shopping centers, glittery new Atlantic City gambling casinos, and luxury resort hotels were 'where the money' was.

During the speculative boom of most of the Reagan years, the money also flowed in from abroad to finance this wild spree. No one seemed to mind that in the process, by the mid 1980s, the United States had within five short years passed from being the world's largest creditor to becoming a net debtor nation, for the first time since 1914. Debt was 'cheap,' and it grew geometrically. Families went into record levels of debt for buying houses, cars, video recorders. Government went into debt to finance the huge loss of tax revenue and the expanded Reagan defense buildup. Budget deficits under the Reagan 'recovery' revealed the true underlying health of the U.S. economy. It was sick.

By 1983, annual government deficits began to climb to an unheard-of level of $200 billion. The national debt expanded, along with the deficits, all paying Wall Street bond dealers and their clients record sums in interest income. Interest payments on the total debt by the U.S. government doubled in six years, going from $52 billion in 1980, when Reagan was elected, to more than $142 billion by 1986—a sum equal to one-fifth of all government revenue. But despite such warning signs, money flowed in from Germany, from Britain, from Holland, from Japan, to take advantage of the high dollar and the speculative gains in real estate and stocks.

To anyone with a sense of history or a long memory, it was all too familiar. It had all happened during the 'Roaring '20s'—until the 1929 market crash brought the roulette wheel to an abrupt halt.

When storm clouds began to gather on the U.S. economic horizon during 1985, threatening the future presidential ambitions of Vice President George Bush, it was once again oil which was to come to the 'rescue'; only this time, in a very different way from the Anglo-American oil shocks of the 1970s. Washington apparently reasoned, 'If we can run the price up, why can't we run it down when it's convenient to our priorities?' So Saudi Arabia was persuaded to run a 'reverse oil shock' and flood the depressed world oil market with its abundant oil. The price of OPEC oil dropped like a stone, to below $10 per barrel by spring of 1986, from an average of nearly $26 only some months earlier. Magically, Wall Street economists proclaimed the final 'victory' over inflation, while conveniently ignoring the role of oil in creating the inflation of the 1970s or in reducing it in the 1980s.

Then, when a further fall in oil prices threatened to destabilize vital interests of the large British and American oil majors themselves, not merely the small independent rival producers, George Bush made a quiet trip to Riyadh in March 1986, where he reportedly told King Fahd that he should stop the price war. Saudi Oil Minister Sheikh Zaki Yamani was made the convenient scapegoat for a policy authored in Washington, and oil prices stabilized at a low level of around $14–16 per barrel. Texas and other oil-producing states were plunged into depression, but speculation in real estate took off elsewhere in the United States at a record pace, while the stock market began a renewed climb to record highs.

This 1986 oil-price collapse unleashed what was comparable to the 1927–29 phase in the U.S. speculative bubble. Interest rates dropped even more dramatically, as money flowed in to make a 'killing' on the New York stock markets. A new financial perversion became fashionable on Wall Street, the 'leveraged buyout.' With money costs falling and stock prices apparently ever rising, and a Reagan administration which promoted the religion of the 'free market,' anything was allowed. A sound 100-year-old industrial company, which had been conservatively managed, producing tires, or machines or textiles, for example, might become the target for the new corporate 'raiders,' as the Wall Street scavengers were called. Colorful personalities such as T. Boone Pickens, Mike Milken, and Ivan Boesky became billionaires on paper, as frontmen in the leveraged buyouts. A new corporate management philosophy was proclaimed from august institutions such as the Harvard Business School to rationalize this madness in the name of market 'efficiency.'

In a typical corporate leveraged buyout raid, a raider such as Boone Pickens would line up a promise of borrowed money to buy control of stock in a company many times his worth, such as Union Oil of California, or even Gulf Oil. His buying of stock in the victim company drove prices up. If he succeeded, he took over a huge company, almost entirely with borrowed money. This debt was then repaid, if all went well, by 'below investment grade' bonds issued by the new debt-loaded company, appropriately known as 'junk bonds.' If the company became bankrupt, the bonds were just so much 'junk' paper. But in the 1980s, stock market and real estate prices were climbing, so no one paid much attention to this risk. The Reagan tax reforms made it more 'profitable' for a company to be saddled with huge debts than to issue stock equity.

Interest rates paid by these 'junk bonds' were very high, to attract buyers. The 'sharks,' as these raiders were called, moved quickly to 'strip' the assets of the new company, sell off the pieces for a quick profit, and run to the next victim corporation, like so many piranha fish. During the last half of the 1980s, such actions consumed Wall Street and pushed the Dow upwards, driving corporations into the highest levels of debt since the 1930s depression. But this debt was not undertaken to invest in modern technology or new plant and equipment. It was the cancerous result of the financial speculation process permitted during the free-market years of the Reagan and Bush administrations.

Over the decade of the Reagan years, almost $1 trillion flowed into speculative real estate investment, a record sum, almost double the sums of previous years. Banks, desiring to secure their balance sheets against troubles in Latin America, for the first time went directly into real estate lending rather than traditional corporate lending.

Savings and loan banks, established as separately regulated banks during the depression years to provide a secure source of long-term mortgage credit to family homebuyers, were 'deregulated' in the early 1980s as part of Treasury Secretary Donald Regan's Wall Street free-market push. They were allowed to 'bid' for wholesale deposits, termed 'brokered deposits,' at a high cost. The Reagan administration removed all regulatory restraints in October 1982, with passage of the Garn–St. Germain Act. This act allowed savings and loan (S&L) banks to invest in any scheme they desired, with full U.S. government insurance of $100,000 per account guaranteeing the risk in case of failure.

Prophetically, as he signed the new Garn–St. Germain Act into law, President Reagan enthusiastically told an audience of invited S&L bankers, 'I think we've hit the jackpot.' This 'jackpot' was the beginning of the collapse of the $1.3 trillion savings and loan banking system.

The new law opened the doors of the S&Ls to wholesale financial abuses and wild speculative risks as never before. Moreover, it made S&L banks an ideal vehicle for organized crime to launder billions of dollars from the growing narcotics business in 1980s America. Few noticed that it was the former firm of Donald Regan, Merrill Lynch, whose Lugano office was implicated in laundering billions of dollars of Mafia heroin profits in the so-called 'pizza connection.'

The wild and woolly climate of deregulation created an ambience in which normal, well-run savings banks were surpassed by fast-track banks which catered to dubious monies with no questions asked. Banks laundered funds for covert operations of the CIA, as well as covert operations of the Bonano or other organized crime families. The son of the vice president, Neil Bush, was a director of the Silverado Savings and Loan in Colorado, later indicted by the government for illegal practices. Son Neil had the good taste to 'resign' the week his father received the Republican nomination for president in 1988.[9]

In order to compete with the newly deregulated banks and S&Ls, the most conservative of all financial sectors, life insurance companies, began to go into speculative real estate in a major way during the 1980s. But unlike banks and S&Ls, insurance companies, perhaps because they had been so conservative in the past, had never been placed under national supervision. There was no national government insurance fund to protect policy holders of insurance companies, as there was for banks. By 1989, insurance companies were holding an estimated $260 billion of real estate on their books, an increase from some $100 billion in 1980. But by then, in the worst depression since the 1930s, real estate was collapsing, forcing failures of insurance companies for the first time in postwar history, as panicked policyholders demanded their money.

The simple reality was that New York financial power had so overwhelmed all other national interests since the oil shocks of the 1970s that almost no other voice was heard in Washington after the Mexico crisis of 1982. Debt grew by astonishing amounts. When Reagan won the election in late 1980, total private and public debt of the United States stood at $3,873 billion. By the end of the decade, it touched $10 trillion, or $10,000 billion. This meant an increased debt burden of more than $6,000 billion during this brief span.[10]

With the debt burden carried by the productive economy rising, and U.S. industrial plant and the labor force deteriorating, the cumulative effects of two decades of neglect began to become manifest in wholesale collapse of the vital public infrastructure of the nation. Highways cracked for lack of regular maintenance; bridges became structurally unsound and in many cases collapsed; in depressed areas such as Pittsburgh, water systems were allowed to become contaminated; hospitals in major cities fell into disrepair; housing stock for the less wealthy decayed dramatically. By 1989, the association for the construction industry, Associated General Contractors of America, estimated that a net investment of $3.3 trillion was urgently needed merely to rebuild America's crumbling public infrastructure to modern standards. No one in Washington listened. By 1990, the Bush administration proposed free-market private initiative to solve the problem. Washington was in a budget crisis. The unequal distribution of the benefits from the Reagan 'recovery' was indicated by U.S. government figures on the number of Americans living 'below the poverty level.' In 1979, when Paul Volcker had begun his monetary shock in the midst of the second oil crisis, the government recorded 24 million Americans below the poverty level, defined as an annual income of $6,000. By 1988, the figure had expanded by more than 30 per cent, to 32 million Americans. Reagan–Bush tax policies had concentrated wealth into a tiny elite, as never before in U.S. history. Since 1980, according to a study carried out by the U.S. House Ways and Means Committee of Congress, real income for the top 20 per cent increased a full 32 per cent.

Costs of American health care, a reflection of the strange combination of 'free enterprise' and government subsidy, rose to the highest levels ever, and as a share of GNP, to double that of the United Kingdom; yet 37 million Americans had no health insurance whatever. Health levels in large American cities, with impoverished ghettoes of black and Hispanic unemployed, resembled those of a Third World country, not what was supposed to be the world's most advanced industrial nation.

Thatcher's eleven-year rule in Britain had produced equally disastrous results. Real estate speculation and a vastly increased financial services 'industry' in the City of London obscured the fact that Thatcher's economic policy severely discriminated against industrial investment, and against modernization of the nation's deteriorating public infrastructure, such as railways and highways. The financial deregulation of the City of London in 1986, appropriately termed the 'Big Bang,' was among Thatcher's proudest 'accomplishments.' But by the end of the 1980s everything was unravelling: interest rates again climbed to double digits, industry went into a deep slump and later a depression worse than any since the war, and inflation rose to the level it had been at when Thatcher took office in 1979.

On its own terms, Thatcher economics had failed, as had its twin sister, Reagan economics. But the powerful oil and finance interests of London and New York were not the least deterred. Their domain in this 'postindustrial' imperium was global, not parochial. They demanded financial deregulation everywhere—Frankfurt, Tokyo, Mexico City, Paris, Milan, São Paulo.

### 'WE'LL GET BY WITH A LITTLE HELP FROM OUR FRIENDS'

On October 19, 1987, the bubble burst. On that day the prices on the Dow Jones Index traded at the New York Stock Exchange collapsed more than in any single day in history, by 508 points. The bottom had fallen out of the Reagan 'recovery.' But not out of the strategy of the Thatcher–Bush wing of the Anglo-American establishment. They were determined to ensure that sufficient funds kept the bubble afloat until the new Bush presidency could impose the grand strategy for the century's end.

While many comments have since been made about how the October 1987 crash proved that depressions of the 1930s sort were a thing of the past, it did indeed signal the beginning of the end of the deregulated financial speculation which had kept the Anglo-American century afloat since the early 1970s.

George Bush, facing a presidential election the following November 1988, enlisted the efforts of his former campaign manager and close friend, Treasury Secretary James Baker, along with a powerful faction of the American establishment, to guarantee that, despite the implications of the October 1987 crash, foreign capital would continue to flow into U.S. bond and stock markets to keep the illusion of a Reagan–Bush economic recovery alive in the minds of voters.

Direct Washington appeals to the Japanese government of Prime Minister Nakasone, arguing that a Democratic president such as Gephardt would damage Japanese trade to the U.S., were successful. Nakasone pressed the Bank of Japan and the Ministry of Finance to be accommodating. After October 1987, Japanese interest rates fell progressively lower, making U.S. stocks and bonds, as well as real estate, appear 'cheap' by comparison. Billions of dollars flowed out of Tokyo into the United States. During 1988, the dollar remained strong and Bush was able to secure his election against his Democratic opponent, Dukakis. To secure this support, Bush gave private assurances to senior Japanese figures that a Bush presidency would improve U.S.–Japanese relations.

The Bush presidency was intended to be the first direct rule by an insider of the monied East Coast establishment since Franklin D. Roosevelt in the early 1940s. Bush's task was to steer the American century through its most dangerous waters since 1919. In his first weeks in office, he gave the appearance of decisiveness in tackling some of the nation's most urgent problems. He proposed a drastic reorganization of the nation's collapsing savings and loan banking system, and he used the popular outcry following a bizarre accident of the *Exxon Valdez* oil tanker to win approval for a radical new series of punitive laws which would, for the first time since Jimmy Carter, make environmentalism a priority of the presidency. Both initiatives later turned out to be catastrophes, but the all-important message in the early months was that, unlike the aging Reagan, in George Bush, America finally had a president who was personally on top of world events.

The actual plan of the new Bush administration was to direct pressures onto select U.S. allies for increased 'burden sharing' to manage the huge U.S. debt burdens. The argument was put forward that the Soviet Union was collapsing and that, as a result, only one superpower with overpowering military might and size remained— the United States. In this situation, the argument was offered that Germany, Japan and other major economic and military allies of America should increase their financial support to maintain this superpower. It was a thinly veiled attempt at blackmail.

It soon became clear that Bush's call for a 'kinder and gentler America' was little more than a rhetorical appeal to an aging voting population. The Bush who occupied the White House moved quickly to establish his 'tough guy' policies, by creating a major media pretext for a military invasion of a tiny central American republic, Panama, during the Christmas days of his first year as President, December 1989. According to eyewitness accounts, upwards of 6,000 Panamanians, mostly poor civilians, were killed as U.S. Special Forces and U.S. bombers invaded the small country on the pretext of arresting the de facto ruler, General Manuel Noriega, on charges of being a drug cartel kingpin.

Bush's attorney general, Richard Thornburgh, who as governor of Pennsylvania played such a controversial role during the Three Mile Island nuclear emergency, had formulated an incredible new U.S. doctrine. The Thornburgh Doctrine stipulated that the American FBI and the Justice Department had authority to act on foreign territory, if deemed necessary, 'in the course of extraterritorial law enforcement.' Translated, this meant that the U.S. government, by executive fiat, using the pretext of tracking international narcotics or terrorist criminals, had declared its unilateral right to come into Germany, France, Panama or any other place it deemed necessary, without concern for the laws of the sovereign country involved. But the Panama invasion, incredible as it was, produced a stony silence from the moral conscience of the civilized world. It was considered an 'American affair.'

By September 1989, CIA Director William Webster publicly unveiled a bold new intelligence mandate for U.S. intelligence. Pointing to the increasing signs that Gorbachev's Soviet Union was eager to reach a mutual disarmament agreement with NATO, and especially with the United States, Webster told an elite gathering of the Los Angeles World Affairs Council on September 19 that year that his CIA was retooling itself for new tasks in the post-cold war era. Webster told his audience, 'economic issues I mentioned—trade imbalances and technological development—illustrate a point that is becoming increasingly clear: our political and military allies are also our economic competitors.' The new mission of U.S. intelligence worldwide was to be economic espionage and other acts against key industrial 'allied' nations, rather than hunting communist operations and subversion.

## THE FALL OF A WALL PANICS SOME CIRCLES

Then, in November 1989, events in eastern Europe took a most dramatic, and to many in Washington and London, a wholly unexpected turn. Mikhail Gorbachev had privately met with the old-guard Honecker communist leadership in East Germany, and had more or less ordered them to give way to the enormous popular movement for freedom sweeping East Germany since that spring. Within weeks, the old order in the DDR was swept aside in a genuine popular revolution. Moscow had apparently realized that continuing its old efforts to maintain a costly and inefficient empire through force was likely to cause the destruction of the Soviet Union itself.

The collapse of the world oil price in 1986 had perhaps been the final fatal blow to Moscow's illusions that reform within the rotten communist bureaucracy could work. Soviet export earnings from its oil sales to the West, the major source of its hard currency earnings since the early 1970s, collapsed after 1986, just when popular demand for change prompted Gorbachev to promise far more than he was able to deliver. The economic chaos which ensued was the major factor motivating the Moscow leadership to cut its ties with its east European satellites of the Warsaw Pact. Moscow hoped that a united Germany, under the strong economic direction of West Germany, could provide a suitable partner to help rebuild the collapsing Soviet system.

But while official Washington put on a face of public approval for the dramatic end to 40 years of communist domination in eastern Europe, privately, Bush, himself a former CIA director whose view of world politics was shaped by the clandestine world of U.S. intelligence, was dead set against success of the revolution in eastern Europe. In Britain, Margaret Thatcher's wing of the Tory party was equally alarmed at the prospect of what some there even called a 'German Fourth Reich.'

A well-placed British establishment voice, Peregrine Worsthorne, editor of the influential London *Sunday Telegraph*, articulated the thoughts of the Thatcher faction of the Tories towards the emerging new Germany. Worsthorne was the the stepson of the former Bank of England governor, Montagu Norman. Norman had maintained personal ties with Hitler's finance minister Hjalmar Schacht, during the war, and had worked intimately with J.P. Morgan Bank in New York after 1919 to impose the Dawes reparations atrocities on defeated Germany.

In his lead editorial on July 22, 1990, titled 'The Good German Problem,' Worsthorne cynically recalled Montagu Norman. 'My stepfather, Montagu Norman, who as Governor of the Bank of England had done so much to help the German economy after the First World War, lived just long enough to see the earliest beginnings of the German economic miracle.' Worsthorne recalled Norman's comment shortly before his death: 'I always knew we would beat the bad Germans; but I wish we could be so sure that we will do as well against the good Germans.'

Then Worsthorne came to his point.

> Let us assume that a united Germany is going to be a good giant, what then? Let us assume a united Germany teaches Russia to become a good giant, what then? ... In truth, the threat could be more dangerous, rather than less. For how on earth can any effective defense be put up against a united Germany that intends to win by obeying the rules? Germany is going to be very powerful and, as Lord Acton taught us, power corrupts ... Germany is marvellously well placed, at long last, to be the principal agent to bring Slavdom back into the comity of nations.

Worsthorne's *Sunday Telegraph* was owned by an Anglo-American holding, the Hollinger Corporation, on whose board sat Dr. Henry Kissinger and former British Foreign Secretary Lord Carrington, who was also a business partner in Kissinger's New York Kissinger Associates consultancy firm.

Referring to controversial comparisons made by Thatcher government Trade Minister Nicholas Ridley, who had just been forced to resign for publicly comparing the Kohl government to Hitler's Reich, Worsthorne concluded his telling diatribe against the implications of a reunified Germany:

> Mr. Ridley was talking nonsense, but perhaps there was more method in his nonsense than is dreamt of ... Perhaps Britain's role should be to preserve enough independence to be free, at the right moment, to make use of these grievances. In the course of doing good, Germany will make just as many enemies as ever it did in doing harm, and America may well be one of the enemies ... Sooner or later it is going to be balance of power politics all over again. This could be an opportunity for Britain which knows about the balance of power ...

That summer, according to London reports, the Thatcher government formed a new unit of British intelligence, to significantly upgrade its activities in Germany. Moreover, the Bush administration moved to improve its ability to control the German developments. In a select Washington meeting in the spring of 1990 of the Association of Former Intelligence Officers, a former senior CIA official, Theodore Shackley, the man who had previously been involved in the destabilization of the Shah of Iran and the illegal Iran–Contra guns-for-drugs operations, told fellow American intelligence professionals they should begin to recruit from disaffected former East German Stasi and related ranks and to build up U.S. intelligence assets in Berlin, for the conditions of the new Germany.

The long-term implications of the fall of the Berlin Wall and the opening up of the potential to modernize the underdeveloped economic potentials of eastern Europe and the Soviet Union around the emerging unified Germany were alarmingly clear for policy strategists in London and New York. Writing a weekly report to investor clients, as well as the general financial community, David Hale, a U.S. economist with reported ties to the Bush Treasury Department, warned in January 1990 of the strategic 'dangers' for the U.S. financial markets if German unity were to succeed:

> One of the most extraordinary features of Wall Street economic research during recent weeks is its complacency about the potential consequences of eastern European economic developments for the

global financial equilibrium which permitted America to borrow over a trillion dollars externally during the 1980's.

Hale then noted:

Indeed, when the financial history of the 1990's is written, analysts may look upon the fall of the Berlin Wall as a financial shock comparable to the long-feared Tokyo earthquake. The destruction of the Wall symbolized an upheaval which could ultimately divert hundreds of billions of dollars capital towards a region which had not only been a minor factor in the world credit markets for six decades.

Hale concluded, in a message he reportedly was asked to circulate by influential Washington circles:

Nor should Americans take comfort from the fact that Germany itself has been only a modest investor in the U.S. during recent years. The biggest investor in the U.S. since 1987 has been Britain (over $100 billion of takeover bids) and the British could not have undertaken such large investments without access to surplus German savings.[11]

On November 29, 1989, days after the collapse of the Berlin Wall, highly professional assassins blew up the protected car of Deutsche Bank head Alfred Herrhausen, a key adviser of the Kohl government who only days before had told the *Wall Street Journal* of his plans for reconstruction of East Germany into Europe's most modern economic region within a decade.

Herrhausen's assassination was seen by knowledgeable Germans as a direct echo of the assassination more than 60 years earlier of Walther Rathenau, architect of the Rapallo plan to industrialize Russia with German industrial technology. But the Bonn government proceeded with plans to unify Germany, and with discussions to assist the economic rebuilding of the collapsing Soviet economy as part of the terms for Moscow's agreeing to German unification.

The German chancellor spoke to the nation that late November about his dream of constructing a modern rail link connecting Paris, Hanover and Berlin, on to Warsaw and finally to Moscow, as the foundation for the infrastructure of the emerging new Europe. The old de Gaulle concept of a Europe economically cooperating from the 'Atlantic to the Urals' was suddenly a real possibility for the first time since 1948.

In this climate, observers in the City of London noted a dramatic increase in the number of French and British informal contacts, on the level of senior business and diplomatic persons. British strategy was to play on latent French fears of a strong Germany. Mitterrand, the socialist French president with a lifelong personal Anglophile inclination, was a ready listener. Britain began quietly to rebuild the old dual alliance of the pre-1914 era and to set the stage for a new Entente Cordiale against the 'German threat.' But the actual strategic battle was to be waged far from central Europe.

The decision had been made sometime during 1989 to make a bold offensive, using the Middle East and its vast oil reserves as the staging ground. Again, as during the 1970s, U.S. and British strategists determined that the serious threat of an economically expanding Continental Europe must be countered through using the Anglo-American 'oil weapon.' But the form this was to take was soon to astonish the entire world.

## SADDAM AND OPERATION DESERT STORM

Senior circles in the Thatcher and Bush governments had determined to create a manufactured pretext which would allow the United States and Britain to establish a direct military presence at the choke point of the world's, and especially Continental Europe's, petroleum supplies.

The domestic economic and financial plight of both Britain and the United States during early 1990 added a special note of desperation to the plan. Thatcher's economic 'revolution' was rapidly collapsing, after the October 1987 stock market debacle and rising British interest rates forced the worst real estate, industrial and banking crisis of the postwar period. In the United States, George Bush faced an out-of-control federal budget deficit, collapsing banks, soaring unemployment and an overall depression, privately likened by some inside the White House to the 1930s Great Depression.

Iraq, a nation of 16 million people, had just emerged from eight years of a fruitless war against Iran, which had accomplished little other than to provide Western arms manufacturers with a vast market for arms sales to the Middle East. Washington had secretly encouraged Saddam Hussein to invade Iran in 1980, falsely feeding him intelligence data indicating early success. By 1989, the economy of Iraq was in shambles and investment in industry and agriculture had been largely halted during the war, which had cost an estimated total of one million or more lives.

But Iraq, unlike Khomeini's Iran, emerged from the costly war with an enormous foreign debt burden. In 1988, she owed an estimated $65 billion to various creditors. Kuwait and Saudi Arabia were owed a large part of this debt, as was the Soviet Union and the countries of eastern Europe, which had expected to be repaid in Iraqi oil. The remainder was owed largely to French, British and American banks. France was Iraq's second largest supplier of arms, after the USSR.

The Anglo-American gameplan was to lure Saddam Hussein into a trap he could not resist, in order to provide a pretext for military intervention from the United States and Britain, professedly to secure the safety of world oil supplies. In June 1989, a top-level delegation from an organization known as the United States–Iraq Business Forum, which included Kissinger Associates' Alan Stoga and senior executives of Bankers' Trust, Mobil Oil, Occidental Petroleum and other large U.S. multinationals, came to Baghdad at the request of Saddam Hussein. He wanted to discuss an Iraqi postwar plan to develop his country's agricultural and industrial potential.

Iraq had a five-year $40 billion plan to complete the large Badush Dam irrigation project, which would have enabled her to become self-sufficient in food production; Iraq at that time depended on U.S. Government Commodity Credit Corporation grain imports for as much as $1 billion worth of grain in 1989. In addition, Iraq proposed to the U.S. group major investment in building up its petrochemicals industry, agriculture fertilizer plants, an iron and steel plant, and an auto assembly plant, as part of an effort to develop the country. The American businessmen told Saddam he must first restructure his foreign debts, and in return agree to privatize Iraq's national oil resources, or a major portion of it. According to best British and American geophysical calculations, Iraq was perhaps the largest unexplored oil region in the world, with the possible exception of the Soviet Union.[12]

Predictably, Saddam refused the American 'offer' to surrender sovereignty over Iraqi petroleum in exchange for vague assurances on future loans. By late 1989, some $2.3 billion in Bush administration-authorized credits for Iraq, which had been deliberately channeled through the Atlanta, Georgia, subsidiary of the Italian Banco Nationale del Lavoro (BNL), were abruptly cut. The cutoff of credit followed a series of sensational allegations in the London *Financial*

*Times*, which claimed that the monies were secretly being used by Iraq to build its war machine.

The combined effect of the Stoga talks and the BNL exposés was a total Western bank credit cutoff to Iraq by early 1990. At this critical juncture, the emir of Kuwait, an ally of Her Majesty's Foreign Office ever since the end of the previous century, entered the picture. The emir had earlier been instructed by London and Washington to funnel credits from Kuwait's vast oil revenues in order to keep Iraq from suing for peace during the eight-year Iran–Iraq War. The cynical Anglo-American purpose at that time, as later scandals were to reveal, was to keep the Iran–Iraq War simmering and to maintain a sufficient 'strategy of tensions' to absorb large Western arms deliveries to both Iran and Iraq.

But in early spring of 1990, Kuwait's 'mission' had changed. She was told to flood OPEC markets with her oil, in violation of OPEC production ceilings which had been agreed in order to stabilize world oil prices following the debacle of 1986–87. By the summer of 1990, Kuwait had succeeded in drawing oil prices from their precarious level of some $19 per barrel down to little more than $13 per barrel. Iraq and other OPEC members made repeated diplomatic efforts to persuade the emir, Sheikh al-Sabah, and the oil minister, Ali Khalifa al-Sabah, to stop the deliberate economic pressure on Iraq and the other economically hard-pressed OPEC producers. The appeal fell on deaf ears. By July, oil traders were predicting a repeat of 1986, with price levels of less than $10 per barrel in sight. Iraq was not even able to service its old debt or finance much-needed food imports.

The previous February, in Amman, Jordan, Iraqi President Saddam Hussein had told fellow members of the Arab Cooperation Council, which included the presidents of those two countries plus Egypt and North Yemen, that the strategic implications of the collapse of the old communist order in eastern Europe, and the apparent emergence of the United States as the only military 'superpower,' presented the Arab world with special dangers.

Saddam pointed, with concern, to the fact that despite the clear end to the Iran–Iraq War one year earlier, U.S. military forces and warships in the Gulf had not shown any signs of pulling back. Rather, he noted with foreboding, 'the United States makes many statements that it is staying.' He noted the increasing preoccupation of the Soviet Union with its internal problems. 'When the Soviet Union is involved with its own internal affairs, the [Iran–Iraq] war has ended, no direct threat exists, and the United States especially at this time is still repeating that it will stay, then this is something that warrants attention.'

Saddam's conclusion in his remarks that February was that oil-wealthy Arab countries should join forces and make use of their 'possession of an energy source unparalleled in the world ... I think we should forge relationships with Europe, Japan, and the Soviet Union in a manner that will make us benefit from this element as soon as possible.'[13]

If anything had stiffened the resolve of leading Anglo-American establishment circles to go ahead with plans for a dramatic new Middle East military action, it was this speech of Saddam's. On July 27, 1990, when tensions between Iraq and Kuwait over oil prices were at a peak, the U.S. Ambassador to Baghdad, April Glaspie, asked for a meeting with Saddam Hussein in Baghdad to discuss the tense situation. According to official Iraqi transcripts of the exchange, later released by the Baghdad government and confirmed by U.S. Congress almost a year later, Glaspie told Saddam that Washington would not take a position on the dispute between Iraq and Kuwait. Less than one week later, Iraqi forces occupied Kuwait City. The Kuwaiti al-Sabah royal family had fled well in advance, able to escape with their Rolls-Royces, their gold and other valuables, because, according to one bitter former Kuwaiti government official in exile in Europe, 'the CIA informed the royal family in good time to get out, but the Al-Sabahs "conveniently" forgot to inform the country's military of their information that Kuwait was about to be invaded.'

Within hours of the Kuwait occupation, the Bank of England and the U.S. government acted to freeze all Kuwaiti assets, held in what is believed to be the world's largest single investment fund, the Kuwait Investment Office, based in London. Its total asset portfolio is kept secret, but was reliably reported to be well beyond $100–150 billion in value.

What followed during the ensuing six months was one of the most cynical calculated acts of recent history. Despite initial claims that the United States, immediately backed by Thatcher's British government, would send military forces only to defend Saudi Arabia against an allegedly threatened Iraqi invasion (the threats were later revealed to have been fabricated in Washington), President Bush, who had been together with Thatcher during the initial hours of decision in early August, appropriately at Aspen, Colorado, proclaimed what he soon referred to as his 'New World Order.'

On September 11, Bush declared:

> Out of these troubled times a New World Order can emerge, under a United Nations that performs as envisioned by its founders. We stand at a unique and extraordinary moment. This crisis in the Persian Gulf, as grave as it is, also offers us a rare opportunity to move toward an historic period of cooperation. Today that New World Order is struggling to be born. A world quite different from the one we've known.

Further evidence that George Bush and Margaret Thatcher never intended anything other than a military 'solution' to the Iraq–Kuwait crisis was given in the personal account of the Soviet special Middle East envoy, Yevgeni Primakov, some months later. In an extensive personal interview published in *Time* magazine on March 4, 1991, some days after the end of the devastating bombardment of Iraq, Primakov, as personal envoy of President Gorbachev, recounted his meeting in Baghdad in the early days of October 1990 with Saddam Hussein and his foreign minister, Tariq Aziz, which convinced Primakov that a war 'could have been averted.' Primakov recounted for *Time* his subsequent October 19 mediation mission to Washington, where he met with George Bush, Secretary Baker and other top officials at the White House. The Moscow envoy reported that Bush listened with apparent interest, but that some hours later he sent the clear message to Primakov that Washington was not interested in exploring the new opening further.

After leaving Washington, Primakov received instructions to stop over in London to deliver the same report to Prime Minister Margaret Thatcher. Primakov's account is revealing:

> The Prime Minister received us at her country residence, Chequers. She listened attentively to the information I presented her, without interrupting. But then, for a good hour, she allowed no one to interrupt her monologue, in which she outlined in a most condensed way a position that was gaining greater momentum: not to limit things to a withdrawal of Iraqi forces from Kuwait but to inflict a devastating blow at Iraq, 'to break the back' of Saddam and destroy the entire military, and perhaps industrial potential of that country.

After months of careful bribing and pressuring of key member nations of the United Nations Security Council, Arab states, Turkey and other nations, not only to impose total economic embargo against Iraq, but to authorize the use of force to liberate Kuwait, Bush told the U.S. Congress, on January 29, 1991, in his State of the Union address, 'The world can therefore seize the opportunity of the present Persian Gulf crisis to fulfill the long-held promise of a New World Order ...'

But, as the largest military buildup since the Vietnam War took place in Saudi Arabia, in preparation for offensive saturation bombing of Iraq in the early days of January 1991, more than a few informed voices inside the Washington establishment began to express grave doubts as to the ultimate wisdom of Bush's clear military intent. In a November 12, 1990, television interview, a former Reagan administration navy secretary, James H. Webb, declared, 'The purpose of our presence in the Persian Gulf is to further the Bush Administration's New World Order, and I don't like it.'

Webb took the occasion of a January 31 *Wall Street Journal* commentary some ten weeks later to repeat the point:

> The Bush Administration aided by editorial onslaughts from many sides ... has relentlessly maneuvered our nation into a war. One must reach back to William Randolph Hearst urging us into the Spanish–American War to find a parallel to the editorial pressure that preceded our present conflict. One must go even further, perhaps to the Mexican War, to find a president so avidly desirous of putting the nation at risk when it has not been attacked.

The former U.S. ambassador to Saudi Arabia, James Akins, a respected Washington expert on Middle East affairs, also came out publicly against the Bush war plan against Iraq. Akins pointed out, in a signed article published in the *Los Angeles Times* of September 12, only days after the decision of President Bush to send U.S. troops to 'defend' Saudi Arabia against threatened Iraqi invasion, that the White House had an 'ulterior motive.' Akins charged that U.S. Defense Secretary Cheney had deliberately misled Saudi King Fahd on the likelihood of such an invasion in order to be allowed to station U.S. troops on Saudi soil, something fiercely resisted by the Saudis for decades. In 1975, Akins related, plans to find a pretext to send U.S. troops to occupy vital Mideastern oilfields had been encouraged by Secretary of

State Henry Kissinger. He noted that Kissinger, then Akins' superior, had opposed Akins' adamant attacks on such ideas.

> Henry Kissinger, then U.S. Secretary, had another view, and my career in the Foreign Service did not extend much beyond that point ... There are those in the Bush Administration who will point out that conditions are more propitious now than in 1975 ...

Notably, in 1990, the former Kissinger Associate president, Lawrence Eagleburger, was deputy secretary of state under James Baker, and former Kissinger employee Brent Scowcroft was Bush's White House national security adviser during this period, ensuring that the Kissinger view was dominant in the formulation of U.S. foreign policy during the Gulf War buildup. Furthermore, Kissinger was calling in the media for war against Iraq during this period. The domestic voices of opposition were effectively drowned out by the president's war mobilization in the media.

## THE TARGET: AN INDEPENDENT EUROPE AND JAPAN

Within a brief period, it became clear to thinking people in Europe and elsewhere that George Bush, indeed, had quite another objective than merely defending U.S. or even Western oil interests in Saudi Arabia. Bush's incredibly vulgar public pronouncements, taunting Saddam Hussein, and comparing Iraq's president to 'a modern-day Adolf Hitler,' were made quite deliberately.

An unprecedented Washington and London propaganda and pressure offensive was unleashed against Iraq's Western supporters during the war and its six-month-long buildup, but not against the Soviet Union or France, which had been the major suppliers of Iraq's armaments. The target was Germany—more precisely, German high-technology industry, which was vital for the reconstruction of eastern Europe and the Soviet Union. France and the USSR, which together with China, the United States and Britain, comprised the five permanent members of the UN Security Council, had agreed to vote with Washington and Britain for going to war after the ultimatum deadline of January 17. Their role in Iraq was discreetly ignored by various Washington-linked exposés.

Instead, through channels directly linked to British and American intelligence, Hamburg's *Der Spiegel* and influential Republican senators such as Jesse Helms began an all-out offensive against

Germany, alleging that German exports of what were dubbed 'dual use' technologies had enabled Saddam's military to fire Soviet Scud missiles on Israeli targets.

A stunned Bonn government, itself in the midst of the complexities of dealing with reunification of the former East Germany, was forced to divert precious time, attention and financial resources from that pressing task, to focus on George Bush's and Thatcher's New World Order. In late January, U.S. Secretary of State James Baker went on one of the most high-pressure financial fund-raising missions in history, extracting pledges from Germany, Japan, Kuwait and Saudi Arabia to guarantee a total of $54.5 billion to pay the costs of what was called Operation Desert Storm.

In one of many tragic footnotes to the history of the war, the London *Times* reported on February 6, some three weeks into the Operation Desert Storm bombings of Iraq, that the 'Berlin–Baghdad railway, once a thriving network has been devastated in the Gulf war. The relentless allied bombing of Iraqi bridges, junctions and marshalling yards leaves in ruins one of the few extensive railway networks in the Middle East,' they noted, adding, with understatement, 'The old Berlin–Baghdad railway was a focus of strategic rivalry between Britain and Germany.'

After the conclusion of fighting, a former U.S. assistant secretary of defense in the Reagan administration, Lawrence J. Korb, revealed in an early April press conference in Washington that the U.S. government deliberately hid the actual Gulf War costs in order to offset domestic budget cuts, by using allied contributions in an 'off-budget' fund. Informed estimates were that the United States had come out of the entire Gulf War affair with a net 'profit' of perhaps $19 billion, when all allied war contributions were counted. The huge inflows of foreign money during the first months of 1991, with fully $6.6 billion paid in cash by Germany, created a strong upward pressure on the U.S. dollar, which only weeks before had fallen to an all-time postwar low of 1.46 Deutschmarks. Moreover, aggressive U.S. arms contracts with Mideastern countries began to be signed before the war had ended, much to the anger of European arms makers.

The Bush administration triumphantly proclaimed that America had proved itself the strongest power in the world. His boast rang hollow to those at home standing in ever longer unemployment lines, or those in eastern Europe denied the prospect of needed billions of Western capital to rebuild infrastructure and modernize their economies.

Eastern European economies were devastated by the combined impact of Operation Desert Storm and the initial huge run-up in world oil prices during late 1990 to more than $30 per barrel, caused by the disruption of agreed oil deliveries from Iraq. Formerly, before January 1991, the countries of eastern Europe, through their trade ties with the Soviet Union, paid for their needed oil imports in a form of barter trade of industrial and agricultural goods with Moscow. After January 1, that system came to an end and Western dollars were needed to buy Russian oil. Iraq had over $1 billion in oil commitments to Bulgaria, Hungary and other countries of the east, which became unpayable as a result of the Gulf War.

In March 1990, the Italian magazine *30 Days* interviewed an Italian professor with ties to Washington, Gianfranco Miglio. Miglio told the journal:

> The U.S. saw that to avoid falling into a decline similar to that of the Soviet Union, it had to keep pace with potential adversaries of the future. They include Japan and the Continent of Europe united around German economic power ... The United States could not accept the idea of Europe as it is today, a Continent that not only can manage quite happily without America, but one which is economically and technologically more powerful.

For this reason, Miglio declared, 'The Americans turned their attention on the Middle East, on gaining control of the Arab oil tap on which Japan and Germany depend.'

From France, Charles de Gaulle's former minister of agriculture, Edgar Pisani, head of the Institut du Monde Arabe in Paris, told a German interviewer in *Die Tageszeitung* on February 18, at the height of the bombing of Iraq by U.S., British and French planes:

> I wish it were not so. I am deeply shocked over the fact, that a nation is powerful only because it has the weapons. The USA, which in its economic affairs has extreme difficulties, has managed to silence Japan and Europe, because they are militarily weak. How long will the World accept that various countries must pay one Gendarme to enforce their own World Order. Japan, Germany and the oil-rich states finance this Gendarme ...

In a clear if veiled reference to the tragic follies of the British-led balance-of-power politics, German President Richard von Weizsäcker told the Berlin daily *Der Tagesspiegel* shortly after the Gulf War, 'We have earlier had the policy of balance of power of European nations, which ended in the perversion of National Socialism and resulted in two world wars. Then came the time of dominance by the two Superpowers.' Von Weizsäcker made an appeal for Europe to take advantage of the unique chance finally to end such balance-of-power follies, through realizing the 'unfulfilled vision of de Gaulle, for a Europe from the Atlantic to the Urals.'

Operation Desert Storm and the Bush–Thatcher Gulf War did incomprehensible damage to Iraq and its people, to Kuwait and to the world economy, but there were signs that it had not accomplished its prime objective of reinserting Continental Europe into George Bush's and Margaret Thatcher's New World Order.

# 12
# From the Evil Empire to the Axis of Evil

With the collapse of the Soviet Union at the beginning of the 1990s, hopes were high in many quarters that the world might see a new era of peace and prosperity. The decade that followed disappointed, to put it mildly. Far from an end to geopolitics and cold war, the stage merely shifted. As sole surviving superpower, Washington set about shaping its New World Order, though the term was quickly dropped by George H.W. Bush after it drew critical attention in his 1991 State of the Union speech. It provoked too many questions as to whose order it was and what priorities it might have.

The years from the end of the cold war in the late 1980s to the dawn of a new war on terrorism at the beginning of the new millennium were anything but peaceful or stable. In Washington, the geopolitical focus shifted from Ronald Reagan's 'Evil Empire,' the Soviet Union, to the young George W. Bush's 'Axis of Evil,' a vague domain conveniently embracing the Eurasian continent from Iraq and Iran to North Korea. What remained unspoken in that shift was the thin red thread of American geopolitics, which shaped the most significant world events. Oil and the dollar played a decisive role in that transition.

American cold war dominance of the noncommunist world had been based on the perceived global threat of Soviet and potentially Chinese communist aggression. Once that threat ended at the end of the 1980s, as Washington well knew, restraints on its major military allies were gone. The allies were potential economic rivals. Japan and east Asia, as well as the European Union, were emerging as major economic challengers to American hegemony. That economic challenge was to be the focus of U.S. geopolitics after 1990.

Armed with the gospel of free-market reform, privatization and dollar democracy, and backed by the powerful Wall Street financial firms, the Clinton administration began a process of extending the dollar and U.S. influence into domains which had previously been closed to them. The near religious campaign to win those areas to Washington's peculiar brand of market economy was to target not just the former communist economies of eastern Europe and the Soviet Union—it was to target any and every major part of the world that continued to try to develop its own resources, independently of the mandate of the IMF and the dollar world. The process also involved bringing every major oil region of the world under more or less direct U.S. control, from the Caspian Sea to Iraq, from West Africa to Colombia. It was an ambitious undertaking. Critics termed it imperial; the Clinton administration called it the extension of market economy and human rights. It was definitely not what most of the world were hoping for as the cold war drew to an end.

The Clinton administration and its Wall Street allies had brought one region after the other into its direct orbit during the 1990s, with the promise of the free market as the road to wealth and prosperity. The catch word was 'globalization,' and in reality it was the globalization of American power, consolidated through American banking and finance and corporate power.

Few realized that it might be part of a well thought-out strategy until the process was well advanced. Free trade had traditionally been demanded by the superior economic power of its weaker partners. By the time it became clear what the Washington agenda was, America had largely disarmed potential opponents and built a new ring of military bases around the world to defend its gains, a guarantee that the new converts to the free market did not lose the faith and try to revert to older economic forms.

In the 1950s, under the cold war and the Eisenhower doctrine, the United States had declared itself prepared, with armed force if necessary, to assist any Middle Eastern country asking for help to resist any incursion backed by international communism. This doctrine was used repeatedly by Washington during the four decades after 1945 by painting countless nationalist leaders, from Mossadegh to Nasser, with a red brush. The red taint justified military or other action.

After 1990, Washington faced a significant problem. What bogeyman could it find to justify such acts of foreign policy in the future, now that the danger of godless communism could no longer be used as a rationale? Finding the answer was to take until the new millennium, more than a decade.

In the meantime, the U.S. establishment had prepared a full plate to dish out to an unsuspecting world, starting in Japan. Washington knew that its continued global dominance depended on how it dealt with Eurasia, from Europe to the Pacific. Former presidential adviser and geostrategist, Zbigniew Brzezinski, put it bluntly:

> ... in terminology that hearkens back to the more brutal age of empires, the three grand imperatives of imperial geostrategy are to prevent collusion and maintain security dependence among the vassals, to keep tributaries pliant and protected, and to 'keep the barbarians from coming together.'

It was an ambitious agenda.

## JAPAN: WOUNDING THE LEAD GOOSE

One of the most pressing challenges to the U.S. role in the post-cold war world was the enormous new economic power of its Japanese ally over world trade and banking. Japan had built up its economic power during the postwar period through careful steps, always with an eye to its military protector, Washington.

By the end of the 1980s, Japan was regarded as the leading economic and banking power in the world. People spoke about the 'Japan that can say no,' and the 'Japanese economic challenge.' American banks were in their deepest crisis since the 1930s, and U.S. industry had become overindebted and undercompetitive. This was a poor basis on which to build the world's sole remaining superpower, and the Bush administration knew it.

Prominent Japanese intellectual and political figures, such as Kinhide Mushakoji, were keenly aware of the special nature of the Japanese model. 'Japan has industrialized but not Westernized,' he noted. 'Its capitalism is quite different from the Western version, and is not based on the formal concepts of the individual. It has accepted selectively only the concepts associated with the state, economic wealth accumulation and technocratic rationalism.' In short, the Japanese model, which was tolerated during the cold war as a geopolitical counterweight to Chinese and Soviet power, was a major problem for Washington once that cold war was over. How major, Japan was soon to learn.

No country had supported the Reagan era budget deficits and spending excesses during the 1980s more loyally and energetically than Washington's former foe, Japan. Not even Germany had been so supportive of Washington's demands. As it appeared to Japanese eyes, Tokyo's loyalty, and its generous purchases of U.S. Treasury debt, real estate and other assets, were rewarded at the beginning of the 1990s by one of the most devastating financial debacles in world history. Many Japanese businessmen privately believed that this was the result of a deliberate Washington policy to undercut Japanese economic influence in the world. At the end of the 1980s, Harvard economist and later Clinton Treasury secretary, Lawrence Summers, warned, 'an Asian economic bloc with Japan at its apex is in the making ... raising the possibility that the majority of American people who now feel that Japan is a greater threat to the U.S. than the Soviet Union, are right.'

The Plaza Hotel accord of the G-7 industrial nations in September of 1985 was officially designed to bring an overvalued dollar down to more manageable levels. To accomplish this, the Bank of Japan was pressured by Washington to take measures that would increase the yen's value against the U.S. dollar. Between the Plaza accord, the Baker–Miyazawa agreement a month later, and a Louvre accord in February 1987, Tokyo agreed to 'follow monetary and fiscal policies which will help to expand domestic demand and thereby contribute to reducing the external surplus.' James Baker, the Treasury secretary, had set the stage.

As Japan's most important export market was the United States, Washington was able to put Japan under intense pressure. And it did. Under the 1988 Omnibus Trade and Competitiveness Act, Washington listed Japan for 'hostile' trade practices and demanded major concessions.

The Bank of Japan cut interest rates to a low of 2.5 per cent by 1987, where they remained until May 1989. The lower interest rates were intended to spark more Japanese purchases of U.S. goods, something which never happened. Instead, the cheap money found its way into quick gains on the rising Tokyo stock market, and soon a colossal bubble was inflating. The domestic Japanese economy was stimulated, but above all, the Nikkei stock market and Tokyo real estate prices were pumped up. In a preview of the later US 'New Economy' bubble, Tokyo stock prices rose 40 per cent or more annually, while real-estate prices in and around Tokyo ballooned, in some cases by 90 per cent or more, as a new goldrush fever gripped Japan.

Within months of the Plaza accord, the yen had appreciated dramatically. It rose from 250 to only 149 yen to a dollar. Japanese export companies compensated for the yen's impact on export prices by turning to financial speculation, dubbed 'zaitech,' to make up for currency losses in export sales. Japan overnight became the world's largest banking center. Under new international capital rules, Japanese banks could count a major share of their long-held stocks in related companies, the *keiretsu* system, as bank core assets. As the paper value of their stock holdings in other Japanese companies rose, bank capital rose with it.

By 1988, as the stock bubble roared ahead, the ten largest banks in the world all had Japanese names. Japanese capital flowed into U.S. real estate, golf courses and luxury resorts, into U.S. government bonds and even into more risky U.S. stocks. The Japanese obligingly recycled their inflated yen into dollar assets, thereby aiding the presidential ambitions of George H.W. Bush, who succeeded Ronald Reagan in 1988. Commenting on Japan's success during the 1980s, New York financier George Soros remarked, '... the prospect of Japan's emerging as the dominant financial power in the world is very disturbing ...'

But Japanese euphoria over becoming the world's financial giant was short-lived. The inflated Japanese financial system, with banks awash with money, led as well to one of the world's greatest stock and real-estate bubbles, as stocks on the Nikkei index in Tokyo rose 300 per cent in a space of three years after the Plaza accord. Real-estate values, the collateral of Japanese bank loans, rose in tandem. At the peak of the Japan bubble, the value of Tokyo real estate in dollar terms was greater than that of real estate in the entire United States. The nominal value of all stocks listed on the Tokyo Nikkei stock exchange accounted for more than 42 per cent of world stock values, at least on paper. Not for long.

By late 1989, just as the first signs of the collapse of the Berlin Wall surfaced in Europe, the Bank of Japan and Ministry of Finance began a cautious effort to slowly deflate the alarming Nikkei stock bubble. No sooner did Tokyo act to cool down the speculative fever, than the major Wall Street investment banks, led by Morgan Stanley and Salomon Bros., began using exotic new derivatives and financial instruments. Their aggressive intervention turned the orderly decline of the Tokyo market into a near panic sell-off, as the Wall Street bankers made a killing on shorting Tokyo stocks in the process. The result was that no slow, orderly correction by the Japanese authorities was possible.

By March 1990, the Nikkei had lost 23 per cent or well over $1 trillion from its peak. Japanese government officials privately recalled a May 1990 Washington meeting of the IMF Interim Committee, where a heated debate over Japanese proposals to finance the economic reconstruction of the former Soviet Union was drawing strong opposition from Washington and the Bush Treasury Department. They saw that meeting as a possible reason behind the speculative Wall Street attack on Tokyo stocks. It was only partly true.

The Japanese Ministry of Finance had issued a report to the IMF, arguing that, far from being a problem, as argued by Washington, Japan's huge capital surplus was urgently required by a world needing hundreds of billions of dollars in new rail and other economic infrastructure investment following the end of the cold war. Japan proposed its famous MITI model for the former communist economies. Washington was unenthusiastic, to put it mildly. The MITI model involved a heavy role for the state in guiding national economic development. It had proved remarkably successful in South Korea, Malaysia and other east Asian countries. When the Soviet Union collapsed, many began eagerly looking to Japan and South Korea as better alternatives to the U.S. free-market model. That was a major threat to Washington plans as the cold war drew to an end.

The Bush administration was less than eager to accept a leading role from Japan in rebuilding eastern Europe and the Soviet Union. Washington had other plans for its former cold war adversary, and the creation of a Japanese-financed economic bloc with Russia was not on the list. To drive the point home, George Bush sent his defense secretary, Dick Cheney, to Tokyo in early 1990 to 'discuss' drastic U.S. troop reductions in the Asia–Pacific rim, a theme calculated to raise Japanese military security anxieties. Cheney's barely concealed blackmail mission followed on the heels of a January trip by Japan's Prime Minister Kaifu to western Europe, Poland and Hungary, to discuss the economic development of the former communist countries of eastern Europe. The message was clear—'Do as Washington says, or we leave you poorly defended.'

By the time the Japanese prime minister met the American president in Palm Springs that March, he had got the point. Japan was not to compete with American dollars in eastern Europe. Within months, Japanese stocks had lost nearly $5 trillion in paper value. Japan Inc. was badly wounded. Little more was heard about a Japanese challenge to American financial plans in eastern Europe. Washington economists proclaimed the end of the Japanese model. Privately, Tokyo politicians often used the analogy of a flight of geese, with Japan flying as the lead goose and the smaller economies of east Asia following in its path. By 1990, Washington had badly wounded the lead goose. Now it turned its attentions to the flock following—the Tiger economies—for the second phase of its new dollar order.[1]

## PHASE TWO: SHOOTING ASIAN TIGERS

The second phase of breaking up the Japan model involved destroying the east Asian economic sphere, a highly successful model that challenged the American dictates of rugged free-market individualism. The Japanese model, as Washington knew well, was not limited to Japan. In the postwar period it had been nurtured in South Korea, Thailand, Malaysia, Indonesia and other east Asian economies. In the 1980s, these fast-growing economies were labeled the Tiger states.

East Asia had been built up during the 1970s and especially the 1980s, by Japanese state development aid, large private investment and MITI support. While this had happened with little fanfare, in effect the booming economies of east Asia in the 1980s owed much to a deliberate regional division of labor, with Japan at the center and Japanese companies outsourcing manufacturing processes to east Asian centers. These were referred to in Asian business circles as the yen bloc countries because of their close ties to Japan's economy.

The Tiger economies were a major embarrassment to the IMF free-market model. Their very success in blending private enterprise with a strong state economic role was a threat to the IMF free-market agenda. So long as the Tigers appeared to succeed with a model based on a strong state role, the former communist states and others could argue against taking the extreme IMF course.

In east Asia during the 1980s, economic growth rates of 7–8 per cent per year, rising social security, universal education and a high worker productivity were all backed by state guidance and planning, albeit in a market economy—an Asian form of benevolent paternalism. Even more than Soviet central planning, the self-sufficient Asian Tiger economies were an obstacle to the global spread of the dollar free-market system being demanded by Washington in the 1990s.

Beginning in 1993, at the Asia Pacific Economic Cooperation (APEC) Summit, as Japan's banks struggled with the collapse of their stock and real-estate markets, Washington officials began to demand that east Asian economies open up their controlled financial markets to free capital flows, in the interest of 'level playing fields,' they argued. Previously, the debt-free economies of east Asia had avoided reliance on IMF loans or foreign capital, other than direct investment in manufacturing plants, usually as part of a long-term national goal.

Now they were told to open their markets to foreign capital flows and short-term foreign lending. Given the rhetoric of 'level playing fields,' many Asian officials wondered privately whether Washington was talking about cricket or about their economic future. They soon learned.

Once capital controls were eased and foreign investment was allowed to flow freely, in and out, South Korea and the other Tiger economies were awash with a sudden flood of foreign dollars. The result, between 1994 and the onset of the attack on the Thai baht in May 1997, was the creation of speculative bubbles in luxury real estate, local stock values and other assets.

Once the east Asian Tiger economies had begun to open up to foreign capital, but well before they had adequate controls in place over possible abuses, hedge funds went on the attack. These secretive funds first targeted the weakest economy, Thailand. American speculator George Soros acted in secrecy, armed with an undisclosed credit line from a group of international banks including Citigroup. They gambled that Thailand would be forced to devalue the baht and break from its peg to the dollar. Soros, head of Quantum Fund, Julian Robertson, head of the Tiger Fund and reportedly also of the Long-Term Capital Management (LTCM) hedge fund, whose management included former Federal Reserve deputy David Mullins, unleashed a huge speculative attack on the Thai currency and stocks. By June, Thailand had capitulated, its currency was floated, and it was forced to turn to the IMF for help. In swift succession, the same hedge funds and banks hit the Philippines, Indonesia and then South Korea. They pocketed billions, as the populations sank into economic chaos and poverty.

Chalmers Johnson described the result in blunt terms: 'The funds easily raped Thailand, Indonesia and South Korea, then turned the shivering survivors over to the IMF, not to help the victims, but to insure that no Western bank was stuck with non-performing loans in the devastated countries.'

A European Asia expert, Kristen Nordhaug, summed up the Clinton administration policy towards East Asia in 1997. Clinton had developed a major economic strategy, using the new National Economic Council, initially headed by Robert Rubin, a Wall Street investment banker. East Asian emerging markets were targeted for an offensive. 'The Administration actively supported multilateral agencies such as the IMF ... to promote international financial liberalization,' Nordhaug noted. 'As ... the strategy of targeting

East Asian markets [was] in place, the U.S. Administration was in a strong position to take advantage of the financial crisis to promote liberalization of trade, finance and institutional reforms through the IMF.'

The impact of the Asia crisis on the dollar was notable. The general manager of the Bank for International Settlements, Andrew Crockett, noted that while the east Asian countries had run a combined current account deficit of $33 billion in 1996, as speculative hot money flowed in, '1998–1999, the current account swung to a surplus of $87 billion.' By 2002, it peaked at $200 billion. Most of that surplus returned to the United States in the form of Asian central bank purchases of U.S. Treasury debt, in effect financing Washington policies. Japan's Finance Ministry had made a futile effort to contain the Asia crisis by proposing a $30 billion Asian Monetary Fund. Washington made clear that it was not pleased. The idea was quickly dropped. Asia was to become yet another province of the dollar realm through the IMF. Treasury Secretary Rubin euphemistically termed it America's 'strong dollar policy.'[2]

## WASHINGTON REVISITS HALFORD MACKINDER

Even as it was destroying the Japanese economic model during the 1990s and reshaping east Asia to suit its own interests, Washington placed the highest priority on the dismantling of the Soviet Union.

By the beginning of the 1990s, as the Berlin Wall came down and the Soviet Union with it, Washington faced no apparent rival for global hegemony. In the euphoria of the day, few expressed alarm or concern that one country held so much power over the planet. After all, it was democratic, and it was America. With no more threat of Soviet military action, NATO countries, above all the United States, could begin to shift their trillion dollar annual expenditure as a world military sector into civilian uses.

A new era of peaceful development, market reforms and capitalist prosperity was the dream of millions in the former communist states of the Warsaw Pact. Those dreams were short-lived. The U.S. establishment was preparing to secure global hegemony for America, as the sole superpower, all the while trying to lull the rest of the world into a sense of false complacency. Deception played a strategic role in Washington policy during the 1990s. The greatest deception, it soon became clear, was the impression that Washington was groping for ideas about where to go after the end of the Soviet threat.

The collapse of the Soviet Union was an event of signal importance in the history of the past century. Little understood was the cold calculation of policy makers in the Bush administration in the early 1990s regarding the future of Russia and its former satellite states. Russia was to be brought into the U.S. economic orbit through imposition of 'market reforms.'

In effect, it was to be dollarized. How that was to work was complex and differentiated. The end effect, however, was to prop up the United States as the sole remaining superpower and the sole issuer of the world reserve currency, the dollar—with all the benefits that gave Washington. The instrument for Washington's new Russian policy was to be the International Monetary Fund.

At the same time, Russia was to be systematically surrounded by a ring of U.S. and NATO military bases, and an eastward expansion of NATO which, when completed, would prevent any future strategic alliance between the Russian and Continental European powers that potentially might challenge America's supremacy. The trick for Washington would be to persuade a nuclear-armed Moscow elite to accept such a complete dismantling of its power.

Washington policy was classic geopolitics, as outlined almost a century earlier by Sir Halford Mackinder. Mackinder had warned a British elite that an alliance of the major Eurasian powers of the time, including Germany, Russia and central Asian states, held the potential to become the dominant global power, since it would be geographically coherent and would possess all the necessary economic raw materials and a sufficient population to challenge any rivals.

At the end of the First World War, Mackinder had stated, 'Who rules Central Europe, commands the Heartland; Who rules the Heartland, commands the World Island; Who rules the World Island, commands the world.' In other words, if the nations around Germany and France in Europe were to dominate the Russian-centered Eurasian 'Heartland,' as Mackinder termed it, that combination would hold the potential, the resources and the geographic advantage to dominate the entire world.

Washington establishment strategists such as Zbigniew Brzezinski, a former White House National Security Council head, who had held top national security posts under several administrations, worked with Henry Kissinger, and advised the first Bush presidency, openly acknowledged the role of Mackinder's geopolitical thinking on U.S. strategic policy. 'It is imperative that no Eurasian challenger emerges capable of dominating Eurasia and thus of also challenging

America,' Brzezinski stated in his book *The Grand Chessboard*. He added, 'Mackinder pioneered the discussion early in this century with his successive concepts of the Eurasian "pivot areas."'

This policy involved identifying any potential power able to upset the balance of power, and as Brzezinski put it, 'to formulate specific U.S. policies to offset, co-opt and or control the above.' Eurasia, as he drew the map, included the oil wealth of the Middle East, the central Asian region, the industrial potentials of Europe and Japan, the resources of China, India and Russia. He warned, 'control over Eurasia would almost automatically entail Africa's subordination, rendering the Western Hemisphere and Oceania geographically peripheral to the world's central continent.'

Just how Washington acted on this imperative was not at first clear to the rest of the world as the cold war came to an end. It was clear, however, to Russian strategic thinkers in and around the Soviet Academy of Sciences. They had carefully studied Mackinder and Anglo-Saxon theories of geopolitics. In the collapse of the Soviet Union, however, their voices were drowned out. The market economy and the prospect of fabulous wealth had momentarily diverted the energies of Russia's elite.[3]

From the side of Washington, the strategy for reshaping its cold war adversary into a tool of American hegemony was clear from the outset—albeit not without risk, given the remaining Soviet nuclear arsenal. The Russian bear may have been economically bankrupt in 1990, but she still had a few nuclear teeth. The process of restructuring had to be done carefully.

## RUSSIA GETS THE IMF THIRD WORLD CURE

In July 1990, at a meeting of the G-7 industrial nations in Houston, Texas, U.S. Secretary of State James Baker played the key policy role regarding the future of the Soviet Union. Baker, the man who five years earlier as Treasury secretary had brought Japan to the Plaza accord, told his G-7 allies that the United States wanted the central role in the economic reform of the Soviet economy to be carried out by the IMF. The final G-7 communiqué stated, 'We welcome the efforts underway in the Soviet Union to liberalize and to create a more open, democratic and pluralistic Soviet society, and to move toward a market-oriented economy.' The declaration added, 'We have agreed to ask the IMF ... to undertake a detailed study of the Soviet economy ... to make recommendations for its reform.'

The aim of Washington's IMF 'market reforms' in the former Soviet Union was brutally simple: destroy the economic ties that bound Moscow to each part of the Soviet Union, from Uzbekistan to Kazakhstan, from Georgia to Azerbaijan, from Estonia to Poland, Bulgaria or Hungary. Though it was never stated, IMF shock therapy was intended to create weak, unstable economies on the periphery of Russia, dependent on Western capital and on dollar inflows for their survival—a form of neocolonialism.

By placing the U.S.-dominated IMF in the key economic policy role, James Baker and the Bush administration had ensured that any and all Western economic investment in or support for the Soviet economy would first have to pass a Washington veto. The Russians were to get the standard Third World treatment, much as an African former colony or a banana republic—IMF conditionalities and a plunge into poverty for the population. A tiny elite were allowed to become fabulously rich in dollar terms, and manipulable by Wall Street bankers and investors.

Harvard economists, such as Jeffrey Sachs, armed with their theories of 'shock therapy,' were flown to Moscow to assist in the destruction of the old central state apparatus. IMF technocrats demanded that Russian oil and gas, aluminum, manganese and other raw materials be sold at world market prices, that state subsidies for food, health and other essentials be ended, and that the Russian industry be 'privatized.'

In 1992 the IMF demanded a free float of the Russian ruble as part of its 'market-oriented' reform. The ruble float led within a year to an increase in consumer prices of 9,900 per cent, and a collapse in real wages of 84 per cent. For the first time since 1917, at least during peacetime, the majority of Russians were plunged into existential poverty. That was but the start of IMF-style capitalism for the Russians.

Under IMF direction, Washington could in effect dictate which sector of Russian industry would survive, which not. The 'world market,' was defined by Washington and IMF technocrats, trained in the ways of Milton Friedman's free market. Neither Russian national priority nor the general welfare of the population would be the criterion.

The dictates of the IMF 'global market' were to replace the Stalin-era dictatorship of the proletariat for the peoples of Russia and the former Soviet region. Never mind that the level of economic freedom in the United States, ostensibly the model, was a complex product of an evolution of more than 350 years, in some cases reaching back to the English Civil War. Under the IMF, countries like Russia and Ukraine were told to immediately adopt the U.S. version of market economy, with no adequate preparation. The results were predictable and well planned. The goal was not a stable, prosperous Russia.

As most Russians soon realized, the effects of the IMF reform were catastrophic. Instead of the hoped-for American-style prosperity, two-cars-in-every-garage capitalism, ordinary Russians were driven into economic misery. Industrial production fell to half its earlier level as inflation passed levels of 200 per cent. Average life expectancy for men dropped to 57 years by 1994, the level of Bangladesh or Egypt.

The West, above all the United States, clearly wanted a deindustrialized Russia, to permanently break up the economic structure of the old Soviet Union. A major area of the global economy, which had been largely closed to the dollar domain for more than seven decades, was to be brought under its control. Behind the nice rhetoric of market-oriented reform, the region was being carved up in much the manner the European powers had colonized and divided Africa 100 years before.

For Washington's Clinton administration, it mattered little that the Russian privatization of key state industrial assets was controlled by a Russian elite, the so-called oligarchs. The prime point was that Russian industry was tied for the first time since Lenin to the future of the dollar. The new oligarchs were 'dollar oligarchs,' and most of their new wealth came from the export of oil and gas.

The partner for the United States and the point man for the IMF during the Yeltsin era was Anatoly Chubais, minister for privatization. The IMF granted Russia a $6 billion loan in 1996, on the condition that Chubais be put in charge of economic policy. In 1997, George Washington University Professor Peter Reddaway wrote in the *Washington Post* that Chubais had been accused in Russia of 'censoring the media, undermining democracy, engaging in dubious personal dealings, taking orders from Washington and building a criminalized form of capitalism.' This was apparently enough to win the backing of the deputy Treasury secretary, Lawrence Summers. Summers, who also funneled millions of taxpayer dollars into U.S. support for Harvard 'shock therapy' economist and Russia adviser, Jeffrey Sachs, hailed Yeltsin's 1997 naming of Chubais as first deputy prime minister. Making Chubais responsible for the economy, Summers argued, created 'a re-energized presidency and an economic dream team.' For most Russians, the dream was a nightmare.

Ukraine, which had been a major industrial, military and grain-producing center of the USSR, was put through the same brutal process as Russia. There, after IMF 'reforms' began in October 1994, the collapse was equally dramatic. The IMF ordered an end to state foreign exchange controls and the currency collapsed. The IMF then demanded state subsidies be ended. The price of bread shot up by 300 per cent, electricity by 600 per cent, and public transportation by 900 per cent. The population was now forced to buy local goods in prices set in dollar terms, a result of the IMF demands. With sky-high electricity costs and no bank credit, state industries were forced into bankruptcy. Foreign speculators were free to pick the jewels among the rubble at dirt-cheap prices. Ukranian agriculture was deregulated on IMF and World Bank demands. The result was that Ukraine, once the breadbasket of Europe, was forced to beg food aid from the U.S., which dumped its grain surpluses on Ukraine, further destroying local food self-sufficiency.

Russia and the states of the former Soviet Union were being treated like the Congo or Nigeria, as sources of cheap raw materials, perhaps the largest sources in the world. With the collapse of the Warsaw Pact, those mineral riches were now within the reach of Western multinationals for the first time since 1917. Above all, the oil and gas riches of the former Soviet Union came into view of the large U.S. and British oil multinationals. In the eyes of the Washington planners, a modern, thriving Russian industrial economy would only be a hindrance to such plundering of its raw material wealth.

In the early 1990s, the Clinton administration held out to Moscow the term, 'the mature strategic partnership.' Many Russians naively assumed this would mean that U.S. aid and capital would flow into Russia to restructure a vibrant economy, that Russia would be treated as an equal partner in some form of 'global condominium' with the United States, and that its historical hegemony over the states of the former Soviet Union would be respected by Washington. But by the time it had become brutally clear in Moscow that the 'partnership' was a hollow slogan, designed to deceive, it was too late. The Russian industrial complex had been largely dismembered. Its population was enmiserated by IMF reforms, and its ability to influence events on its perimeter was severely diminished. That suited Washington just fine.

The IMF shock treatment for Russia after 1991 not only reduced the former superpower to a Third World economy. It also opened up the potential for American and allied oil companies to control what had been the world's largest oil and natural gas producer. That process was to take a while, however.

Under the controlled and manipulated privatizations of the Chubais era, Russia's prized oil and gas interests were given away for a song to select Yeltsin and Chubais cronies. An IMF report in 1998 estimated that 17 Russian oil and gas companies, with a fair market value of at least $17 billion, had been sold by Chubais for a total of $1.4 billion. Moreover, 60 per cent of the state gas monopoly, Gazprom, the world's largest gas producer, was sold to private Russian groups for some $20 million. The market value was about $119 billion. Companies such as Lukoil, Yukos, Sibneft and Sidanko were created. Oligarchs such as Mikhail Khodorkovsky, Boris Berezovsky and Viktor Chernomyrdin dominated the Russian economy as no communist-era bureaucrat ever had. In a November 1996 interview, Berezovsky, as deputy secretary of the Russian Security Council as well as an oil oligarch, boasted that seven men controlled 50 per cent of the country's vast natural resources. Their hard currency profits were all dollar denominated, he might have added.

By summer of 1998, the dollarization of Russia had almost got out of hand. In August, the IMF extended an emergency loan of $23 billion to support the ruble and protect the speculative investments of Western banks, which had made millions investing in Russian state bonds. The IMF bailout of the banks came too late.

On August 15, Russia announced that it would default on its dollar loans. For New York and other major banks, the unthinkable had taken place. A major debtor, despite IMF aid, had decided to default. For a few nervous weeks, the entire dollar edifice shook at the foundations. LTCM, the world's largest hedge fund, had bet heavily on the Russian market as well as on most of the world bond markets. Its directors included a former Federal Reserve deputy governor, David Mullins, leading Wall Street investors and Nobel Prize economists. The sudden default threatened the fund with bankruptcy and a chain-reaction collapse of trillions of dollars in financial derivatives contracts, and ultimately a chain of bankruptcies which could bring down the entire global financial house of cards. The Federal Reserve called an extraordinary closed-door meeting with 15 of the world's most powerful bankers and arm-twisted a rescue operation. Russia, far too valuable strategically, was quietly forgiven its default and soon the dollarization resumed, if at a less fevered pace.[4]

## YUGOSLAVIA GETS THE SHOCK THERAPY

Well before the Soviet Union was treated to American-made economic 'shock therapy,' the Balkans had been targeted for U.S. intervention. The importance of destroying the Yugoslav economic model was a major reason for Washington's early focus on Yugoslavia. As events developed into the mid 1990s, the strategic position of Yugoslavia in regard to the potential oil sources of central Asia became increasingly important for Washington. Oil and the dollar in effect played decisive roles in Washington's Balkan politics through the latter half of the 1990s, though not in the simplistic way critics in the West suspected.

Well before the fall of the Berlin Wall, Washington was busy at work in what was then Yugoslavia, working in tandem with the IMF once again. Balkan nationalism was being manipulated from the outside to transform the map of Eurasia into what it had been in the years before the First World War, when British and other interests, intent on dismantling the Ottoman Empire and stopping Germany's Baghdad railway dreams, had intervened.

The obvious aim now was to fragment Yugoslavia into dependent, tiny states, and to open a foothold for NATO and the United States at the crossroads between western Europe and central Asia. Oil and geopolitics were again in the forefront for Washington.

Ironically, with the dismantling of the Warsaw Pact in the early 1990s, the very reason for the continued existence of NATO appeared to vanish. What threat could justify continuation of the 1949 cold war alliance, or a permanent U.S. military presence across western Europe, let alone a further extension to the east? Many hoped NATO might be dismantled once it was clear the Soviet threat had gone. But Washington strategists had begun to devise a new mission for NATO, even before the collapse of the Soviet regime.

The new proposed NATO mandate was termed 'NATO out of area deployment,' meaning well beyond the borders of NATO member states. This new mandate was later coupled, in 1994, with a Washington 'Partnership for Peace,' a scheme to integrate the military defense of former Warsaw Pact members, stepwise, into a U.S.-led NATO. Republican Senator Richard Lugar posed the dilemma facing the U.S.-dominated NATO at the end of the cold war with the phrase, 'NATO: out of area, or out of business.' Conveniently, the Balkan wars were to give Washington a much-needed argument to extend NATO. The process was to last more than a decade.

For over 40 years, Washington had quietly supported Yugoslavia, and the Tito model of mixed socialism, as a buffer against the Soviet Union. As Moscow's empire began to fall apart, Washington had no more use for a buffer—especially a nationalist buffer which was economically successful, one that might convince neighboring states in eastern Europe that a middle way other than IMF shock therapy was possible. The Yugoslav model had to be dismantled, for this reason alone, in the eyes of top Washington strategists. The fact that Yugoslavia also lay on a critical path to the potential oil riches of central Asia merely added to the argument. Yugoslavia must be brought, kicking and screaming if need be, into the IMF version of free-market reform. NATO would secure the deal.

Already in 1988, as it became clear that the Soviet system was on its last legs, Washington had sent in advisers to Yugoslavia from a curious, private, non-profit organization with the high-sounding name, the National Endowment for Democracy, or NED as it was known in Washington circles. That 'private' organization began handing out generous doses of dollars in every corner of Yugoslavia, financing opposition groups, buying up hungry young journalists with dreams of a new life, and financing trade union opposition, pro-IMF opposition economists such as the G-17, and human rights NGOs.

Speaking in Washington in 1998, ten years later, and one year before NATO began bombing Belgrade, NED director Paul McCarthy boasted, 'NED was one of the few Western organizations, along with the Soros Foundation and some European foundations, to make grants in the Federal Republic of Yugoslavia, and to work with local NGO's and independent media throughout the country.' During the cold war, such internal intervention in a foreign country would have been labeled a CIA destabilization. In Washington newspeak, it was called, 'the fostering of democracy.' The result, for the living standard of Serbs, Kosovans, Bosnians, Croats and others, was disastrous.

What ensued in Yugoslavia after 1990 was understood by only a few insiders for what it was. Washington, using the NED, George Soros's Open Society Foundation and the IMF, introduced economic chaos into Yugoslavia as an instrument of geopolitical policy. In 1989, the IMF demanded that the prime minister, Ante Markovic, impose structural reform on the economy. For whatever reasons, he did.

Under the IMF policies, the Yugoslavian GDP sank in 1990 by 7.5 per cent, and by another 15 per cent in 1991. Industrial production plunged 21 per cent. The IMF demanded wholesale privatization of state enterprises. The result was the bankruptcy of more than 1,100 companies by 1990, and more than 20 per cent unemployment. The economic pressure on the various regions of the country created an explosive cocktail. Predictably, amid growing economic chaos, each region fought for its own survival, against its neighbors. Leaving nothing to chance, the IMF ordered all wages to be frozen at 1989 levels, while inflation rose dramatically, leading to a fall in real earnings of 41 per cent by the first six months of 1990. By 1991, inflation was over 140 per cent. In this situation, the IMF ordered full convertibility of the dinar and the freeing of interest rates. The IMF explicitly prevented the Yugoslav government from obtaining credit from its own central bank, crippling the ability of the central government to finance social and other programs. This freeze created a de facto economic secession, well before the formal declaration of secession by Croatia and Slovenia in June 1991.

In November 1990, under pressure from the Bush administration, the U.S. Congress passed the Foreign Operations Appropriations Act. The new U.S. law provided that any part of Yugoslavia failing to declare independence from Yugoslavia within six months of the act would lose all U.S. financial support. The law demanded separate elections, supervised by the U.S. State Department, in each of the six Yugoslav republics. It also stipulated that any aid go directly to each republic, and not to the central Yugoslav government in Belgrade. In short, the Bush administration demanded the self-dissolution of the Yugoslav Federation. They were deliberately lighting the fuse to an explosive new series of Balkan wars.

Using groups such as the Soros Foundation and NED, Washington financial support was channeled into often extreme nationalist or former fascist organizations that would guarantee a dismemberment of Yugoslavia. Reacting to this combination of IMF shock therapy and direct Washington destabilization, the Yugoslav president, Serb nationalist Slobodan Milosevic, organized a new Communist Party in November 1990, dedicated to prevent the breakup of the federated Yugoslav Republic. The stage was set for a gruesome series of regional ethnic wars which would last a decade and result in the deaths of more than 200,000 people.

The economic heat was being turned up on the tiny but strategic Balkan country, and the Bush administration was doing the turning. In 1992 Washington imposed a total economic embargo on Yugoslavia, freezing all trade and plunging the economy into chaos, with hyperinflation and 70 per cent unemployment as the result. The Western public, above all in the United States, was told by establishment media that the problems were all a result of a corrupt Belgrade dictatorship. The American media chose rarely if ever to mention the provocative Washington actions, or the IMF policies which were driving events in the Balkans.[5]

In 1995, the Dayton accord brought an end to the war in Bosnia. This coincided with the point at which the Clinton administration became convinced of the strategic importance of Caspian oil, and the extent of EU efforts to secure that oil for Europe via Balkan pipelines. Washington decided apparently that peace in the region was needed to develop oil routes from the Caspian into Europe. But it was to be 'peace' on Washington's terms.

After Dayton, Bosnia, once multiethnic, was established as a de facto Muslim state, in effect a client state under control of the IMF and of NATO. The Clinton administration had largely financed the arming of the Bosnian Muslim army. The depiction of the war in the international media maximized the impression of European Union powerlessness to settle a major war on its borders without America's intervention. Washington's argument for extending NATO eastward advanced significantly in the process. Hungary, Poland and the Czech Republic became prospective NATO partners, something inconceivable just five years earlier.

Soon the Clinton administration went to work on the next stage of dismantling any nationalist residue in the Balkans that might have a different agenda for the region than that of Washington. American and British oil companies scrambled to exploit the potentially vast oil reserves believed to lie under the Caspian Sea off Baku, and bordering Kazakhstan in central Asia. Geologists spoke of a 'new Kuwait or Saudi Arabia' there. The U.S. government estimated oil reserves could be in excess of 200 billion barrels—if true, the largest oil discovery in decades. Zbigniew Brzezinski, a well-paid Washington lobbyist, represented the interests of BP, the Anglo-American oil giant with a major stake in the Caspian oil region.

## U.S. OIL GEOPOLITICS IN THE BALKANS

No sooner had the Berlin wall come down than the European Union, backed by France, Italy and Holland, announced a major EU energy security strategy. The stability of the Balkans was a central part of that strategy. In a June 1990 EU summit, the Dutch prime minister, Ruud Lubbers, unveiled a proposal for a European energy community, to bind the countries of the 'European Economic Community with the USSR and the countries of Central and Eastern Europe.' The Lubbers Plan was just the first of a series of aid programs for EU energy security in the post-cold war period.

By 1992, the EU had created the Energy Charter Treaty to give a legal framework for EU investment in the oil and energy resources of the now dissolved Soviet Union. The newly independent states of the Caspian, above all Azerbaijan and Kazakhstan, were high on the priority list for future EU energy security. But the new Clinton administration seemed preoccupied with other problems and paid little note to Caspian oil at that point. That slowly began to change, however.

In December 1994, when the EU hoped to secure the ratification of its energy charter by 49 countries, among them the United States and Russia, Washington abruptly refused on flimsy technical grounds. The EU proceeded without U.S. support, and in December 1998 a transit working group was established by the countries signing the energy charter. The secretary-general of that conference stressed the importance of new oil and gas regions, 'such as the Caspian Sea region. Ensuring the security of supply from such areas is a key strategic task for governments.' The EU spoke of building a 'milestone in East–West energy co-operation.'

From 1990 until the bombing of Serbia in 1999, the EU had created a series of little-heralded initiatives, including aid to upgrade the port of Azerbaijan near Baku 'to allow up to 500,000 barrels a day of oil shipments from the eastern Caspian,' according to one U.S. Energy Department report. In 1995, the EU had initiated the Interstate Oil and Gas Transport to Europe (INOGATE) program with the goal, 'to promote the security of energy supplies.' In February 1999, just before the Clinton administration began bombing Belgrade, EU commissioner Hans van der Brock stated the goal of INOGATE to be 'to help free the huge gas and oil reserves of the Caspian Basin by overcoming ... bottlenecks which have impeded access to local and European markets.' The biggest bottleneck was about to come: a NATO strike on Belgrade.

Western European governments clearly saw the region from the Balkans to the Caspian Sea as a strategic focus for investment in alternative oil and gas supplies, a potential step to greater energy independence, especially as North Sea oil reserves began to decline. That was definitely not the vision of leading policy circles in Washington in 1999.

By the mid 1990s, partly through the active lobbying of Brzezinski and the major U.S. oil companies, the Clinton administration had begun to recognize the Caspian oil issue as a strategic priority. In July 1996, Washington created the Southern Balkan Development Initiative to discuss pipeline cooperation with Bulgaria, Macedonia and Albania. It backed two Caspian pipeline routes. One would go from Baku through Georgia to the Turkish port of Ceyhan. In 1997, former Bush secretary of state James Baker wrote an op-ed in the July 21 *New York Times* titled 'America's Vital Interest in the "New Silk Road."' Baker, who would later emerge as a major figure in a later Bush administration, argued that it 'was in the strategic interests of the United States to build the strongest possible economic, cultural and political ties to Georgia,' a country between the Caspian oil and Western markets. 'Caspian oil may eventually be as important to the industrialized world as Middle East oil is today,' he added. At the time, Baker was also attorney for the Baku interests of BP–Amoco.

A second pipeline route, AMBO or Albanian Macedonian Bulgarian Oil Pipeline Corp., backed by the U.S. government and First Boston Bank, had been on ice for several years. Before it could move ahead, Washington decided it had to eliminate the obstacle of the Milosevic regime.

Slobodan Milosevic, the elected Yugoslav president, a former banker who had once, when it was thought he might play the IMF game, enjoyed the backing of Washington, became a new 'Adolf Hitler' in the U.S. media. Numerous accounts from the region and from impartial outside observers confirmed that by the mid 1990s, all sides in the destabilized former Yugoslavia were guilty of atrocities— Bosnian Muslims, Croatian Catholics and Serb Orthodox Christians. Washington and NATO-scripted media reports concentrated, however, on only one side: the recalcitrant Serb president Milosevic. So long as a well-defended enclave remained in the middle of the Balkans, which rejected IMF 'reform' and the presence of NATO, the long-term geopolitical agenda of Washington for the control of the Caspian pipeline routes and central Asia was blocked.

By early 1999, the Clinton administration had decided the time was right to change all that. An indignant Milosevic rejected a U.S. demand at Rambouillet, the infamous Appendix B, mandating that he allow NATO troops to occupy Kosovo, and potentially Serbia, 'for humanitarian reasons of preventing genocide.' Milosevic's predictable rejection was used to justify war. Washington began a massive bombing campaign, ignoring the niceties of international law, the

UN Charter (and indeed any involvement at all of the UN in the process), the NATO charter (which specifies a purely defensive role), the 1975 Helsinki accords, and even the U.S. constitution (which mandates that only Congress has the power to declare war). President Clinton cited 'humanitarian' reasons and the threat of imminent genocide against Kosovo Albanians, and began a merciless bombing of civilian Serb targets.

Thousands of tons of bombs later, and after an estimated $40 billion of destruction to the economy and infrastructure of Serbia, the Pentagon began the construction of one of the largest U.S. military bases anywhere in the world. Camp Bond Steel near Gnjilane in southeast Kosovo, a fortress housing 3,000 soldiers, an airfield and state-of-the-art telecommunications, gave the United States a commanding and clearly permanent military presence in the strategic Balkans, within reach of the Caspian Sea.

In June 1999, as soon as the bombing of Serbia was over, the U.S. government announced it was funding a feasibility study for the AMBO pipeline. Referring to the imposition of NATO control over Serbia and Kosovo, a senior U.S. government official, Joseph Grandmaison, declared, 'The prospect that the U.S. government would guarantee security in the region and also provide financial guarantees, now makes it (AMBO) a much more attractive proposition.'

The AMBO engineering feasibility study had been undertaken by Halliburton Corporation's Brown & Root, when Dick Cheney was head of Halliburton. When the new study was published in May 2000, U.S. Ambassador Richard Armitage, later to become deputy secretary of state in the Bush administration, stated:

> In what one could term a 'bombing dividend' or a *quid pro quo* to the support provided by these surrounding states to NATO during the Kosovo conflict, Albania, Macedonia and Bulgaria now seek economic compensation from the West for their support.[6]

Much as the Baghdad railway represented the efforts of Continental Germany, before the First World War, to open a trade route to the Arabian Gulf, which would be independent of British naval control so a new series of pipelines through the Balkans could potentially offer the EU diversity of oil supply and a degree of energy independence from U.S. and Russian controlled energy sources. In the wake of the Kosovo war, the United States had preempted such possible energy independence, imposing NATO and U.S. control over possible pipeline routes and sources. As Belgrade dug out from the bombing and rubble of the Kosovo war, the U.S. appeared to be in firm control over any potential pipeline routes to the EU.

The military control of Eurasia by the sole superpower had taken a giant step forward by the end of the Kosovo war. Dollar democracy had marched ahead once more. The flag of the free market was firmly planted in a destroyed Yugoslavia. By 2001, Washington was in uncontested military control of the Balkans. The new U.S. ambassador to the Court of St. James in London, William Farish, son of a wealthy Texas oil family, pointed to the vast oil riches of the Caspian area as a major reason for American interest in the Balkans.

In a September 23, 2001, interview with the *Sunday Times*, Farish told of his planned trip to the Balkans, an unusual foray for an ambassador to Britain, to say the least. Farish was a trusted friend of the Bush family, an heir to the Standard Oil fortune, who understood oil geopolitics—no doubt the real reason he was at the Court of St. James as ambassador. He spoke of a strengthening of the NATO presence in the Balkans, as a consequence of the terror attacks on the United States that month, referring to the Balkans as a possible 'buffer zone against unstable regimes to the east.' He also mentioned the strategic importance of the Caspian energy resources and the pipeline routes.

As the new decade opened, Washington was the uncontested economic superpower, with its military dominance playing a less visible role. Within a few short months those roles had shifted dramatically. It took a Wall Street stock collapse, economic recession and unbelievable events in New York and Washington to bring about that shift. The consequences were to be significant for Americans and for the world.

# 13
# A New Millennium
# for Oil Geopolitics

## BUSH BRINGS BIG OIL BACK TO WASHINGTON

The Clinton Presidency ended in impeachment scandals and the deflation of the world's greatest financial bubble, the New York stock market. More than $7 trillion of paper vanished in a matter of months. The myth of a New Economy disintegrated, along with the pension hopes of millions of Americans and hundreds of billions in losses for foreign investors who had been lured by the prospect of fantastic gains. The presidential election campaign in 2000 pitted Vice President Al Gore against a largely unknown governor from Texas, a former oilman, whose main attribute appeared to be his ignorance of world politics.

George W. Bush took office in January 2001 after the most hotly contested election in modern history. He won on the basis of an extraordinary 5–4 Supreme Court intervention into the Florida vote, despite a clear popular-vote mandate for his rival, Gore. The Clinton focus on economic policy as the basis for extending American hegemony was no longer to be the focus of Washington policy.

Bush's leading cabinet choices were notable. Someone in a time machine could well have thought the clock had turned back to the time of father Bush, twelve years earlier. All the top cabinet posts were held by old cronies of George H.W. Bush, including Vice President Dick Cheney, Defense Secretary Donald Rumsfeld, Secretary of State Colin Powell, and even National Security Adviser Condi Rice. Cabinet choices were decided for the president by Cheney and James Baker, an immensely important figure who always seemed to appear in critical situations.

The oil background of Bush's inner circle was undeniable. Cheney had been chief executive of the world's leading geophysics and oil services company, Halliburton Inc. Rice had served on the board of Chevron Oil. Bush himself had extensive oil experience, and Commerce Secretary Don Evans was also an oilman. In short, the Bush administration which took office in January 2001 was steeped in oil and energy issues as no administration in recent U.S. history had been. Oil and geopolitics were back at center stage in Washington.

Clinton's era had been personified by his Treasury secretary, the Wall Street investment banker Robert Rubin and his 'strong dollar.' With an emphasis on multilateral cooperation, free-market economic policies and the IMF, Clinton had pushed a ruthless agenda of corporate globalization, to American advantage. He downplayed military spending, as well as oil geopolitics, until quite late.

By the start of the new century, powerful circles in the U.S. establishment had decided it was time for a change in emphasis. If the Treasury had been the symbol of power in the Clinton era, the Defense Department was to become the focal point of the Bush era. And, as during most of the cold war, its agenda was directly tied to oil geopolitics.

Dick Cheney's first job as Bush's vice president was to carry out a comprehensive review of U.S. energy policy. Cheney, who was clearly making most major policy decisions for the neophyte president, had acquired more power than any vice president in history.

Cheney turned for help to James Baker III, an old friend and mentor. After leaving Washington in 1992, Baker had endowed a major think tank, the Baker Institute, at Houston's Rice University. The Baker Institute energy group was notable. It included Kenneth Lay, head of the soon-to-be infamous Enron Corp., and one of Bush's most generous financial supporters. It included a board member of Shell, a top executive of BP, and the head of ChevronTexaco. Oil consultant Matthew Simmons was also in the group, and the Baker Institute board included the former Kuwaiti oil minister, Sheikh Saud Nasir al-Sabah.

Sheikh al-Sabah's daughter, in a curious postscript to the first Iraq war, was later identified as the Kuwaiti woman who had told the U.S. Congress in October 1990 that she had witnessed Iraqi soldiers taking Kuwaiti babies from their incubators. Her shocking testimony had been a major factor in getting U.S. popular support for Operation Desert Storm. That incident was later exposed as a PR stunt, fabricated by Hill & Knowlton, a Washington firm close to the Bush administration. The exiled Kuwaiti government had paid Hill & Knowlton $10.8 million to win friends for Kuwait in Washington on going to war with Iraq. Hill & Knowlton's Washington office was run at the time by Craig Fuller, former chief of staff to Vice President George Bush.

A California electricity crisis, soaring natural gas and oil prices, and a chaotic U.S. electricity grid were the publicly stated reasons for the president's asking Cheney to make proposals on a national energy strategy. The Cheney National Energy Policy Report gave a clear signal of what the new administration was about. Its message was buried in partisan debate and ignored. It should have been studied more carefully as a clue to the Bush agenda.

## 'WHERE THE PRIZE ULTIMATELY LIES'

The Baker Institute's energy strategy report formed the basis of the official Cheney task force recommendations to the president, the National Energy Policy Report of April 2001. Both the Baker and Cheney reports projected a dramatic increase in U.S. dependency on imported oil over the coming two decades. Baker's group identified growing shortages of world oil, and singled out Iraq for attention: 'Iraq remains a de-stabilizing influence to ... the flow of oil to international markets from the Middle East,' the Baker study declared. They didn't explain why. They simply called on Washington to 'restate goals with respect to Iraq policy.'

The Baker Institute study also recommended that Cheney's Energy Policy Group include 'representation from the Department of Defense.' The U.S. military and energy strategy were in effect to be one. The Baker report concluded, as a portent of what was to come, 'Unless the United States assumes a leadership role in the formation of new rules of the game, U.S. firms, U.S. consumers and the U.S. government [will be left] in a weaker position.' Cheney and the new administration did not hesitate to assume the leadership role, though few could imagine at that point just how the new rules would be formed.

Cheney's report emphasized a growing dependency of the United States economy on oil imports, and looked well into the future. After a passing mention of domestic energy alternatives, the core of the recommendations dealt with how the United States might secure new foreign oil sources. In this regard, the report noted a problem. Many of the areas in the world holding the largest oil resources were in the hands of national governments whose interests were not necessarily to help the U.S. energy agenda. Cheney's report noted that these 'foreign powers do not always have America's interests at heart.' What he meant was that a nationalist government with control of its own energy resources and with its own ideas of national development might not share the agenda of ExxonMobil or ChevronTexaco or Dick Cheney.

Cheney, Baker and others in the top policy circles of Washington had serious long-term concerns. They were privately alarmed at the state of world oil supplies, a theme which, for good reasons was rarely mentioned in public discussion. They were also thinking of how to get their hands on what remained.

Back in autumn 1999, at a private London Institute of Petroleum meeting, Cheney, then CEO of Halliburton, had told leading international oil executives that the Middle East would become an even more vital strategic center of needed oil reserves over the coming decades. In a preview of his 2001 energy report, Cheney told the oilmen:

> by 2010 we will need on the order of an additional fifty million barrels a day. So where is the oil going to come from? Governments and the national oil companies are obviously controlling about ninety percent of the assets. Oil remains fundamentally a government business.

The figure of 50 million barrels a day was almost two-thirds of total world oil output then at the time, a huge volume, equal to more than six times the total oil production of Saudi Arabia. The fact that Cheney also saw it as a problem that governments controlled their oil was highly significant, as Saddam Hussein and other heads of oil states were soon to learn.

Where would the world find six new Saudi Arabias? Cheney answered, 'While many regions of the world offer great oil opportunities, the Middle East, with two-thirds of the world's oil and the lowest cost, is still where the prize ultimately lies …' A year earlier, at a Texas oil meeting, Cheney hinted at what would be the focus of Bush administration oil geopolitics. Talking about the dangers and instability in Kazakhstan, Cheney, who was still CEO at Halliburton, retorted, 'You've got to go where the oil is … I don't worry about it a lot.' He had clearly thought about it a lot, though.

With undeveloped oil reserves perhaps even larger than those of Saudi Arabia, Iraq had become an object of intense interest to Cheney and the Bush administration very early on. Paul O'Neill, a Bush cabinet member who had been fired in late 2002 for not being a good team player, later revealed that, as president, Bush had decided to make Iraqi regime-change a top goal well before the September 11, 2001, terror attacks.

In a January 11, 2004, interview for *60 Minutes*, a popular U.S. TV program, the former Bush Treasury secretary stated that early in 2001, Bush began to focus on how to topple Iraq's government. 'From the very beginning, there was a conviction that Saddam Hussein was a bad person, and that he needed to go,' O'Neill recalled. 'For me, the notion of preemption, that the U.S. has the unilateral right to do whatever we decide to do is a really huge leap.' O'Neill, known for his stubborn honesty if not for his diplomacy, claimed that ten days after Bush took office, 'topic A' was Iraq. Eight months before Osama bin Laden and the war on terrorism were in the forefront, Bush and Cheney and the cabinet were looking at military options for removing Saddam Hussein.

Baker's group was by no means the first to put the spotlight on the need for regime change in Iraq. Nor were the attacks of September 11, 2001, the first occasion for senior U.S. industry, military, energy and political elites to discuss how to maintain their unique global hegemony.[1]

## 'THE NEW AMERICAN CENTURY'

A little-known Washington think tank issued a policy paper in September 2000, weeks before the U.S. presidential elections and a year before 9/11. The paper, titled 'Rebuilding America's Defenses,' was clearly meant to shape the policy of the next administration. The document had been prepared by an influential Republican group calling itself the Project for the New American Century, or PNAC.

Among the members of the PNAC were the same men who were to shape policy in the coming administration. The group included Halliburton chief Cheney, Don Rumsfeld and Paul Wolfowitz, who later became Rumsfeld's deputy defense secretary and a leading Iraq war hawk. It also included Cheney's later chief of staff, Lewis Libby, and Karl Rove, who went on to become George W. Bush's most powerful political strategist. Senior executives, such as Bruce Jackson of Lockheed Martin, one of the world's biggest defense firms, Richard Perle, and Florida Governor Jeb Bush, were involved too. The PNAC chairman was William Kristol, who had built a hawkish media empire around his *Weekly Standard*, with the help of a generous $10 million from London *Times* publisher Rupert Murdoch. Given these powerful backers, the PNAC report was worth careful reading. Few did so before September 11.

That PNAC report began with a simple question: 'Does the United States have the resolve to shape a new century favorable to American principles and interests?' They declared:

> The United States is the world's only superpower ... At present the United States faces no global rival ... America's grand strategy should aim to preserve and extend this advantageous position as far into the future as possible. There are, however, potentially powerful states dissatisfied with the current situation and eager to change it, if they can ...

The report made it clear that they had in mind various Eurasian powers, from Europe to the Pacific.

The Project for the New American Century praised a 1992 strategic white paper that Wolfowitz had written for Cheney, back when Cheney had been defense secretary during the first Iraq war, stating, 'The Defense Policy Guidance drafted in the early months of 1992 provided a blueprint for maintaining U.S. pre-eminence, precluding the rise of a great power rival and shaping the international security order in line with American principles and interests.' Bush ordered that 1992 policy paper to be buried. It became far too hot after a copy was leaked to the *New York Times* in early 1992. It had called for precisely the form of preemptive wars, to 'preclude' a great power rival, that George W. Bush made official as the U.S. national security strategy, the Bush doctrine, in September 2002.

Cheney and company now restated that 1992 imperial agenda for America in the post-cold war era. They declared that the United States 'must discourage advanced industrial nations from challenging our leadership, or even aspiring to a larger regional or global role.'

The PNAC group were not content only to dominate the earth, proposing that Washington create a 'worldwide command and control system.' They also called for the creation of 'U.S. space forces' to dominate space, for total control of cyberspace, and for the development of biological weapons 'that can target specific genotypes and may transform biological warfare from the realm of terror to a politically useful tool.' Biological warfare as a politically useful tool? Even George Orwell would have been shocked.

With uncanny prescience, that September 2000 PNAC report went on to identify what later became immortalized by George W. Bush as the 'Axis of Evil.' It singled out three regimes—North Korea, Iran and Iraq—as posing a special problem for the New American Century.

Months before the world, courtesy of CNN, witnessed the attacks on the World Trade Center and the Pentagon, or had even heard of Osama bin Laden, Cheney's PNAC had targeted Saddam Hussein's Iraq for special treatment, stating bluntly that U.S. policy should be to take direct military control of the Arabian Gulf. The report declared:

> The United States has for decades sought to play a more permanent role in Gulf regional security. While the unresolved conflict with Iraq provides the immediate justification, the need for a substantial American force presence in the Gulf transcends the issue of the regime of Saddam Hussein.

That sentence, on the 'need for a substantial American force presence in the Gulf,' was later read and reread in many quarters around the world, in the months before the bombing of Baghdad. Iraq was simply a useful excuse for Cheney, Wolfowitz and others to justify 'the need for a substantial American force presence in the Gulf ...' There was no talk of Iraqi weapons of mass destruction, or of its ties to terrorists.[2]

## FROM KABUL TO BAGHDAD: WAR ON TERROR OR WAR ON OIL?

If the Bush administration had been unprepared for the shock of September 11, 2001, they certainly wasted no time in preparing their response, the war on terror. Terror was to replace communism as the new global image of 'the enemy.' The new terrorists could be anywhere and everywhere. Above all, as the war was defined in Washington, they were mostly to be found in the Islamic regions which also happened to control most of the world's oil reserves. Old 'cold warriors' were galvanized again into action. Defense Secretary Donald Rumsfeld, now in his seventies, was in the center of global power politics as never before.

According to the account of *Washington Post* editor Bob Woodward in his book *Bush at War* (for which he got access to sensitive National Security council documents), one day after the collapse of the World Trade towers, on September 12, 2001, Secretary Donald Rumsfeld and Deputy Defense Secretary Paul Wolfowitz began to urge the president that Iraq should be 'a principal target of the first round in the war against terrorism.' This was even before any conclusive evidence had been presented as to who was behind the terror attacks.

With the support of Cheney, Secretary of State Colin Powell, who, as chairman of the Joint Chiefs of Staff, had been in charge of the first Gulf War, reportedly persuaded Bush that 'public opinion has to be prepared before a move against Iraq is possible.' Not that Powell was any dove. In 1992, he had declared that the United States needed sufficient power to 'deter any challenger from ever dreaming of challenging us on the world stage.' The impending campaign to remove the Taliban from Afghanistan was just to be the warm-up for the bigger fight. At the same time as the Afghan campaign was taking shape, Woodward reported that Bush was already ordering secret plans for an Iraq invasion.

Afghanistan, under the fundamentalist Islamic Taliban, had given sanctuary to a Saudi named Osama bin Laden. Bin Laden's organization, Al Qaida, was to be the first military target in Bush's newly-proclaimed war on terror. On September 18, 2001, the BBC quoted Niaz Niak, former Pakistani foreign secretary. Niak told the BBC he had been informed by senior U.S. officials at a mid-July Berlin meeting that 'military action against Afghanistan would go ahead by the middle of October.'

Washington had initially considered the Taliban government as a possible pipeline business partner. Taliban representatives were invited by Unocal to Texas in late 1997 to talk turkey, though no agreement was reached. Another Texas company, this one intimately close to Bush and Cheney, was also quietly negotiating possible pipeline routes through Afghanistan for Caspian oil and gas. The company was Enron, which collapsed in November 2001, in the largest case of corporate bankruptcy and fraud in U.S. history.

The company that Enron had asked to build the multibillion-dollar Afghan pipeline was Cheney's old Halliburton Company. There were indications that secret talks between Vice President Cheney and Enron chief and Bush financial backer Ken Lay involved Washington backing for the Enron pipeline through Afghanistan. Curiously, Cheney refused to release documents of his secret talks with Enron to the Congress General Accounting Office, forcing a court showdown. By that time, Enron's financial house of cards was collapsing.

The Taliban fell out of favor in Washington in July 2001, when U.S. negotiators proposed conditions for their pipeline, reportedly telling the Taliban leaders, 'Either you accept our offer on a carpet of gold, or we bury you under a carpet of bombs.' The Taliban was demanding U.S. aid to rebuild the Afghan infrastructure. They wanted the pipeline not only to be a transit line to India and beyond, but also to serve Afghan needs for energy. Washington rejected the demands. September 11, 2001, gave Washington the excuse to deliver its carpet of bombs to Kabul.

Unocal had broken off negotiations with the Taliban over possible pipeline routes. President Bush's national security adviser on Afghanistan and central Asia at the time was Zalmay Khalilzad, an Afghan close to the exiled Afghan king. Khalilzad was subsequently to be Bush's envoy to Afghanistan and later Iraq. He had also worked for Unocal on Afghan pipelines.

The Pentagon, with a touch of both the poetic and the patriotic, called the bombing of Afghanistan 'Operation Enduring Freedom.' The freedom seemed to be freedom for American troops to destroy what they deemed necessary in Afghanistan, a point later noted by disappointed Afghans with biting irony. How enduring it would be was open to doubt.

The Afghan military campaign ended with little fighting. The Taliban regime collapsed in early 2002. Most soldiers surrendered after getting generous CIA handouts of dollars. Khalilzad then recommended that Bush name another former Unocal consultant, Hamid Karzai, to be provisional Afghan president in the postwar ruins of Afghanistan.

Several years earlier, in February 1998, before a U.S. House of Representatives committee on international relations, a Unocal vice president, John Maresca, had urged Washington to back an Afghan pipeline route for the vast oil and gas reserves of central Asia. He spoke of the possible routes and declared, 'a route through Afghanistan appears to be the best option ... the one that would bring Central Asian oil closest to Asian markets.' It would proceed from northern Turkmenistan, through Afghanistan, into Pakistan and on to the Indian Ocean. From there it could serve the huge oil and gas markets of India, China and Japan. 'The territory across which the pipeline would extend is controlled by the Taliban,' he noted. After February 2002, the Taliban was no longer an obstacle.

The military attack on Afghanistan, the first strike in the new war on terror gave Washington many things. It gave it the pretext for a huge Pentagon budget increase to nearly $400 billion a year, and for building a ring of permanent U.S. military bases from Uzbekistan to Afghanistan and Kyrgyzstan, places deep inside the former Soviet Union territory. (The latter point was not lost on Russian thinkers around President Putin.) The U.S. removal of the Taliban also gave the world a flood of heroin, as old warlords suppressed by the Taliban were able to resume poppy cultivation.

The U.S. ambassador to Pakistan, Wendy Chamberlain, in January 2002 met with Usman Aminuddin, Pakistan's oil minister. The talks were about how to continue plans for a north–south pipeline to Pakistan's Arabian Sea oil terminal. In May 2002, according to a BBC report, Karzai announced plans to hold talks with Pakistan and Turkmenistan on a $2 billion gas pipeline from Turkmenistan to India. A deal was quietly signed in early January 2003, with no international press fanfare.

No sooner had Washington installed Karzai in Kabul than Bush and Cheney began beating the drums of war against Saddam Hussein, Washington's new Adolf Hitler, replacing Slobodan Milosevic in the gallery of evil tyrants. Washington set out to apply the Bush doctrine, regardless of whether the UN Security Council agreed. And they didn't.[3]

### 'YOU'VE GOT TO GO WHERE THE OIL IS'

Washington prepared its military attack on Baghdad in 2002 without UN Security Council backing, in violation of the UN Charter and without the support of most of its major allies, apart from Britain's Blair, Portugal and Spain, Poland and a few others. Russia, China, France and even Germany openly opposed the U.S. decision to go to war with Iraq. Russian Foreign Minister Igor Ivanov issued an official statement that Moscow was opposed to any U.S. military operation against Iraq. Russia's Lukoil and two Russian government companies had a 23-year contract to develop Iraq's West Qurna oilfield. China also was against war. Its China National Petroleum Company held a potentially huge oil contract in western Iraq. France too held rights to exploit Iraqi oil under the Saddam regime. All three powers knew that a unilateral U.S. war could end their Iraqi oil dreams for good.

China by then was well on its way to replace Japan as the world's second largest oil importer after the United States. Within ten years, at present growth rates, it would easily become the world's largest consumer of oil, almost all imported. It had not been able to find enough domestic oil. China knew its very future as an economic power depended on securing its oil. Now the most promising sources were about to be firmly put under American military control. In Beijing, the message was clear and very alarming.

As the countdown for Bush's Iraq war proceeded, despite pleas from the world community, the large unanswered question for much of the world was, Why? Why would the United States risk its entire standing as a force for peace and stability, its so-called 'soft power'? Why would it risk creating instability in the entire oil-producing world, perhaps even triggering a new oil price shock and a global economic depression, in order to strike Iraq? The official Washington answer was that Saddam Hussein had an arsenal of weapons of mass destruction and that he had ties to Al Qaida terrorists. Was that sufficient to explain the clear obsession of George W. Bush, Dick Cheney, Donald Rumsfeld, Paul Wolfowitz and others in Washington for a new Iraq war? Many were not convinced. Their skepticism was confirmed, but only after 130,000 American troops had been firmly entrenched in Iraq.

The military phase of the attack on Iraq, Operation Shock and Awe, was predictably over within weeks. It was no contest. Fighting was officially declared over in May 2003. There had been only token resistance, and no Iraqi use of dreaded weapons. Perhaps never in history had such a small land been hit with such devastating force and destruction. CNN and Rupert Murdoch's Fox Network made sure the message was seen around the world in graphic clarity. America was not to be treated lightly. The clear message was that the United States meant what George Bush had said, 'You are either with us or you are against us.'

Washington had insisted repeatedly that the justification for going to war had been to remove the imminent threat to the United States of Iraq's alleged arsenal of chemical, biological and even nuclear weapons. When UN inspectors found no weapons, they shifted, arguing that the real reason was that Saddam Hussein had forged an alliance with Osama bin Laden and the elusive Al Qaida terror group. Later, the argument was floated that it was desirable to replace a dictator with a democratic regime. After the war, Bush made the democracy theme the 'forward strategy of freedom' for U.S. policy in the Middle East. Ominously, buried in his January 2004 State of the Union address, Bush called for a doubling of the budget for the National Endowment for Democracy in order to develop 'free elections, free markets, free press and free labor unions in the Middle East.' Just as in Yugoslavia and across eastern Europe, Washington clearly planned to soften up the existing regimes for a change. The implications were enormous.

Once U.S. troops held control of the country, the weapons and terrorism arguments for war fell away, one-by-one. Tony Blair was exposed as having staked his political future on a fraudulent case. At times it appeared that his Washington allies had set Blair up to be a fall guy. Soon after U.S. occupation of Baghdad and Iraq's oilfields, various Washington officials began to admit that the reasons had not been what they had said.

The most brazen was Deputy Defense Secretary Paul Wolfowitz, author of the 1992 white paper calling for preemptive wars, coauthor of the September 2000 Project for the New American Century report and leading war hawk. In June 2003, less than a month after Bush officially declared an end to the fight for Iraq, Wolfowitz told delegates to a Singapore security conference, 'Let's look at it simply. The most important difference between North Korea and Iraq is that economically, we just had no choice in Iraq. The country swims on a sea of oil.' The fact that North Korea had admitted developing nuclear warheads and missiles was apparently of little concern to Wolfowitz and others in the Pentagon. Iraq was their goal.

By the end of December 2003, Washington had quietly removed a 400-man U.S.-led task force that had spent months searching for any clue of Iraqi weapons of mass destruction. They had come up with nothing. By January 2004, Colin Powell was forced to admit that the United States had no proof of Iraq–Al Qaida links, feebly insisting that the 'possibility' of such links had existed and that that was enough. Powell argued that Bush went to war because 'he believed that the region was in danger, America was in danger.' A respected Washington think tank, the Carnegie Endowment for International Peace, accused the administration of 'systematically misrepresenting' the danger of the alleged Iraqi weapons. The Powell comments left many wondering why Washington had risked so much on no firm evidence of imminent danger.

The Pentagon was in control of postwar reconstruction, not the State Department as would have been normal. The Pentagon's Wolfowitz made clear that only the administration's good friends would get lucrative contracts for the Iraqi oil industry. Cheney's Halliburton Corp. was at the top of the list, along with Bechtel and U.S. and British oil companies. Adding insult to injury, Washington then asked its allies in Europe, Russia and elsewhere to forgive their old debts to Iraq. As Washington had almost none, it stood to gain. It also asked foreign troops to take the burden, while refusing to allow UN control of peacekeeping. All in all, Washington's attitude seemed more imperial than democratic. George Bush had spoken piously of America's dream of bringing democracy to Iraq and other despotic Arab lands. Not surprisingly, democracy from the barrel of an Abrams tank was not the dream of most Iraqis.

Michael Meacher, a former Blair cabinet minister, who had resigned in June, just after the war, told the London *Guardian*, 'Bush's cabinet intended to take military control of the Gulf region whether or not Saddam Hussein was in power.' Meacher went on to make a shocking charge: '[I]t seems that the war on terror is being used largely as a bogus cover for achieving wider U.S. strategic geopolitical objectives.' Meacher also referred to the Cheney PNAC plan and the Baker Institute energy reports as providing the evident blueprint for Washington policy. The allegations of weapons of mass destruction and Al Qaida links were, for Meacher, just a smokescreen.

He saw a different possible explanation. The real issue, he argued, was, 'that the U.S. and UK are beginning to run out of secure hydrocarbon energy supplies ... The UK could be facing severe gas shortages by 2005.' The former cabinet minister pointed out that Britain, especially British oil majors BP and Shell, were keen not to be left out of the grab for the remaining world oil. Meacher recalled that 'Lord Browne, chief executive of BP, warned Washington not to carve up Iraq for its own companies in the aftermath of war.' Meacher had been UK environment minister and presumably knew of an unusual memo submitted to Blair's Cabinet Office just days before September 11.[4]

## THE PEAK OF OIL?

On September 9, 2001, the Cabinet Office of Prime Minister Blair had received a highly alarming memo with a simple title, 'Submission to the Cabinet Office on Energy Policy.' It had been prepared by the Oil Depletion Analysis Centre, a group of leading geologists.

The UK Cabinet Office memo was to the point: 'The world faces severe hydrocarbon supply difficulties.' It stated, 'Global oil supply is currently at political risk ... Large investments in Middle East production, if they occur, could raise output, but only to a limited extent. The main exception is Iraq ...' The Cabinet Office memo went on to forecast that 'global output of conventional oil will soon decline. The date of the peak depends on the size of Middle East reserves ... Best estimates put the global peak between five and ten years away.' The report predicted a global peak for natural gas too, perhaps 20 years away. The authors suggested that the government do the 'relatively straightforward work of checking these calculations.' But the memo was quietly buried.

Blair had well-informed oil advisers. They included BP's chairman, Lord Browne, who was also a close friend of the prime minister. In 1999, more than two years before the UK memo and a year before Bush's election, Mike Bowlin, chairman of the ARCO oil company, part of Lord Browne's BP, stated, 'We've embarked on the beginning of the last days of the age of oil.'

What Bowlin meant would have been quite clear to George W. Bush, James Baker and Dick Cheney. Curiously, such a profound issue, affecting economic stability and security, never once entered the public debate, during or after the 2000 elections campaign.

Many times during the past century, from the 1920s on, the world had been told that oil was near an end, and every time the doomsayers were proved wrong. Chicken Little was always shouting that the sky was about to fall. Why should the new warning be any more real than those of the 1970s?

The short answer is because, this time, there was much evidence to support the case. At the very least, the stakes were great enough to warrant a serious public debate. Curiously, unlike the earlier oil scares, this one generated no open discussion. That was most alarming.

The geologists did not predict that the world would run out of oil in five or ten years. They argued something else, namely, that the present availability of easy, cheap oil would decline dramatically, at a time when global demand, especially from China and other economically emerging regions such as India and Indonesia, would be exploding. They also argued that obvious alternatives, including heavy oil, coal or nuclear energy, would not be able to replace oil. The economic implications of their analysis were staggering. For almost a century, the world economy had been built on cheap, abundant oil.

Very serious independent geologists were behind the claims that world oil was nearing a decisive turning point, a peak as it was technically called. The chief figure at the UK Oil Depletion Analysis Centre, which had prepared the Cabinet Office report of September 9, 2001, was a well-respected geologist, Colin J. Campbell. His estimates were supported by some of the world's leading geologists, from such organizations as the Colorado School of Mines, Princeton University Geology Department, the French Petroleum Institute (IFP), Uppsala University, as well as private energy consultants, such as Douglas-Westwood Ltd. and Petroconsultants in Switzerland.

These prominent geologists argued quite simply that increasing global oil demands, in order to sustain even modest global population and economic growth over the coming decade or more, would coincide with the dramatic decline in oil production from many of the largest fields, such as the North Sea, Alaska's Prudhoe Bay and others in Mexico, Russia and Nigeria.

In a May 2003 conference on the subject of peak oil, Matthew Simmons, an American energy expert and adviser to both Cheney and George Bush, gave alarming testimony. Simmons had been a leading member of the Baker Institute energy group and one of the main authors of the report to Cheney. He was no minor figure, but an insider in the Bush administration energy discussions. Simmons told the international group of geologists and energy specialists at the French Petroleum Institute, 'Five years ago I barely had thought about the question of, "What does peaking mean and when might it occur?"' He then stated, 'The worry is that peaking is at hand, not years away ... If I am right, the unforeseen consequences are devastating ... unfortunately the world has no Plan B if I'm right.'

Simmons went on to describe the implications for the world economy, in terms of transport, food and industry, of a sudden shortage of basic energy at the current low cost. He stated, 'There aren't any good energy solutions for bridges, to buy some time, from oil and gas to the alternatives. The only alternative right now is to shrink our economies.' In so many words, he predicted that the only prospect was for the world to go into deep recession or depression.

In a July 2002 study on the subject of remaining oil reserves, Colin Campbell stated, 'The watershed for oil comes around 2010, followed five years later by the peak of oil and natural gas combined.' He pointed out that oil supplied 40 per cent of all world energy needs and 90 per cent of transportation fuel. 'It is evident the world will have to learn to use less, much less,' Campbell concluded.

The geologists defined oil peaking as the point where at least half a given field's oil has been extracted. After the peak, each additional barrel requires ever more input in terms of pressure to maintain oil extraction. Injecting gas or water into old fields is costly. That implies that as the world's major fields pass their peak, oil costs are likely to explode. This time, the peak predicted was not of one oil field or even one producing country. It was an absolute peak, a worldwide peak in oil.

Campbell predicted, 'Beyond 2005, the energy required to find and extract a barrel of oil will exceed the energy contained in the barrel.'

He added that over the past 20 years, despite more than $1 trillion spent trying to find new untapped oil fields to replace the aging North Sea, Alaska and other fields, oil companies had not been able even to keep up with current consumption. Campbell estimated that for every new barrel discovered, four were being used, an alarming trend.

In another study on the peak oil problem, Matthew Simmons pointed to alarming statistics confirming the dismal rate of new oil discoveries. 'The top 10 public exploration and production companies spent $195 billion between 2000–2002, to grow production from 22.4 to 24.1 million barrels oil equivalent a day.' Acquisitions of existing oil and gas properties were responsible for 93 per cent of that. Simmons went on to predict that rates of decline of existing oil and gas supply would 'consume all of the current base within 10–15 years,' that is, by 2010 or 2015.

Once a major oilfield had peaked, it was only a matter of time before the production declined dramatically, precipitously. Campbell cited examples in the North Sea of older fields, such as Brent, which had lost 90 per cent of its output in the space of four or five years after peaking. That might also explain why the world was unaware of the looming crisis. Many of the major oil sources of the past 30 or so years were at or near peak, while statistics for total reserves gave the illusion of plenty. The major companies and governments all had a vested interest in downplaying the staggering implications of the problem. The Bush administration had more than a passing interest in the question of peak oil. The future of the American century, of Pax Americana itself, was on the line.

In effect, Campbell and other independent geologists confirmed Cheney's 1999 London estimate. Campbell had concluded that the only region of the world which still had significant undeveloped oil, at low cost, was the Middle East.

Campbell and Simmons both pointed to a unique geological formation, a triangle which holds perhaps 65 per cent or more of the world's remaining oil reserves. It encompasses five countries: Iraq, Iran, Saudi Arabia, Kuwait and the Emirates, notably, Qatar. The largest of those undeveloped Middle East oil reserves were reportedly in Iraq. Some U.S. government studies estimated that Iraq might hold as much as 432 billion barrels of unexplored oil resources, far more than Saudi Arabia. The strategic importance of Iraq and the entire Middle East, in a world where other sources of oil had peaked, was preprogrammed to grow exponentially over the next few years. And that oil was still controlled by Arab governments.

The president of ExxonMobil Exploration Company, Jon Thompson, writing in a company magazine in early 2003, indirectly confirmed the basic analysis of the geologists who predicted a global oil crisis by between 2010 and 2015. Thompson was careful not to speak directly of peak oil problems. Yet his message was clear enough.

Thompson wrote:

> We estimate world oil and gas production from existing fields is declining at an average rate of 4–6 per cent a year. To meet projected demand in 2015, the industry will have to add about 100 million oil-equivalent barrels a day of new production. That's equal to about 80 per cent of today's production level. In other words, we will need to find, develop and produce a volume of new oil and gas that is equal to eight out of every 10 barrels being produced today. In addition, the cost associated with providing this additional oil and gas is expected to be considerably more than what industry is now spending.

Those remarks of one responsible for new oil and gas finds for the world's largest energy company were a bombshell. He stated in effect that the world faced a dramatic need for new oil and gas in the coming decade, beyond anything found to date. And the cost of securing new energy would be 'considerably more.' Thompson titled his piece, appropriately, 'A revolutionary transformation.'

If those alarming estimates of an early crisis in the world's present energy supply are accurate, or even close, the implications for the world economy are orders of magnitude greater than the oil shocks of the 1970s. Kenneth Pollack, a former senior Clinton National Security Council Middle East specialist, who backed the Iraq invasion, put it bluntly: '[T]he global economy built over the last 50 years, rests on a foundation of inexpensive, plentiful oil, and if that foundation were removed, the global economy would collapse.'

In short, the looming depletion of a major share of world oil and gas, due to take effect around the end of the first decade of the century, sometime around 2010 or 2015, perhaps even sooner, would explain the drive to unilateral military action in Iraq by the Bush administration, despite the enormous risks. It could also explain much more about U.S. domestic and foreign policy motives under Bush.

If U.S. military control over Iraq and over future Iraq oil flows went unchallenged, Washington would hold the trump cards over all potential economic rivals. Before the war, Iraq's government had signed long-term oil development deals with Russia, France and China. Washington strategists around the Pentagon did not overlook the fact that those three were rivals for oil in any future crisis. Nor did Cheney. Among the documents which Cheney refused to make public at the time of his 2001 Energy Task Force were detailed oilfield maps and lists of just which foreign companies had business in Iraq. The documents were partially made public, but only well after the Iraq occupation had been secured.

As the rubble in Iraq was cleared for oil development in early 2004, Washington declared that oil and reconstruction contracts would go only to those who had helped her take Iraq. The first oil companies to reap the gains were ChevronTexaco, Condi Rice's old company, BP and Shell of the UK, and Cheney's Halliburton.

Even as war in Iraq was being prepared, Doha in Qatar had become the major American military base in the Gulf, allowing reduced reliance on Saudi Arabia's Prince Bandar Air Base. By early 2004, Iraq faced a long U.S. military occupation, perhaps lasting decades. Robert Kagan, an author of the Cheney Project on the New American Century report, which had called for taking Iraq, told the *Atlanta Journal-Constitution*, months after the Iraq war, 'We will probably need a major concentration of forces in the Middle East over a long period of time ... If we have a force in Iraq, there will be no disruption in oil supplies.'

As the world viewed the results of Bush's war in Iraq, the conclusion was inescapable that American military might had been used to secure direct control of the world's largest oil resources. This also explained the lack of concern in Washington over weapons of mass destruction once Iraq had been conquered.[5]

## OIL AND BASES: REMOVING THE OBSTACLES

If the gloomy estimate of the imminent peaking of world oil explained why Washington had been prepared to take such extreme risks to control Iraq, it also offered an explanation for many puzzling new U.S. foreign policy initiatives, from the African west coast to Libya and Sudan, from Colombia and Venezuela to Russia and Georgia, as well as Baku and Afghanistan.

As Bush prepared his bid to secure reelection, a definite pattern to U.S. military policy and to U.S. energy policy was clear. The conclusion was inescapable. U.S. foreign and military policy was now about controlling every major existing and potential oil source and transport route on earth. Such control would be unprecedented. One superpower, the United States, would be in a position to decide who gets how much energy and at what price. On the eve of an approaching supply crisis, whose impact would be potentially devastating to the world's economy and social stability, such power held unimaginable potential. Washington appeared to be waging what one critic called resource wars.

In the face of unexpected and imminent global supply shortages, especially in fast-growing regions like China and India, the United States, as the world's only military superpower, would be in a position to dictate the terms of world economic development. It would have unprecedented power to allow or deny the most economically essential raw material, oil. To be able to control the coming resource crisis, Washington would have to act well before the world realized what was at stake. Deception would be essential. There seemed to be no shortage of that in Bush's Washington.

Another speaker at the same May 2003 Paris peak oil conference was Michael Klare, author of studies on resource. He cited a little-noted remark by Bush Energy Secretary Spencer Abraham to a March 2001 National Energy Summit. The Bush energy official had warned, 'America faces a major energy supply crisis over the next two decades. The failure to meet this challenge will threaten our nation's economic prosperity, compromise our national security, and literally alter the way we lead our lives.' Referring to the Cheney energy report of 2001, Klare remarked, 'The overall emphasis is on removing obstacles—whether political, economic, legal and logistical—to the increased procurement of foreign oil by the United States.' He added, '... the Cheney energy plan will also have significant implications for U.S. security policy and for the actual deployment and utilization of American military forces.'

The prospect of a sudden, unexpected global peaking of present oil and gas supplies, perhaps before the end of the decade, some five to seven years off, would indeed explain Washington's mood of obsessive determination for war. It would also explain why respected establishment media like the *New York Times*, in a January 2003 feature piece by Michael Ignatieff, would argue the case for empire when describing American foreign policy—something that previously would have been inconceivable for that traditional liberal paper.

Over the course of the Bush administration, the United States had managed to extend its military power and presence, step by step, into areas of the globe where this had never before been possible.

The collapse of the Soviet economic structure had prepared the possibilities and permitted the extension of a Washington-controlled NATO presence into what Brzezinski called the 'heartland,' right up to Russia's front door.

Commenting on whether there had been a conscious linkage between Bush's energy policy and his military security strategy, Klare noted:

> ... what is undeniable is that President Bush has given top priority to the enhancement of America's power projection capabilities, while at the same time endorsing an energy strategy that entails increased U.S. dependence on oil derived from areas of recurring crisis and conflict ... One arm of this strategy is aimed at securing more oil from the rest of the world; the other is aimed at enhancing America's capacity to intervene in exactly such locales ...

Klare concluded, 'They have merged into a single, integrated design for American world dominance in the 21st Century.'

In the aftermath of the Iraq war, U.S. bases had been extended to Uzbekistan and Kyrgyzstan in the former Soviet domain and to Afghanistan. From its military position in Afghanistan, U.S. forces could control most of south Asia. Pakistan was dependent on U.S. military pressure. The entire Gulf was now a U.S. military protectorate.

With the military control secure in the wake of the Iraq war, one by one the energy dominoes around the world began to fall, with a hefty push from Washington. Georgia, lying on a key pipeline route from the Caspian to Ceyhan in Turkey, was a de facto U.S. protectorate by the beginning of 2004, when Mikhail Saakashvili, a 36-year-old U.S-educated lawyer, took over the presidency in a 'rose revolution.' The latter was supported by Washington and the Soros Foundation, and aided by the personal intervention of James Baker, whose law firm also represented the Caspian Sea BP oil interests.

In early 2003, while all eyes were on Iraq, the Pentagon prepared a long-term military basing agreement with two tiny Pacific islands, São Tomé and Príncipe, which conveniently were within striking distance of the strategic west African oilfields stretching from Morocco to Nigeria, Equatorial Guinea and Angola. George Bush made a highly unusual tour of west Africa to coincide with the deal. Some analysts in Washington estimated that up to 25 per cent of U.S. oil needs would soon come from west Africa. They called the Gulf of Guinea an area of 'vital interest' to the United States. The Cheney energy policy report had said that west Africa was 'expected to be one of the fastest-growing sources of oil and gas for the American market.' Behind the scenes, the United States had been pushing the French from their traditional role in various African oil regions.

Libya was also falling into the U.S. orbit. In January 2004, Colonel Qaddafi announced his rejection of terror and opening up of Libya to foreign oil investment, in return for a U.S. lifting of sanctions. Remarking on his new embrace of Washington, Qaddafi noted, 'It is the era of globalization, and there are many new factors which are mapping out the world.' Libya still held considerable oil, and Washington wanted to get its hands on it. Libya had begun signing major deals with Japanese, Italian, French and other foreign companies not bound by the U.S. sanctions. It had already signed with China to build oil and gas pipelines. Now that would all change. American oil companies were invited back. Qaddafi had become a survivalist.

In Sudan, the government in Khartoum signed an agreement in January 2004 to share the oil wealth of the rebel south, ending two decades of civil war. Washington was behind the deal. Sudan had been working with Chinese and European oil companies, and U.S. firms were excluded by Washington sanctions policy. Sudan had significant oil reserves and Washington decided the time was ripe to get them too.

Colombian oil and that of neighboring Venezuela were also subject to growing U.S. military presence. The Bush administration announced plans to spend $98 million to provide military training and support in Colombia. This was not intended to stop the flood of cocaine into the United States. It was to resist the guerillas of the FARC and ELN, who threatened the large Occidental Petroleum pipeline there. Colombia had become the seventh-largest oil supplier to the United States. And when the Venezuelan president, Hugo Chavez, tried to take more direct policy control of the Venezuelan state oil company, the Bush administration attempted a covert coup. (U.S. oil imports from Venezuela, Colombia and Ecuador exceeded those from the entire Middle East.) The same applied to the oil and gas of Indonesia: the terror war opened the doors to a new, far stronger U.S. military presence. One American analyst, Zoltan Grossman, remarked, '[E]stablishment of new bases may in the long run be more critical to U.S. war planners than the wars themselves, as well as to the enemies of the U.S.'

By the end of his first term in office, George W. Bush, the neophyte in foreign affairs, had presided over the most dramatic extension of American military power in its history. U.S. military bases allowed it to control the strategic energy routes of all Eurasia as never before. It could control future energy relations with Japan, China, East Asia, India and Russia, as well as the European Union. Belgian author Michel Collon put it bluntly: 'If you want to rule the world, you need to control oil. All the oil. Anywhere.' That was clearly just what Washington was doing.

When an energy-dependent Japan had tried to sign a long-term deal to develop a major oilfield in Iran in August 2003, after the Iraq war, Washington stopped Japan from signing, citing Iran's nuclear program as reason. Tokyo got the message. By October, they were frantically trying to outbid China for Russian oil from the Yukos company, at a time when the Russian company was talking with George H.W. Bush about selling a dominant share of Yukos to ChevronTexaco. The Washington oil radar was monitoring everyone, anywhere.

In the wake of the U.S. occupation of Iraq, it became clear that the United States was determined, one way or another, to lock up every major source of oil and natural gas it could. Small wonder that many outside the United States began to question the motives of the American president and his declared mission of spreading freedom and democracy. His proposal to advance democracy in the Middle East through doubled funding for the National Endowment for Democracy was hardly reassurance.

Anatol Lieven analyzed the U.S. push for war just before the march on Baghdad. Lieven, of the Carnegie Endowment for International Peace in Washington, remarked:

> The basic and generally agreed plan is unilateral world domination through absolute military superiority, and this has been consistently advocated and worked on by the group of intellectuals close to Dick Cheney and Richard Perle since the collapse of the Soviet Union in the early 1990's.

Lieven tied the agenda of the Cheney circle directly to the strategic issue of oil: 'For the group around Cheney, the single most important consideration is guaranteed and unrestricted access to cheap oil, controlled as far as possible at its source.'[6]

'FULL SPECTRUM DOMINANCE'

The stakes in securing military control over Iraqi oil and the entire Arabian Gulf were so high, and the resulting ability to determine the entire economic future of Eurasia and other countries so vital to America's new imperial strategy, that the costs were clearly considered worth risking.

The Bush administration's economic policy was simple: Win reelection in 2004 regardless of what it takes. Washington was running staggering budget deficits of the order of $500 billion a year. Its deficit in trade was just as high. China and Japan and east Asian exporters invested hundreds of billions of their surplus trade dollars in U.S. Treasury and other assets, out of fear of losing exports, becoming more dependent on the United States in the process. They seemed to be caught up in a process from which they could find no exit.

Alarming as the economic data out of Washington was, no one in either the Federal Reserve or the administration appeared concerned. They now controlled the most essential commodity for world economic growth, its oil. And they controlled it not indirectly, through the support of various regimes in oil regions, but directly, militarily. With their firm grip on world oil flows, they now held a true weapon of mass destruction, potential blackmail over the rest of the world. Who would dare challenge the dollar?

The contrast between the first oil shock in the 1970s and the events after the Iraq invasion was dramatic. The 1973 Bilderberg policy, set out in Saltsjöbaden, Sweden, had been to raise oil prices high enough to make the new discoveries in the North Sea, Alaska and other non-OPEC regions profitable. That first oil shock managed to buy some time for the dollar system.

In the 1970s, powerful groups such as the Bilderberg and the Trilateral Commission had been able to postpone the impact of that first oil shock on Europe, Japan, and above all the United States. They did this by imposing the IMF system on the aspirations of most of the emerging world, crushing any nationalist movement for economic development and self-sufficiency.

They called this 'sustainable' growth. It sustained the rich nations of the industrial world and the dollar system for more than three decades, by enforcing 'limits to growth' on the rest of the world. The industrial world was able to live some three decades more under the illusion of abundant, cheap oil supporting a living standard unprecedented in history. That illusion, however, had been bought at the cost of the well-being of the populations of the once-developing world, from Africa to Latin America to Asia. Only through stifling the natural aspirations of most of the rest of the world for economic stability and growth could a small handful of nations, led by the United States, enjoy that illusion of prosperity for a little longer.

The IMF played a central role in making that illusion possible. By artificially depressing the industrialization of most of the planet, Washington could depress the global demand for oil, and allow U.S. imports of cheap oil to continue to fuel their artificial prosperity. American oil output had peaked in the early 1970s. The American way of life depended on an ever rising import of foreign oil.

By the beginning of the new century, even that illusion of abundant, cheap oil was no longer sustainable. The IMF treatment, or its equivalent, was turned on the populations of the industrial world for the first time. As an absolute world oil peak approached, the United States adopted unilateral measures to preserve its power, from rejecting the Kyoto protocol, to refusing to accept the jurisdiction of the International Court of Justice over its soldiers and officials, to the invading of Iraq and beyond.

Thirty years after the first oil shock, the largest new fields had already passed their peak. Washington and the major British and American oil giants no longer had the luxury of counting on regimes with state-owned oil companies to do their bidding. Direct U.S. and British control of world oil and gas assets was the agenda. They preferred to call it promoting democracy in the Middle East. All the evidence pointed to an imminent world peak, an absolute peak, in oil resources, and Washington was leaving little to chance. If 1973 had been a warning call, it was increasingly clear that 2003 was not. It was for real.

At the start of the new millennium, the United Stated held a near monopoly on military technology and might. It commanded the world's reserve currency and with it was able to control the assets of much of the industrial world. Following the occupation of the oil fields of Iraq, one power, the United States, now commanded a near monopoly on future energy resources. The Pentagon had a term for it—'full spectrum dominance.' It meant that the United States should control military, economic and political developments, everywhere. They appeared to be well along in the project.

Critics of the unilateral U.S. hegemony saw America's imperial striving as a consequence of her fundamental weakness, not her strength. Emmanuel Todd, an adviser to the French president, Jacques

Chirac, was one. He projected an alternative coalition of interests between a French and German-centered Europe and Russia, the combination of Eurasian land powers that both Halford Mackinder and Brzezinski had warned against. But by early 2004, that Eurasian coalition was in sad disarray and internal division. The European Union could not even agree on a constitution. Washington appeared to have few serious rivals on the horizon.

The late scholar Edward Said wrote in *Al-Ahram*, just after the invasion of Iraq:

> Every single empire, in its official discourse, has said that it is not like all the others, that its circumstances are special, that it has a mission to enlighten, civilize, bring order and democracy, and that it uses force only as a last resort.

He did not live long enough to see whether or not his words would be borne out with the New American Century.[7]

# Notes

CHAPTER 1

1.  Commenting on the British free-trade policy in 1851, American economist Henry C. Carey, architect of the national economic strategy of Abraham Lincoln, noted,

    > We have thus here a system that is unsound and unnatural, and second, a theory invented for the purpose of accounting for the poverty and wretchedness which are its necessary results. The miseries of Ireland are charged to over-population, although millions of acres of the richest soils of the kingdom are waiting drainage to take their place among the most productive in the world, and although the people of Ireland are compelled to waste more labor than would pay, many times over, for all the cloth and iron they consume ... Over-population is the ready excuse for all the evils of a vicious system, and so will it continue to be until that system shall see its end. To maintain it, the price of labor in England must be kept steadily at a point so low as to enable her to underwrite the Hindoo, the German, and the American, with all the disadvantage of freight and duties ...
    >
    > England had monopolized machinery for so long a time that she had acquired skill that could not readily be rivaled; while she had, by this improper division of her population, kept the price of labor and capital at a lower point ... than among her neighbors. Her establishments were gigantic, and always ready to sink those who might undertake competition; while the unceasing changes in her monetary arrangements, the necessary consequences of the colonial system, were of themselves sufficient to spread ruin among all the nations connected with her.

    Carey cites the experience of America, with bank panics and an economic depression beginning in 1837. After the 1820s, American credit had shifted more and more into the control of the banks of the City of London and away from List's notion of national economy.

    In Britain, on the effects of free trade on labour, he notes, 'Women have been substituted for men, and children of the most immature years for women, and the hours of labor have been so far extended as to render Parliamentary interference absolutely necessary.' He rails at the

    > awful consequences that have resulted from this effort to tax the world by monopolizing machinery. The moral effects are as bad as the physical ones. Frauds of every kind have become almost universal. Flour is substituted for cotton ... The quality of iron and of all other

commodities is uniformly reduced to the point required for preventing other nations from producing such commodities for themselves.

Carey cites the 1846 Corn Laws repeal as the watershed of policy:

> Let us now look to the results [of the 1846 Corn Laws Repeal Act] as exhibited in the immediate dependencies of England. With this vast increase in the importation of food from abroad has come the ruin of the people of Ireland. Deprived of manufacture and commerce, her people were driven to live by agriculture alone, and she was enabled to drag on a miserable existence, so long as her neighbor was content to make some compensation for the loss of labor by paying her for her products higher prices than those at which they might have been elsewhere purchased ...
>
> With the repeal of the Corn Laws, that resource has failed, and the result is a state of poverty, wretchedness and famine, that has obliged the [Irish] landowner to maintain the people, whether they work or not; and thus is one of the conditions of slavery re-established in that unhappy country. From being a great exporter of food, she has now become a large importer. The great market for Indian corn is Ireland—a country in which the production of food is almost the sole occupation of the people ... The whole system has for its object an increase in the number of persons that intervene between the producer and the consumer ... thus it is that Ireland is compelled to waste more labor annually than would be required to produce, thrice over, all the iron, and convert into cloth all the cotton and wool manufactured in England.

Henry C. Carey. *The Harmony of Interests: Agricultural, Manufacturing and Commercial*. Philadelphia: J.S. Skinner, 1851. pp. 60–65.

2.  E. Peshine Smith. *A Manual of Political Economy*. New York: George P. Putnam, 1853. pp. 149–52.
3.  Friedrich List. *The National System of Political Economy* (1885 edition. London: Longman, Green). Reprinted New York: Augustus M. Kelley, 1966.
4.  Peshine Smith. *Political Economy* (emphasis in original).

## CHAPTER 2

1.  Karl Erich Born. *Wirtschafts-und Sozialgeschichte des Deutschen Kaiserreichs (1867/71–1914)*. Stuttgart: Steiner Verlag, 1985.
2.  Knut Borchardt. *Deutsche Wirtschaft seit 1870. (German Economy, 1870 to the Present)*. London: Weidenfeld & Nicholson, 1967.
3.  Ernst Loeb. 'The German Exchange Act of 1896.' *Quarterly Journal of Economics*. Vol. xi. Boston, 1897.
4.  Henri Hauser. *Germany's Commercial Grip on the World* (translated from the French). New York: Chas. Scribner & Sons, 1918. pp.106–8.
5.  Sir Llewellyn Woodward. In *Prelude to Modern Europe*. Norfolk: Methuen, 1971. p. 135.

## CHAPTER 3

1. Anton Mohr. *The Oil War*. New York: Harcourt Brace, 1926.
2. Ibid. p. 124.
3. Frank C. Hanighen. *The Secret War*. New York: John Day, 1934.
4. Karl Helfferich. *Der Weltkrieg: Vorgeschichte des Weltkrieges*. Ullstein: Berlin, 1919. pp. 120–65.
5. R.G.D. Laffan. *The Serbs: The Guardians of the Gate* (1917). Reprinted New York: Dorset Press, 1989. pp. 163–4.
6. Ahmad Mustafa Abu-Hakima. *The Modern History of Kuwait*. London: Luzak, 1983. pp. 188–97.
7. Hanighen. *Secret War*. pp. 22–3.
8. Helfferich. *Weltkrieg*. pp. 165–6.
9. H.G. Wells. *An Experiment in Autobiography*. New York: Macmillan, 1934. pp. 658–9.
10. Gabriel Hanotaux. 'Fashoda: The African Negotiation.' *La Revue des Deux Mondes*. Paris, February 1909. T.H. Von Laue. *Sergei Witte and the Industrialization of Russia*. New York: Atheneum, 1974.

## CHAPTER 4

1. Sir George Paish. 'Memorandum on British Gold Reserves sent to Chancellor.' January 1914. Treasury files of British Public Record Office. T 171 53.
2. Paish. 'Letter to the Chancellor Lloyd George, dated, 2 A.M. Saturday, Aug. 1, 1914.' Public Record Office. T 170 14.
3. Frank C. Hanighen. *The Secret War*. New York: John Day, 1934. pp. 82–3.
4. 'Documents on British Foreign Policy, 1919–1939.' First series. Vol. iv. pp. 245–47.
5. T.E. Lawrence. *Seven Pillars of Wisdom*. London: Cape, 1935. p. 24.
6. J. Nevakivi. *Britain, France and the Arab Middle East, 1914–1956*. London, 1969. p. 264.
7. Z.N. Zeine. *The Struggle for Arab Independence: Western Diplomacy and the Rise and Fall of Faisal's Kingdom in Syria*. Beirut, 1960. p. 59.
8. N.A. Rose. *The Gentile Zionists: A Study in Anglo-Zionist Diplomacy, 1929–39*. London: Frank Cass, 1973.
9. Derek Wilson. *Rothschild: A Story of Wealth and Power*. London: Mandarin, 1990. p. 341.
10. Philip Kerr (Lord Lothian). *Round Table*. August 1911. pp. 422–3.
11. Halford J. Mackinder. *Democratic Ideals and Reality*. New York: W.W. Norton, 1969. p. 89.
12. Carroll Quigley. *The Anglo-American Establishment from Rhodes to Cliveden*. New York: Books in Focus, 1981. p. 5.

## CHAPTER 5

1. R.A. Dayer. 'British War Debts to the United States'. *Pacific Historical Review*. No. 45. November 1976. p. 577.

2. Kathleen Burk. *Britain, America and the Sinews of War: 1914–1918*. London: George Allen & Unwin, 1985.
3. Thomas W. Lamont: 'Foreign Government Bonds.' *Annals of the American Academy*. March 1920. p.121.
4. Carroll Quigley. *The Anglo-American Establishment: From Rhodes to Clivden*. New York: Books in Focus, 1981.
5. Frank C. Costigliola. 'Anglo-American Financial Rivalry in the 1920s.' *Journal of Economic History*. Vol. xxxvii, no. 4. December 1977.
6. Anton Mohr. *The Oil War*. New York: Harcourt Brace, 1926.
7. Frank C. Hanighen. *The Secret War*. New York: John Day, 1934.
8. Mohr. *Oil War*. p. 138.
9. Ibid. pp. 222–3.

CHAPTER 6

1. Stephen V.O. Clarke. 'The Reconstruction of the International Monetary System: The Attempts of 1922 and 1933.' *Princeton Studies in International Finance*. No. 33. November 1973.
2. Frank C. Hanighen. *The Secret War*. New York: John Day, 1934.
3. Gustav Stolper, Karl Häuser and Knut Borchardt. *Deutsche Wirtschaft seit 1870*. Tübingen, 1966.
4. Anton Zischka. *Ölkrieg: Wandlung der Weltmacht*. Leipzig: Wilhelm Goldmann Verlag, 1939. (Zischka draws heavily on the earlier research of Hanighen, though omitting to mention this in the credits. The reason for this is not clear.)
5. Z.N. Zeine. *The Struggle for Arab Independence: Western Diplomacy and the Rise and Fall of Faisal's Kingdom in Syria*. Beirut, 1960. p. 59.
6. Stolper et al. *Deutsche Wirtschaft*.
7. Ibid.
8. Otto Pfleiderer. *Währung und Wirtschaft in Deutschland 1876–1975*. Frankfurt: Deutsche Bundesbank, 1976. p. 194.
9. Carroll Quigley. *Tragedy and Hope: A History of the World in Our Time*. London: Collier-Macmillan, 1966.
10. John M. Blair. *The Control of Oil*. New York: Pantheon Books, 1976.
11. U.S. Federal Trade Commission. 'The International Petroleum Cartel.' Report to U.S. Senate Small Business Committee. 82nd Congress, 2nd Session, 1952. p. 245.
12. Dieter Stiefel. *Finanzdiplomatie und Weltwirtschaftskrise: Die Krise der Creditanstalt für Handel und Gewerbe, 1931*. Frankfurt a.M.: Fritz Knapp Verlag, 1989.
13. Richard H. Meyer. *Bankers' Diplomacy: Monetary Stabilization in the 1920's*. New York: Columbia University Press, 1970.
14. Lars-Jonas Ångström. 'Ivar Kreuger blev mördad!' *Svenska Marknaden*. August 1987. Stockholm.
15. Truman Smith. *Berlin Alert: The Memoirs and Reports of Truman Smith*. Stanford Calif.: Hoover Institution Press, 1984.
16. Among the more useful references for this little-discussed topic are J. and S. Pool. '*Hitlers Wegbereiter zur Macht: Die geheimen deutschen und*

*internationalen Geldquellen, die Hitlers Aufsteig zur Macht ermöglichten.'*
München: Scherz Verlag, 1979; Heinz, Pentzlin. 'Hjalmar Schacht.'
Berlin: Verlag Ullstein GmbH, 1980; Also useful is Harold James. *The
German Slump: Politics and Economics 1924–1936.* Oxford: Clarendon
Press, 1986.

## CHAPTER 7

1. United States National Archive. 'Memorandum of Alling to A.A. Berle
   and Secretary of State Dean Acheson.' December 14, 1942. 890F.24/20.
2. U.S. Senate Select Committee on Small Business. 'ECA and MSA Relations
   with International Oil Companies Concerning Petroleum Prices.' 82nd
   Congress, 2nd session. 1952.
3. David S. Painter. 'Oil and the Marshall Plan.' *Business History Review.* No.
   58. Harvard University, Autumn 1984.
4. Marcello De Cecco. 'International Financial Markets and U.S. Domestic
   Policy since 1945.' *International Affairs.* Vol. 52, no. 1. London, January
   1976.
5. Nasrollah S. Fatemi. *Oil Diplomacy: Powderkeg in Iran.* New York: Whittier
   Books, 1954.
6. Ibid. p. 342.
7. Sepehr Zabih. *The Mossadegh Era.* Chicago: LakeView Press, 1982.
8. Joachim Jösten. *Ölmächte im Wettstreit.* Baden-Baden: Verlag August
   Lutzeyer, 1963.
9. United States National Archives. Department of State. Memorandum on
   'Enrico Mattei and the ENI.' NA RG 59. 865.2553/12–1654. December
   16, 1954.
10. Jösten. *Ölmächte.* pp. 108–12.
11. 'ENI Minus Mattei.' *The Economist.* November 5, 1962. p. 499.

## CHAPTER 8

1. Paul McCracken. 'Towards Full Employment and Price Stability.' A Report
   to the OECD by a group of independent experts. OECD. Paris, 1977.
2. P. Bairoch. 'International Industrialization Levels from 1750 to 1980.'
   *Journal of European Economic History.* Vol. 11. 1982.
3. Charles de Gaulle. *The War Memoirs.* London: Weidenfeld & Nicolson,
   1967. p. 214.
4. Lois P. de Menil. *Who Speaks for Europe? The Vision of Charles de Gaulle.*
   London: Weidenfeld & Nicolson, 1977; Erich Mende. *Von Wende zu
   Wende: 1962–1982.* München: Herbig Verlag, 1986.
5. The November 22, 1963, assassination of President Kennedy marked a
   definitive watershed in U.S. policy, which became evident with Lyndon B.
   Johnson's massive buildup of military expenditure in Vietnam. According
   to a variety of informed accounts, including that of Roger Hilsman,
   shortly before his murder, Kennedy had resolved to wind down the
   CIA's military operations in southeast Asia. Certain investigators point
   to the central presence of McGeorge Bundy at the time. For a useful

recent account of the CIA's role in the Kennedy assassination, see Robert J. Groden and H.E. Livingstone. *High Treason: The Assassination of John F. Kennedy and the New Evidence of Conspiracy.* New York: Berkley Books, 1989; Jim Garrison. *On The Trail of the Assassins.* New York: Warner Books, 1988.

6.  John Ranelagh. *The Agency: The Rise and Decline of the CIA.* London: Weidenfeld & Nicolson, 1986.

7.  Jacques Attali. *A Man of Influence: Sir Siegmund Warburg, 1902–1982.* London: Weidenfeld & Nicolson, 1986.

8.  Marcello De Cecco. 'International Financial Markets and U.S. Domestic Policy Since 1945.' *International Affairs.* London, July 1976.

9.  Jacques Rueff. *Balance of Payments: Proposals for the Resolution of the Most Pressing World Economic Problem of Our Time.* New York: Macmillan, 1967.

10.  De Menil. *Who Speaks for Europe?* p. 174.

CHAPTER 9

1.  Victor Argy. *The Postwar International Money Crisis.* London: George Allen & Unwin, 1981.

2.  'Saltsjöbaden Conference.' Bilderberg meetings, 11–13 May, 1973. The author obtained an original copy of the official discussion from this meeting. Normally confidential, the document was bought in a Paris used bookstore, apparently coming from the library of a member. In a private conversation in September 2000, H.E. Sheikh Yaki Yamani told the author about his conversation with the Shah of Iran in early 1974. When Yamani, on instructions from the Saudi King, asked the Shah why Iran demanded such a large OPEC price increase, the Shah replied, 'For the answer to your question, I suggest you go to Washington and ask Henry Kissinger.' The agenda for the 1973 Bilderberg meeting was prepared by Robert Murphy, the man who in 1922 as U.S. consul in Munich, first met Adolf Hitler and sent back favorable recommendations to his superiors in Washington. Murphy later shaped U.S. policy in postwar Germany as political adviser. Walter Levy, who delivered the Saltsjöbaden energy report, was intimately tied to the fortunes of Big Oil. In 1948, as oil economist for the Marshall Plan Economic Co-operation Administration, Levy had tried to block a government inquiry into charges that the oil companies were overcharging.

3.  Matti Golan. *The Secret Conversations of Henry Kissinger: Step-by-Step Diplomacy in the Middle East.* New York: Bantam Books, 1976.

4.  Henry A. Kissinger. *Years of Upheaval.* Boston: Little, Brown, 1982.

5.  Memorandum reproduced in *International Currency Review.* Vol. 20, no. 6. London, January 1991. p. 45.

6.  James Akins. Private conversations regarding his tenure as Director of Fuels and Energy Office of U.S. State Department at that time; later he was ambassador to Saudi Arabia.

7.  Craufurd D. Goodwin. et al. *Energy Policy in Perspective.* Washington, D.C.: Brookings Institution, 1981.

8. For a revealing view of the intimate interrelation of Mr. Kissinger and the British Foreign Office during the entire period of the early 1970s oil shock, it is useful to cite a section from a remarkably frank address given by Kissinger on May 10, 1982, before the Royal Institute of International Affairs in London. Following several minutes of effusive praise for the two centuries of skillful British 'balance-of-power' diplomacy, Kissinger then approvingly cites the postwar U.S.–British 'special relationship,' adding,

> Our postwar diplomatic history is littered with Anglo-American 'arrangements' and 'understandings,' sometimes on crucial issues, never put into formal documents ... The British were so matter-of-factly helpful that they became a participant in internal American deliberations, to a degree probably never before practiced between sovereign nations. In my period in office, the British played a seminal role in certain American bilateral negotiations ... In my White House incarnation then, I kept the British Foreign Office better informed and more closely engaged than I did the American State Department ...

Kissinger then cites as an example his U.S. negotiations over the future of Rhodesia: 'In my negotiations over Rhodesia, I worked from a British draft with British spelling even when I did not fully grasp the distinction between a working paper and a Cabinet-approved document. The practice of collaboration thrives to our day ...' Henry A. Kissinger. 'Reflections on a Partnership: British and American Attitudes to Postwar Foreign Policy.' Royal Institute of International Affairs, Chatham House, London. May 10, 1982.

9. Ford Foundation Energy Policy Project. 'A Time to Choose: America's Energy Future.' Cambridge, Mass.: Ballinger Publishing, 1974.

10. In June 1973, on the personal initiative of Chase Manhattan Bank chairman David Rockefeller, an influential new international organization, largely built on the foundation of the Bilderberg group, was established. It was called the Trilateral Commission, and its first executive director was Bilderberg attendee Zbigniew Brzezinski. The Trilateral Commission attempted for the first time in postwar Anglo-American history to draw Japanese finance and business elites into the Anglo-American policy consensus formation. In 1976, Henry Kissinger changed places with Brzezinski, becoming Trilateral director while Brzezinski assumed Kissinger's job as National Security Adviser to the new president, Jimmy Carter, himself a member of the semisecret Trilateral Commission group, as were many of his key cabinet secretaries.

11. The background for this part is the result of extensive interviews and corporate industry research by the author, over a period of more than 16 years.

12. For a critique of Malthus' economics, see Friedrich List. *The National System of Political Economy*. New Jersey: Augustus M. Kelley, 1977.

13. U.S. National Archives. 'Implications of Worldwide Population Growth for U.S. Security and Overseas Interests.' National Security Study Memorandum 200. December 10, 1974.

CHAPTER 10

1. Sources: International Iron and Steel Institute. *World Steel in Figures*. Brussels, 1991; *Fearnley's World Shipping* (annual reports). Oslo.
2. Guido Carli. 'Why Banks are Unpopular.' Lecture to the Per Jacobsson Foundation. Stockholm, June 12, 1976.
3. Bank for International Settlements. *Annual Report*. Basle, June 1976.
4. Reproduced in full in *International Currency Review*. Vol. 20, no. 6, January 1991. Letter of Jack F. Bennett to Henry Kissinger, February 1975. 'Subject: Special Arrangements for Purchase of U.S. Government Securities by the Saudi Arabian Government.' The career of Jack F. Bennett is noteworthy in that he was 'loaned' from Exxon in 1971 to the Nixon Treasury Department where he helped Paul Volcker to prepare the monetary side of the coming 'petrodollar' currency system, and the demonetizing of the dollar from gold. Following the 1973–75 oil shock and the successful establishment of the petrodollar recycling process, Bennett returned to Exxon. Similarly, Lord Victor Rothschild went from being head of strategic research at Royal Dutch Shell in 1971 to leading the British prime minister's Central Policy Review staff. In this position he had extraordinary influence over UK energy policy, as he had 'fortuitously' predicted a drastic rise in oil price shortly before the 1973 oil crisis. He was in contact with U.S. National Security Council head Henry Kissinger at this time.
5. Fred Hirsh et al. *Alternatives to Monetary Disorder*. Council on Foreign Relations 1980s project. McGraw-Hill, 1977. p. 55.
6. Not only developing nations, but also industrial ones were trying to develop an alternative to the debt strangulation of the 1970s oil shocks. In a proposal released in early 1977, Masaki Nakajima, chairman of Japan's Mitsubishi Research Institute, proposed the creation of what he termed a Global Infrastructure Fund. He motivated it thus:

> Under the prolonged worldwide recession in the post-oil crisis years, every country around the world is groping for ways to get out of it. What is being proposed herein as a Global Infrastructure Fund is a concept that Japan should consider as one of its international responsibilities ... The proposition is to generate effective demand within this country amounting to more than $500 billion ... under the assumption that all leading advanced industrialized countries and oil-producing countries co-operate to do so ... It aims at developing new sources of energy and increasing food production for the world ... Implementation of the various 'super projects' proposed herein would lead to development of peaceful demand in the manufacturing industry ... technological incentives in the advanced countries in lieu of arms production ... Now is the time for mankind to positively assert a bold and long-range vision.

Nakajima's list of great projects included greening the Sahara for agriculture, a Himalayan hydroelectric project, creation of a central African lake in Chad and the Congo, and development of a series of hydroelectric dams across South America. The Nakajima proposal was revived in 1990 in Davos, Switzerland, at a meeting of the World Economic Forum, with support of the Japanese industrial federation, Keidanren.

7. Refer to the citation in Chapter 9, note 8, regarding Kissinger's admission of his close relations with the British Foreign Office during his tenure as secretary of state.

8. Benazir Bhutto. *Tochter der Macht: Autobiographie*. München: Drömer Knaur, 1989.

9. For background to the creation of the Trilateral Commission, refer to Chapter 9, note 10. This institution was to be a broadening of the initial influence base of the Bilderberg, which was founded explicitly as a vehicle to promote Anglo-American policy in western Europe. The Trilateral Commission was an attempt to address the changing geopolitical reality in which Japan was emerging as an economic giant. The triad was that of North America, Europe and Japan. In Europe, it incorporated a motley group, among them Germany's Graf Lambsdorff. Many European members of the Trilateral Commission had been drawn from long-time friends of Rockefeller and old members of his wartime European business networks. That there were no fundamental policy disagreements between Henry Kissinger and the Democratic Party candidacy of David Rockefeller's protégé Carter is evident from Rockefeller's naming of Kissinger to the Advisory Board of his Chase Manhattan Bank after the latter left government, as well as making Kissinger executive director of his Trilateral group to replace Brzezinski, while the latter was running U.S. foreign policy for Carter.

10. In 1978, the Iranian *Ettelaat* published an article accusing Khomeini of being a British agent. The clerics organized violent demonstrations in response, which led to the flight of the Shah months later. See U.S. Library of Congress Country Studies, Iran. *The Coming of the Revolution*. December 1987. The role of BBC Persian broadcasts in the ousting of the Shah is detailed in Hossein Shahidi. 'BBC Persian Service 60 years on.' *The Iranian*. September 24, 2001. The BBC was so much identified with Khomeini that it won the name 'Ayatollah BBC.'

11. Comptroller General of the United States. 'Iranian Oil Cutoff: Reduced Petroleum Supplies and Inadequate U.S. Government Response.' Report to Congress by General Accounting Office. 1979.

## CHAPTER 11

1. A useful explication of the modern American variant of British liberalism can be found in Noam Chomsky. 'The Struggle for Democracy in a Changed World.' Paper presented to the Catholic Institute for International Relations. London, January 1991.

2. Sam Aaronovitch. *The Road From Thatcherism*. London: Lawrence & Wishart, 1981.

3. International Iron and Steel Institute. *Infrastructure: Problems and Prospects for Steel*. Brussels, 1985.

4. William Greider. *Secrets of the Temple*. London: Simon & Schuster, 1987.

5. Michael Hudson. *Super Imperialism: The Origin and Fundamentals of U.S. World Dominance* (second edition). London: Pluto Press, 2003. Hudson provides an incisive analysis of the IMF process in bringing economies such as that of Mexico under control of the dollar system.
6. The *World Debt Tables* series (World Bank: Washington) for the period through the early 1980s shows the exponential growth of external debt in the period.
7. Hans Kornø Rasmussen. *The Forgotten Generation: A Debate Book Concerning Children and the Debt Crisis.* Copenhagen: Danish UNICEF Committee, 1987. Also useful for background on this debt process is Marko Milivojevic. *The Debt Rescheduling Process.* New York: St. Martin's Press, 1985; in addition, the annual United Nations reports, *Economic Survey of Latin America* provide useful data; the comments from Kuczinski are from a remarkable 1988 documentary on the debt crisis from British Independent Television.
8. Walter Michler. 'Wirtschaftskrieg gegen einen Kontinent.' *Welternährung.* 1. 1991. Bonn.
9. Stephen Pizzo. *Inside Job: The Looting of America's Savings and Loans.* New York: McGraw-Hill, 1989.
10. U.S. Congress Joint Economic Committee. *Economic Indicators.* Washington, 1990.
11. David D. Hale. *The Weekly Money Report.* Chicago: Kemper Financial Services, January 29, 1990.
12. U.S.–Iraq Business Forum. *Bulletin.* New York, August, 1989.
13. Saddam Hussein. Address of 16 February, 1990, to Arab Cooperation Council. Translated from Arabic in U.S. State Department Foreign Broadcast Information Service. Washington, 20 February, 1990.

## CHAPTER 12

1. The Japanese debate with the IMF is found in *World Economic Outlook.* International Monetary Fund. Washington, D.C., May 1990. p. 46. The description of Wall Street derivatives actions to accelerate the Nikkei fall comes from market participants in off-record comments to the author. In a January 1990 private client letter, U.S. economist David D. Hale of Kemper Financial Services noted the bizarre contradictions in Washington's Japan policy of the time. Hale noted that

> The U.S. Treasury is now demanding that Japan liberalize her asset markets and abolish her financial cartels ... Americans must recognize that some of Japan's asset inflation stemmed from monetary policies destined to prop up the U.S. financial markets during the final Reagan years and that too rapid liberalization in Tokyo could inadvertently generate a global financial crisis.

Geoffrey P. Miller ('The Role of a Central Bank in a Bubble Economy.' New York University Center for the Study of Central Banks) usefully details the sequence of events from the Plaza accord to the collapse of the

Tokyo bubble. Chalmers Johnson ('Let's revisit Asia's crony capitalism.' *Los Angeles Times*. June 25, 1999) gives a succinct analysis of the U.S. view of the Japanese economic threat at the end of the cold war, from one of the leading Japan scholars in the United States. See also Kinhide Mushakoji. 'Japan and Cultural Development in East Asia.' *Mushakoji Newsletter*. No. 8. Tokyo, June 1997. The Lawrence Summers quote is in Philip Golub. 'East Asia in the Global Political Economy.' *Le Monde Diplomatique*. London, October 2003; on the origins of the Asia crisis, see Kristen Nordhaug. 'U.S. hegemony, Japan and the Asian financial crisis.' Paper presented in 1999 on the origins of the Asia crisis. www.globasia. dk. An official report of the effect of the east Asia crisis is provided by Andrew Crockett. 'Capital Flows in East Asia since the crisis.' Bank for International Settlements. October 11, 2002. www.bis.org.

2. Zbigniew Brzezinski. *The Grand Chessboard: American Primacy and its Geostrategic Imperatives*. New York: Basic Books, 1997. Brzezinski is one of the longer-serving strategists in the Washington establishment, whose ties go back to David Rockefeller's Trilateral Commission and to service with both Democrat and Republican administrations, including that of George H.W. Bush. The book provides invaluable insight into American strategic thinking. He states:

> For America, the chief geopolitical prize is Eurasia ... A power that dominates Eurasia would control two of the world's three most advanced and economically productive regions. A mere glance at the map also suggests that control over Eurasia would almost automatically entail Africa's subordination, rendering the Western Hemisphere and Oceania geopolitically peripheral to the world's central Continent. About 75 per cent of the world's people live in Eurasia, and most of the world's physical wealth is there as well, both in its enterprises and underneath its soil. Eurasia counts for about 60 per cent of the world's GDP and about three-fourths of the world's known energy resources. (pp. 30–1)

Mackinder's formulation is found in Halford J. Mackinder. *Democratic Ideals and Reality*. New York: Henry Holt, 1919. Mackinder, in one of his last pieces, during the Second World War, wrote a geopolitical proposal for the postwar era, 'The Round World and the Winning of the Peace.' *Foreign Affairs*. Vol. 21, no. 4. New York, July 1943. This article outlined his strategy for the postwar domination of Eurasia, on which Brzezinski clearly draws.

3. Bill Bradley. 'Eurasia Letter: A Misguided Russia Policy.' *Foreign Policy*. Winter 1995/1996. The collapse of Russian living standards after the dissolution of the Soviet Union is widely discussed; the deliberate role of IMF and G-7 policy in deindustrializing Russia is for obvious reasons much less discussed. Graeme Herd ('Robbing Russia?' *World Today*. London, April 1998) described in detail the oligarchs' role. 'U.S. criticized for funding "corporatist" and "criminalized" capitalism' (*Russia Reform Monitor*. No. 308. September 11, 1997) contains details on the Clinton administration's role in backing Chubais and the oligarchs. See also Alastair Macdonald.

'Russian government wins time, but problems abound.' *Reuters*. August 2, 1998. The present author conducted numerous discussions with many of the leading banks involved in Russia at the time of the 1998 crisis. Few of the post-mortem accounts of the LTCM collapse deal with the obvious close links between the Washington financial powers, including the Federal Reserve, and the financial operations of LTCM, perhaps the most interesting aspect.

4.  Paul B. McCarthy. Testimony to the Commission on Security and Cooperation in Europe. Washington, December 10, 1998. McCarthy, then head of the National Endowment for Democracy, outlines in detail the role of the NED in financing various opposition groups, journalists, media and trade unions in former Yugoslavia since 1988. The NED was established during the Reagan administration in 1983 as part of what was termed inside Washington policy circles the 'privatization of intelligence.' Smarting from revelations of CIA funding of front groups during the 1960s and 1970s, Congress agreed to create and fund 'private' agencies such as the NED to do the same, but openly. In a September 21, 1991, interview with the *Washington Post*, NED planner Allen Weinstein explained, 'A lot of what we do today was done covertly 25 years ago by the CIA.' Once-sinister CIA agents were transformed into humanitarian NED 'activists.' Instead of being charged with destabilizing a sovereign country, NED activists charged their opponents in Serbia or Bulgaria or elsewhere with being 'corrupt nationalists.' The NED was being groomed for a key role in the 'democratization' of post-Saddam Iraq by the Bush administration in late 2003. The impact of IMF policies on the political instability of Yugoslavia at the end of the 1980s is detailed in Peter Bachmaier. 'Der Balkan als internationales Protektorat.' *Zeit-Fragen*. Zurich, 21 October, 2002. Susan Woodward (*Balkan Tragedy*. Washington, D.C.: Brookings Instituion, 1995) details the role of IMF policies in triggering unrest in Yugoslavia. A detailed description of the NATO strategy in Yugoslavia is found in the paper by the late Sean Gervasi. 'On the NATO Strategy in Yugoslavia.' International Nino Pasti Foundation, Prague. January 1996. 'NATO Expansion: Flirting with Disaster' (Center for Defense Information. Washington, D.C., November 1995) describes the military issues of NATO expansion. Former German CDU parliamentarian and defense expert, Willy Wimmer, in an open letter to Chancellor Gerhard Schroeder in 2001, described his personal discussions with leading Washington officials about U.S. and NATO objectives in Yugoslavia to justify a new NATO 'out of area' strategic concept. Wimmer described the consequences of the NATO presence in Yugoslavia in April 1999: It gave NATO partners direct access to the raw materials as well as allowing control over the Caspian Sea and Persian Gulf. It completed the military control from the Baltic to Anatolia by a U.S.-led NATO 'not seen since the high point of the Roman Empire,' as Wimmer put it. Rainer Rupp. 'Die imperialen Absichten der USA auf dem Balkan.' *Junge Welt*. 23 June 2001.

5.  'A Meeting of Blood and Oil: The Balkan Factor in Western Energy Security.' *Journal of Southern Europe and the Balkans*. Vol. 4, no. 1. May 2002. pp. 75–89. A simplistic claim was made during the Kosovo war

in 1999 that the war was over oil. In reality it was over the strategic relation of the EU to possible new sources of energy, including oil, and Washington's intervention to control those same sources, a slightly different issue. The issue was strategic control by Washington over possible pipeline routes through the Balkans from the Caspian Sea oilfields, in order to control EU energy security. Aleksandra Trtica. 'Trans-Balkan Oil Pipelines through No-Man's Land.' Banja Luka, Srpska, February 27, 2001.

6. Cited in 'Feasibility Study', AMBO Pipeline Consortium, May 2000, US Department of Commerce NTIS Document no. PB2000106974, p. I-78.

## CHAPTER 13

1. *Strategic Energy Policy: Challenges for the 21st Century.* James Baker. Institute for Public Policy and the Council on Foreign Relations. Houston, April 2001. www.rice.edu. The report states that the world has entered a 'new energy era ... reliance on volatile Middle East oil resources could increase dramatically over the next two decades ...' It further states, well before the second war in Iraq, that 'Iraq has become a key "swing" producer, posing a difficult situation for the U.S. government.' The high-level task force advised Cheney and the Bush administration to forge a 'comprehensive energy policy...'

   The information about the daughter of the Kuwaiti al-Sabah and her faked testimony was detailed by Tom Regan ('When Contemplating War, Beware of Babies in Incubators.' *Christian Science Monitor.* September 6, 2002.) Dick Cheney. 'Autumn Lunch Speech.' London Institute of Petroleum, 1999. www.petroleum.co.uk. The O'Neill statements are reported in 'Mid-East Realities.' Washington, January 10, 2004. www.MiddleEast.org. A day later, the Bush administration threatened possible prosecution of O'Neill for allegedly making available a classified document, 'Plan for Post-Saddam Iraq,' in which the postwar control of the Iraq oil industry was detailed. The Bush White House was clearly not happy with O'Neill's remarks.

2. 'Rebuilding America's Defenses.' The Project for the New American Century. Washington D.C., September 2000. Oliver Burkeman and Julian Borger. 'The Ex-President's Club.' *Guardian.* October 31, 2001. This is one of the few public pieces on what is arguably one of the most influential and secretive corporate groups in the world.

3. Rashid, Ahmed, *Taliban: Militant Islam, Oil and Fundamentalism in Central Asia.* London, I.B. Tauris & Co., 2001. John Pilger in the *Pakistan Daily Times,* 'America's Bid for Global Dominance,' December 15, 2002. The 'carpet of gold' quote and the Unocal role in Afghanistan are detailed in Jean-Charles Brisard and G. Dasquie. *Forbidden Truth: U.S.–Taliban Secret Oil Diplomacy...* New York: Thunders' Mouth Press/Nation Press, 2002. The Karzai Unocal link appeared in *Le Monde,* December 13, 2001. News of the signing of the Afghan pipeline agreement with Pakistan and Turkmenistan was reported in after-words.org/grim, January 3, 2003. Ron Callari. 'The Enron–Cheney–Taliban Connection?' *Albion Monitor.*

February 28, 2002. This report contains many details of the role of Enron (before its collapse) in the Afghanistan pipeline talks.

4.  Michael Meacher. 'The War on Terrorism is Bogus.' *Guardian*. September 6, 2003. The article, from a long-standing senior Blair cabinet member, was greeted with deafening silence in the U.S. media. The report of the removal of the U.S. weapons team is in Raymond Whitaker. 'Powell Withdraws Al Qaida Claim as Hunt for Saddam's WMD Flags.' *Independent*. January 11, 2004. The Wolfowitz remarks are covered in an article by George Wright. 'Wolfowitz: The Iraq War was About Oil.' *Guardian*. June 4, 2003. Timothy Garten Ash ('Next Stop Syria?' *Guardian*. January 22, 2004) notes the Bush call to double NED funding for the spread of democracy in the Middle East.

5.  The Cabinet memo to Blair on oil is titled 'Submission to the Cabinet Office on Energy Policy.' The Oil Depletion Analysis Centre. September 9, 2001. www.cabinet-office.gov.uk. Richard Heinberg. *The Party's Over: Oil, Water and the Fate of Industrial Societies*. New Society Publishers, 2003. Matthew Simmons. Address to Association for the Study of Peak Oil. French Petroleum Institute (IFP). May 27, 2003. www.fromthewilderness. com. Matthew Simmons ('Energy Infrastructure.' Sixth Annual Rice Global Forum. Houston, September 8, 2003) also gives a useful summary of the basic economic and oil arguments. C.J. Campbell. 'Forecasting Global Oil Supply 2000–2050.' M. King Hubbert Center for Petroleum Supply Studies. Colorado School of Mines. July 2002; Michael T. Klare. 'The Bush–Cheney Energy Strategy.' Paris, May 2003; Mano Singham. 'Cheney's Oil Maps.' *Atlanta Journal-Constitution*. July 19, 2003; Charles Arthur. 'Oil and Gas Running Out Much Faster than Expected Says Study.' *Independent*. October 2, 2003. The ExxonMobil article is by Jon Thompson. 'A Revolutionary Transformation.' *The Lamp*. Vol. 85, no. 1. Dallas, 2003.

6.  Simon Romero. 'Coup on Tiny African Islands Felt in Texas Oil Offices.' *New York Times*. July 18, 2003; 'Iran and Japan Close to Signing Deal Despite U.S. Pressure.' Dow Jones. July 3, 2003; Anatol Lieven. 'The Push for War.' *London Review of Books*. Vol. 24, no. 19. October 3, 2002; Wayne Madsen. 'Big Oil and James Baker Target the Western Sahara.' *AllAfrica*. January 9, 2003; 'Turmoil in Georgia Linked to Oil.' *Dawn* Group of Newspapers. Pakistan, November 24, 2003; Africa Oil Policy Initiative Group. 'Africa Oil: A Priority for U.S. National Security.' Institute for Advanced Strategic and Political Studies. Washington, January 2002.

7.  Emmanuel Todd. *After the Empire: The Breakdown of the American Order*. New York: Columbia University Press, 2003. Todd argues that American economic foreign policy is driven by fundamental weakness, not by strength. Edward Said. 'Preface to Orientalism.' *Al-Ahram*. 7–13 August, 2003.

# Appendix I
# Founding Members of the
# Trilateral Commission (1973)

USA:
I.W. Abel
David M. Abshire
Graham Allison
John B. Anderson
E.C. Arbuckle
J. Paul Austin
George W. Ball
Lucy Wilson Benson
W. Michael Blumenthal
Robert R. Bowie
Harold Brown
Zbigniew Brzezinski
Jimmy Carter
Lawton Chiles
Warren Christopher
A.W. Clausen
William T. Coleman, Jr.
Barber B. Conable, Jr.
Richard N. Cooper
John C. Culver
Lloyd N. Cutler
Archibald Davis
Hedley W. Donovan
Daniel J. Evans
Walter F. Mondale
David Rockefeller
Robert V. Roosa
Cyrus Vance
Carroll Wilson
Leonard Woodcock

Belgium:
Baron Leon Lambert

France:
Raymond Barre
Georges Berthoin
Jean Boissonat

Jean Claude Casanova
Baron Edmond de Rothschild
Roger Seydoux

Great Britain:
The Earl of Cromer
Sir Reay Geddes
Lord Harlech
Roy Jenkins
Reginauld Maulding
Julian Ridsdale
Sir Frank K. Roberts
Lord Roll of Ipsden
Sir Kenneth Younger
Sir Philip de Zueleta

Italy:
Gianni Agnelli
Piero Bassetti
Umberto Colombo
Guido Colonna di Paliano
Francesco Forte
Arrigo Levi
Cesare Merlini

Netherlands:
Andre Kloos
Max Kohnstamm
John Loudon

# Appendix II
# Participants at the Saltsjöbaden
# Meeting of the Bilderberg Group
# May 11–13, 1973

Chairman: Prince Bernhard of the Netherlands

France:
René Granier de Lilliac, Compagnie Française des Pétroles
Baron Edmond de Rothschild, banker

Germany:
Egon Bahr (Social Democrat), minister without portfolio
Birgit Breuel (Christian Democrat), Hamburg City Council
Helmut Schmidt (Social Democrat), finance minister
Theo Sommer, publisher of *Die Zeit*
Otto Wolff von Amerongen, German Chambers of Commerce

Italy:
Giovanni Agnelli, FIAT
Il Marchese Cittadini Cesi
Raffaele Girotti, chairman of ENI
Arrigo Levi, *La Stampa*

Netherlands:
F.J. Philips, chairman of Philips NV
Gerrit A. Wagner, president of Royal Dutch Shell
Max Kohnstamm

Sweden:
Olof Palme, prime minister
Marcus Wallenberg, chairman of SE-Banken
Krister Wickman, governor of Riksbank

Great Britain:
Sir Eric Drake, chairman of British Petroleum
Sir Denis Greenhill, director of British Petroleum
Denis Healey, Member of Parliament
Sir Eric Roll, vice-chairman of S.G. Warburg & Co.
Sir Reginald Maulding, Member of Parliament

USA:

James Akins, White House

Robert O. Anderson, chairman of Atlantic Richfield Oil Co.

George Ball, ex-deputy secretary of state, Lehman Bros. merchant bankers

Zbigniew Brzezinski, later security adviser to the president

William P. Bundy, New York Council on Foreign Relations

E. G. Collado, vice president of Exxon Corp.

Arthur Dean, law partner of Sullivan & Cromwell

Henry J. Heinz II, chairman of H.J. Heinz & Co.

Henry A. Kissinger, White House national security adviser

Walter J. Levy, oil consultant, author of Bilderberg paper

Robert D. Murphy, chairman of Corning Glass Co., former U.S. State Department

John G. Tower, U.S. senator

Carroll Wilson, MIT professor

# Notes

*Compiled by Sue Carlton*